Teacher's Resources

Building Life Skills

Publisher
The Goodheart-Willcox Company, Inc.
Tinley Park, Illinois

Contents

Introduction

Building Life Skills is a comprehensive text designed to help teens meet the challenges of their daily lives with confidence. Students will learn basic information and practical skills related to such topics as interpersonal and family relationships, career preparation, life management, healthy living, foods and nutrition, clothing, and housing.

The information that follows will help you use the text as well as other components of the teaching package. *Building Life Skills* learning package includes the *Student Activity Guide, Teacher's Annotated Edition, Teacher's Resource Guide, Teacher's Resource Binder,* and *Test Creation Software.*

Using the Text

The text *Building Life Skills* is designed to help your students learn about life management. They will learn how to prepare for the changes and decisions they will face as they become adults.

The text is divided into eight parts with a total of 47 chapters. The material is organized and presented in a logical sequence of topics for the study of life management. Although the text was written to be studied in its entirety, individual chapters and sections are complete enough to be studied independently.

The text is straightforward and easy to read. Information is brought to life with case studies and special boxed features set apart in colors that make them easy to identify. Hundreds of photographs and charts attract student interest and emphasize key concepts. References to the illustrations are included in the copy to help students associate the visual images with the written material. This helps reinforce learning.

The text includes a brief table of contents as well as an expanded table. This gives students an overview of the wide variety of topics they will be studying. The glossary at the back of the book helps students learn terms related to life management. A complete index helps them find information they want quickly and easily.

Each chapter includes several features designed to help students study effectively and review what they have learned.

Words to Know. A list of vocabulary terms appears at the beginning of each chapter. Terms are listed in the order in which they appear in the chapter. These terms are in bold italic type throughout the text so students can recognize them while reading. Discussing these words with students will help them learn concepts to which they are being introduced. To help students become familiar with these terms, you may want to ask them to

- look up, define, and explain each term
- relate each term to the topic being studied
- match terms with their definitions
- find examples of how the terms are used in current newspapers and magazines, reference books, and other related materials

Objectives. A set of behavioral objectives also are found at the beginning of each chapter. These are performance goals students will be expected to achieve after studying the chapter. Review the objectives in each chapter with students to help make them aware of the skills they will be building as they read the chapter material.

Quotes. Famous quotes spoken by world leaders, writers, and other well-known people of the past and present are scattered throughout each chapter. The quotes may offer students further insight on text copy.

Case Stories. Information throughout the text is brought to life with realistic case stories. These stories are set apart in green type so students can identify them easily.

Online Teen Connection. Each chapter contains at least one of these boxed features, presented as an online chat room. In each "room," teens ask peers to help them solve realistic problems. The unanswered question in each feature should promote discussion in the classroom.

The Daily Skill Builder. These current events newspaper headlines are related to chapter material. The feature presents an event or problem teens may face in their lifetimes. Each headline is followed by critical thinking questions. One of these features appears in every chapter.

Review It. Review questions at the end of each chapter are included to cover the basic information presented. This section consists of a variety of true/false, completion, multiple choice, and short essay questions. It is designed to help students recall, organize, and use the information presented in the text. Answers to these questions appear in the front section of the *Teacher's Annotated Edition* as well as in the *Teacher's Resource Guide* and *Teacher's Resource Binder*.

Apply It. Suggested activities at the end of each chapter offer students opportunities to increase knowledge through firsthand experiences. These activities encourage students to apply many of the concepts learned in the chapter to real-life situations. Suggestions for both individual and group work are provided in varying degrees of difficulty. Therefore, you may choose and assign activities according to students' interests and abilities.

Think More About It. These questions at the end of each chapter encourage critical thinking. Thought-provoking questions require students to apply chapter material to their own lives. The use of imagination and problem-solving techniques are promoted.

Getting Involved. A suggested activity for applying chapter concepts to community volunteer work is included in each chapter.

Using the Student Activity Guide

The *Student Activity Guide* designed for use with *Building Life Skills* helps students recall and review material presented in the text. It also helps them apply what they have learned as they prepare for adulthood.

The activities in the guide are divided into chapters that correspond to the chapters in the text. The text provides the information students will need to complete many of the activities. Other activities will require creative thinking and research beyond the textbook.

You may want to use the exercises in the *Student Activity Guide* that are directly related to text material as introductory, review, or evaluation tools. Ask students to do the exercises without looking in the book. Then they can use the text to check their answers and to answer questions they could not complete. The pages of the *Student Activity Guide* are perforated so students can easily turn completed activities in to you for evaluation.

The *Student Activity Guide* includes different types of activities. Some have specific answers related to text material. Students can use these activities to review as they study for tests and quizzes. Answers to these activities appear in the *Teacher's Resource Guide* and *Teacher's Resource Binder*.

Other activities, such as case studies and surveys, ask for students' thoughts or opinions. Answers to these activities cannot be judged as right or wrong. These activities allow students to form their own ideas by considering alternatives and evaluating situations thoughtfully. These thought-provoking exercises can often be used as a basis for classroom discussion by asking students to justify their answers and conclusions.

The use of each activity in the *Student Activity Guide* is described in the *Teacher's Resource Guide* and *Teacher's Resource Binder* as a teaching strategy under the related instructional concept. Activities are identified by name and letter.

Using the Teacher's Annotated Edition

The *Teacher's Annotated Edition* for *Building Life Skills* is a special edition of the student text. It is designed to help you more effectively coordinate materials in the *Student Activity Guide* and *Teacher's Resource Guide/Binder* with text concepts. It also provides you with additional suggestions to help you add variety to your classroom teaching.

Annotations are located throughout the text. Numbers are placed in the right and left side margins that correspond with annotations located at the bottom of each page. The following chart details the annotations used in the annotated edition.

In addition to annotations placed throughout the student text, the *Teacher's Annotated Edition* includes a special front section on colored paper. It begins with a detailed introduction explaining how to use the various components in the teaching package for *Building Life Skills*. This section also contains several features designed to help you prepare meaningful lessons for your students.

■ Teaching Suggestions

A number of suggestions are given to help you increase the effectiveness of your classroom teaching. This information includes suggestions for teaching students of varying abilities, evaluating students, communicating with students, and promoting your program.

■ Scope and Sequence Chart

A *Scope and Sequence Chart,* located at the end of the introduction, identifies the major concepts presented in each chapter of the text. This special resource is provided to help you select for study those topics that meet your curriculum needs.

■ Teaching Aids

The last item in the front section of the annotated text is a chapter-by-chapter teaching aids resource. It is designed to assist you in developing lesson plans and evaluating student learning. The following aids are included for each chapter of the text:

Chapter Outline. An outline of the chapter's main points is provided to give you an overview of the content and organization of chapter material.

Annotation Term	Annotation Description
Vocabulary	These annotations are placed alongside the list of chapter terms and elsewhere within the chapter. They suggest vocabulary reinforcement activities, such as defining terms, using terms in sentences, looking up terms in the glossary, or comparing important new terms. They may also provide interesting and meaningful information about the origins of words.
Discuss	These annotations provide discussion questions to reteach or reinforce learning. Questions may also relate to charts in the chapter.
Reflect	These annotations provide questions to ask students to think about regarding the concepts presented, often by applying the content to their lives. These questions are often more personal than are the discussion questions.
Activity	These annotations suggest activities that would reteach and reinforce text concepts. (Math or science activities are designated as either Math Activity or Science Activity.)
Note	These annotations provide additional points the instructor might want to make regarding the topic, or to spark student interest in the topic discussion. Points might include statistics, interesting facts, or historical notes. These may also be notes to the instructor regarding the subject matter.
Example	These annotations provide one or more examples to use in illustrating an important point in the chapter material.
Enrich	These annotations suggest activities that demonstrate the concept, but are more involved and challenging for students. Examples include role-playing, research topics, debates, surveys, bulletin boards, field trips, or guest speakers.
Resource	These annotations refer to activities in the *Student Activity Guide* and reproducible masters in the *Teacher's Resource Binder* that relate to chapter material.
Answers	These annotations indicate where answers to questions may be found.

Answer Key. Answers for the *Review It* questions at the end of each chapter are supplied to assist you in clarifying student understanding of chapter concepts.

Using the Teacher's Resource Guide

The *Teacher's Resource Guide* for *Building Life Skills* suggests many methods of presenting the concepts in the text to students. It begins with some of the same helpful information found in the *Teacher's Annotated Edition,* including teaching suggestions and a *Scope and Sequence Chart.*

■ Basic Skills Chart

Another feature of the *Teacher's Resource Guide* is a *Basic Skills Chart.* This chart has been included to identify those activities that encourage the development of the following basic skills: verbal, reading, writing, mathematical, scientific, and analytical. (Analytical skills involve the higher-order thinking skills of analysis, synthesis, and evaluation in problem-solving situations.) The chart includes activities from the "Apply It" section of the text, activities from the *Student Activity Guide,* and strategies from the *Teacher's Resource Guide/Binder.* Incorporating a variety of these activities into your daily lesson plans will provide your students with vital practice in the development of basic skills. Also, if you find that students in your classes are weak in a specific basic skill, you can select activities to strengthen that particular skill area.

■ Chapter-by-Chapter Resources

Like the *Student Activity Guide,* the *Teacher's Resource Guide* is divided into chapters that match the chapters in the text. Each chapter contains the following features:

Objectives. These are the objectives that students will be able to accomplish after reading the chapter and completing the suggested activities.

Teaching Materials. A list of materials available to supplement each chapter in the text is provided. The list includes the names of all the activities contained in the *Student Activity Guide* and all the masters contained in the *Teacher's Resource Guide/Binder.*

Introductory Activities. These motivational exercises are designed to stimulate your students' interest in the chapter they will be studying. The activities help create a sense of curiosity that students will want to satisfy by reading the chapter.

Strategies to Reteach, Reinforce, Enrich, and Extend Text Concepts. A variety of student learning strategies is described for teaching each of the major concepts discussed in the text. Each major concept appears in the guide in bold type. The student learning experiences for each concept follow. Activities from the *Student Activity Guide* are identified for your convenience in planning daily lessons. They are identified with the letters SAG following the title and letter of the activity. (*Changes,* Activity A, SAG.)

The number of each learning strategy is followed by a code in bold type. These codes identify the teaching goals each strategy is designed to accomplish. The following codes have been used:

RT identifies activities designed to help you *reteach* concepts. These strategies present the chapter concepts in a different way to allow students additional learning opportunities.

RF identifies activities designed to *reinforce* concepts to students. These strategies present techniques and activities to help clarify facts, terms, principles, and concepts, making it easier for students to understand.

ER identifies activities designed to *enrich* learning. These strategies help students learn more about the concepts presented by involving them more fully in the material. Enrichment strategies include diverse experiences, such as demonstrations, field trips, guest speakers, panels, and surveys.

EX identifies activities designed to *extend* learning. These strategies promote thinking skills, such as critical thinking, creative thinking, problem solving, and decision making. Students must analyze, synthesize, and evaluate in order to complete these activities.

Answer Key. This section provides answers for review questions at the end of each chapter in the text, for activities in the *Student Activity Guide,* for the reproducible masters in the *Teacher's Resource Guide/Binder,* and for the chapter quizzes.

Reproducible Masters. Several reproducible masters are included for each chapter. These masters are designed to enhance the presentation of concepts in the text. Some of the masters are designated as *transparency masters* for use with an overhead projector. These are often charts or graphs that can serve as a basis for class discussion of important concepts. They can also be used as student handouts. Some of the masters are designed as *reproducible masters.* Each student can be given a copy of the activity. These activities encourage creative and critical thinking. They can also serve as a basis for class discussion. Some masters provide material not contained in the text that you may want students to know.

In every chapter, a journal activity entitled *My Personal Journal* has been included. These reproducible masters offer insightful questions that help students consider their personal lives. These activities are not to be discussed with the rest of the class. You may instruct students to turn them in without writing their names on them. You might also have students keep all their journal activities together in a three-ring binder.

Chapter Quiz Masters. Individual quizzes with clear, specific questions that cover all the chapter topics are provided. True/false, multiple choice, and matching questions are used to measure student learning about facts and definitions. Essay questions are also provided in the chapter quizzes. Some of these require students to list information, while others encourage students to express their opinions and creativity. You may wish to modify the quizzes and tailor the questions to your classroom needs.

Using the Teacher's Resource Binder

The *Teacher's Resource Binder* for *Building Life Skills* combines the *Teacher's Resource Guide* with a *Transparency Packet.* All these materials are included in a convenient three-ring binder. Reproducible materials can be removed easily. Handy dividers included with the binder help you organize materials so you can quickly find the items you need.

Color transparencies for *Building Life Skills* add variety to your classroom lecture as you discuss topics included in the text with your students. You will find some transparencies useful in illustrating and reinforcing information presented in the text. Others will provide you with an opportunity to extend learning beyond the scope of the text. Attractive colors are visually appealing and hold students' attention. Suggestions for how the transparencies can be used in the classroom are included.

Comprehensive tests for each of the eight parts of the text are also provided in the *Teacher's Resource Binder.* These tests consist of true/false, multiple choice, matching, and essay questions. An answer key is included for each test. The number after the answer identifies the chapter to which each question relates.

Using Other Resources

Much student learning in your class can be reinforced by allowing students to see, analyze, and work with examples. Your providing samples of materials, pictures, demonstration samples, and articles related to a variety of family and consumer sciences topics can greatly enhance student learning. Students can use these items in many activities related to the text.

You may be able to acquire some items through local stores. Old pattern catalogs, fabric remnants, and other items can often be purchased inexpensively. Many stores may be willing to donate items. You may be able to obtain pamphlets and project ideas by contacting consumer product manufacturers.

Magazines, catalogs, and sales brochures are excellent sources of photos. Having a large quantity available for clipping and mounting photos will be helpful to students. Students may analyze and discuss the pictures in a variety of activities.

Current magazines and journals are also good sources of articles on various family and consumer sciences topics. Having copies in the classroom will encourage students to use them for research and ideas as they study family and consumer sciences. The following publications may be helpful to you or your students:

American Health
Better Homes and Gardens
Choices Magazine
Consumer Reports
Creative Ideas for Living
Journal of Family and Consumer Sciences
Newsweek
Seventeen
Sew It Seams
Sew News
Time
What's New in Family and Consumer Sciences

The following is a list of various companies, associations, and government groups that may serve as resources for additional teaching materials. Most provide videos and/or computer software. Many provide printed materials. Contact these organizations for their latest catalogs.

AAVIM
  220 Smithonia Road
  Winterville, GA 30683
  (800) 228-4689
  (software, videos, and publications)

AGC Educational Media
  1560 Sherman Ave.
  Suite 100
  Evanston, IL 60201
  (800) 323-9084
  FAX: (708) 328-6706

American Association of Family and Consumer
  Sciences
  1555 King St.
  Alexandria, VA 22314

American Gas Association
  1515 Wilson Blvd.
  Arlington, VA 22209

American Home Sewing Association
  1375 Broadway, 4th Fl.
  New York, NY 10018

American Society of Interior Designers
  1430 Broadway
  New York, NY 10018

American Textile Manufacturers Institute, Inc.
  1101 Connecticut Ave., N.W.
  Washington, DC 20036

Bergwall Productions, Inc.
  540 Baltimore Park
  PO Box 2400
  Chadds Ford, PA 19317
  (800) 645-3565

Bureau for At-Risk Youth
  135 Dupont St.
  Plainview, NY 11803
  (800) 999-6884
  (guidance and life skills programs, videos, and handouts)

Cambridge Educational
  PO Box 2153
  Charleston, WV 25328-2153
  (800) 468-4227
  (videos, software, CD-ROM, printed materials in all areas of family and consumer sciences)

Concept Media
  2493 Dubridge Ave.
  Irvine, CA 92606
  (800) 233-7078

Creative Educational Video
  PO Box 65265
  Lubbock, TX 79464-5265
  (800) 922-9965

Distinctive Home Video Productions
  391 El Portal Rd.
  San Mateo, CA 94402
  (415) 344-7756

Durrin Productions
  1748 Kaorama Rd.
  NW Washington, DC 20009
  (800) 536-6843

ETR Associates
  PO Box 1830
  Santa Cruz, CA 95061-1830
  (408) 438-4060

FHA/HERO
  1910 Association Dr.
  Reston, VA 22091

Films for the Humanities and Sciences
PO Box 2053
Princeton, NJ 08543
(800) 257-5126

Human Relations Media Video (HRM)
175 Tompkins Ave.
Pleasantville, NY 10570
(800) 431-2050
(family living, guidance, health, drug education, and conflict resolution)

Injoy Videos
3970 Broadway
Suite B4
Boulder, CO 80304
(800) 326-2082
(videos on pregnancy, birth, and early parenting)

Karol Media
350 N. Pennsylvania Ave.
Wilkes Barre, PA 18773
(800) 526-4773
(videos in family and consumer sciences)

The Learning Seed
330 Telser Road
Lake Zurich, IL 60047
(847) 540-8855
(videos, software, and audiovisuals for family and consumer sciences)

Media International
5900 San Fernando Rd.
Glendale, CA 91202
Owtonna, MN 55060
(800) 477-7575
(videos on personal, social, and sexual issues, character education, relationships, and substance abuse)

Meridian Education Corp.
236 E. Front St.
Bloomington, IL 61701
(800) 727-5507
(videos/multimedia for foods/nutrition, clothing, child development, and relationships)

Midwest Agribusiness Services, Inc.
4565 Highway 33 W.
West Bend, WI 53095-9108
(800) 523-3475
www.hnet.net/midwest
(software and videos on child development, parenting, and foods)

Nasco
901 Janesville Ave.
Dept. EN701-A
Fort Akinson, WI 53538-0901
(800) 558-9595

National Cattlemen's Beef Association
444 N. Michigan Ave.
Chicago, IL 60611

NIMCO, Inc.
PO Box 9102 Highway 81 North
Calhoun, KY 42327
(800) 962-6662
(502) 273-5844
(textbooks, videos, and slides)

RMI Media Productions
2807 West 47th Street
Shawnee Mission, KS 66205
(800) 821-5480
(educational videos)

Sax Family & Consumer Sciences
PO Box 510710
New Berlin, WI 53151
(800) 558-6696
(a complete line of family and consumer sciences teaching aids)

Sunburst Communications, Inc.
101 Castleton St.
Pleasantville, NY 10570
(800) 431-1934
(videos on family living, conflict resolution, sexual education, and anger management)

Teen-Aid
723 E. Jackson
Spokane, WA 99207-2647
(509) 482-2868
FAX: (509) 482-7994
(videos, teaching modules, lesson plans, pamphlets, overheads, and posters)

United Fresh Fruit and Vegetable Association
727 N. Washington St.
Alexandria, VA 22314

USDA, Food Safety and Inspection Service
Room 1180-South Building
14th & Independence Avenue, SW
Washington, DC 20250
(202) 690-0351

U.S. Food and Drug Administration
5600 Fishers Lane
Rockville, MD 20857
(301) 443-3170
www.fda.gov

Teaching Techniques

You can make the study of life management exciting and relevant by using a variety of teaching techniques. Below are some principles that will help you choose and use different teaching techniques in your classroom.

- Make learning stimulating. One way to do this is to involve students in lesson planning. When possible, allow them to select the modes of learning they enjoy most. For example, some students will do well with oral reports; others prefer written assignments. Some learn well through group projects; others do better working independently. You can also make courses more interesting by presenting a variety of learning activities and projects from which students may choose to fulfill their work requirement.

- Make learning realistic. You can do this by relating the subject matter to issues that concern young people. Students gain the most from learning when they can apply it to real-life situations. Case studies, role-playing, and drawing on personal experiences all make learning more realistic and relevant.

- Make learning varied. Try using several different techniques to teach the same concept. Make use of outside resources and current events as they apply to material being presented in class. Students learn through their senses of sight, hearing, touch, taste, and smell. The more senses they use, the easier it will be for them to retain information. Bulletin boards, films, tapes, and transparencies all appeal to the senses.

- Make learning success-oriented. Experiencing success increases self-esteem and confidence. Guarantee success for your students by presenting a variety of learning activities. Key these activities to different ability levels so each student can enjoy both success and challenge. You will also want to allow for individual learning styles and talents. For instance, creative students may excel at designing projects, while analytical students may be more proficient at organizing details. Build in opportunities for individual students to work in ways that let them succeed and shine.

- Make learning personal. Young people become more personally involved in learning if you establish a comfortable rapport with them. Work toward a relaxed classroom atmosphere in which students can feel at ease when sharing their feelings and ideas in group discussions and activities.

Following are descriptions of various teaching techniques you may want to try. Keep in mind that not all methods work equally well in all classrooms. A technique that works beautifully with one group of students may not be successful with another. The techniques you choose will depend on the topic, your teaching goals, and the needs of your students.

One final consideration concerns students' right to privacy. Some activities, such as autobiographies, journals, and opinion papers, may invade students' privacy. You can maintain a level of confidentiality by letting students turn in unsigned papers in these situations. You may also encourage students to pursue some of these activities at home for personal enlightenment without fear of evaluation or judgment.

■ Helping Students Gain Basic Information

Many teaching techniques can be grouped according to different goals you may have for your students. One group of techniques is designed to convey information to students. Two of the most common techniques in this group are reading and lecture. Using a number of variations can make these techniques seem less common and more interesting. For instance, students may enjoy taking turns to read aloud as a change of pace from silent reading. Lectures can be energized by the use of flip charts, overhead transparencies, and other visual materials. Classroom discussions of different aspects of the material being presented get students involved and help impart information.

Other ways to present basic information include the use of outside resources. Guest speakers, whether speaking individually or as part of a panel, can bring a new outlook to classroom material. Guest lectures can be videotaped to show again to other classes or to use for review. In addition to videotapes, students also enjoy films and filmstrips related to material being studied.

■ Helping Students Question and Evaluate

A second group of teaching techniques helps students develop analytic and judgmental skills. These techniques help your students go beyond what they see on the surface. As you employ these techniques, encourage students to think about points raised by others. Ask them to evaluate how new ideas relate to their attitudes about various subjects.

Discussion is an excellent technique for helping students consider an issue from a new point of view. To be effective, discussion sessions require a great deal of advance planning and preparation. Consider the size of the discussion group and the physical arrangement. Since many students are reluctant to contribute in a large group, you may want to divide the class into smaller groups for discussion sessions. Participation will also be enhanced if the room is arranged so students can see each other.

Discussion can take a number of forms. Generally it is a good idea to reserve group discussions involving the entire class for smaller classes. Buzz groups consisting of two to six students offer a way to get willing participation from students who are not naturally outgoing. They discuss an issue among themselves and then appoint a spokesperson to report back to the entire class.

Debate is an excellent way to explore opposite sides of an issue. You may want to divide the class into two groups, each to take an opposing side of the issue. You can also ask students to work in smaller groups and explore opposing sides of different issues. Each group can select students from the group to present the points for their side.

■ Helping Students Participate

Another group of teaching techniques is designed to promote student participation in classroom activities and discussion. There are many ways to involve students and encourage them to interact. Case studies, surveys, opinionnaires, stories, and pictures can all be used to boost classroom participation. These techniques allow students to react to or evaluate situations in which they are not directly involved. Open-ended sentences often stimulate discussion. However, it is wise to steer away from overly personal or confidential matters when selecting sentences for completion. Students may be reluctant to deal with confidential issues in front of classmates.

The *fishbowl* can be a good way to stimulate class discussion. An interactive group of five to eight students is encircled by a larger observation group. The encircled students discuss a given topic while the others listen. Observers are not permitted to talk or interrupt. Positions can be reversed at the end of a fishbowl session to allow some of the observers to become the participants.

One of the most effective forms of small group discussion is the *cooperative learning group.* The teacher has a particular goal or task in mind. Small groups of learners are matched for the purpose of completing the task or goal, and each person in the group is assigned a role. The success of the group is measured not only in terms of outcome, but in the successful performance of each member in his or her role.

In cooperative learning groups, students learn to work together toward a group goal. Each member is dependent upon others for the outcome. This interdependence is a basic component of any cooperative learning group. The value of each group member is affirmed as learners work toward their goal.

The success of the group depends on individual performance. Groups should be mixed in terms of abilities and talents so there are opportunities for the students to learn from one another. Also, as groups work together over time, the roles should be rotated so everyone has an opportunity to practice and develop different skills.

The interaction of students in a cooperative learning group creates a tutoring relationship. While cooperative learning groups may involve more than just group discussion, discussion is always part of the process by which cooperative learning groups function.

■ Helping Students Apply Learning

Some techniques are particularly good for helping students use what they have learned. Simulation games and role-playing allow students to practice solving problems and making decisions under nonthreatening circumstances. Role-playing allows students to examine others' feelings as well as their own. It can help them learn effective ways to react or cope when confronted with similar situations in real life.

Role-plays can be structured, with the actors following written scripts, or they may be improvised in response to a classroom discussion. Students may act out a role as they themselves see it being played, or they may act out the role as they presume a person in that position would behave. Roles are not rehearsed and lines are composed on the spot. The follow-up discussion should focus on the feelings and emotions felt by the participants, and the manner in which the problem was resolved. Role-playing helps students consider how they would behave in similar situations in their own lives.

■ Helping Students Develop Creativity

Some techniques can be used to help students generate new ideas. For example, brainstorming encourages students to exchange and pool their ideas and to come up with new thoughts and solutions to problems. No evaluation or criticism of ideas is allowed. The format of spontaneously expressing any opinions or reactions that come to mind lets students be creative without fear of judgment.

You can also promote creativity by letting students choose from a variety of assignments related to the same material. For example, suppose you wanted students to know how to manage money to reach financial goals. You could give students the option of preparing a budget based on their actual income and expenses. They might also choose to interview a financial planner about the importance of budgeting and saving for the future. A third alternative would be for students to play a simulation game allowing them to purchase various needs and wants with play money. Any teaching techniques you use to encourage students to develop their own ideas will foster their creativity.

■ Helping Students Review Information

Certain techniques aid students in recalling and retaining knowledge. Games can be effective for drills on vocabulary and factual information. Crossword puzzles can make the review of vocabulary terms more interesting. Structured outlines of subject matter can also be effective review tools. Open-book quizzes, bulletin board displays, and problem-solving sessions all offer ways to review and apply material presented in the classroom.

Teaching Students of Varying Abilities

The students in your classroom represent a wide range of ability levels. Special-needs students who are mainstreamed require unique teaching strategies. Gifted students must not be overlooked. They need to be challenged up to their potential. All the students in between will have individual needs to consider also. Often you will be asked to meet the needs of all these students in the same classroom setting. It is a challenge to adapt daily lessons to meet the demands of all your students.

To tailor your teaching to mainstreamed and lower-ability students, consider the following strategies:

- Before assigning a chapter in the text, discuss and define the key words that appear at the beginning of each chapter. These terms are defined in the glossary at the back of the text. Ask students to write out the definitions and to tell what they think the terms mean in their own words. You might want to invite students to guess what they think words mean before they look up the definitions. You can also ask them to use new words in sentences and to find the sentences in the text where the new terms are used.

- When introducing a new chapter, review previously learned information students need to know before they can understand the new material. Review previously learned vocabulary terms they will encounter again.

- Utilize the "Introductory Activities" section in the *Teacher's Resource Guide/Binder* for each chapter. Students who have difficulty reading need a compelling reason to read the material. These introductory activities can provide the necessary motivation. Students will want to read the text to satisfy their curiosity.

- Break the chapters into smaller parts, and assign only one section at a time. Define the terms, answer the *Review It* questions, and discuss the concepts presented in each section before proceeding to the next. It often helps to rephrase questions and problems in simple language and to repeat important concepts in different ways. Assign activities in the *Student Activity Guide* that relate to each section in the book. These reinforce the concepts presented. In addition, many of these activities are designed to improve reading comprehension.

- Ask students, individually or in pairs, to answer the *Review It* questions at the end of each chapter in the text. This will help them focus on the essential information contained in the chapter.

- Use the buddy system. Pair nonreaders with those who read well. Ask students who have mastered the material to work with those who need assistance. It may also be possible to find a parent volunteer who can provide individual attention where needed.

- Select a variety of educational experiences to reinforce the learning of each concept. Look for activities that will help reluctant learners relate information to real-life situations. It helps to draw on the experiences of students at home, in school, and in the community.

- Give directions orally as well as in writing. You will need to explain assignments as thoroughly and simply as possible. Ask questions to be certain students understand what they are to do. Encourage them to ask for help if they need it. You will also want to follow up as assignments proceed to be sure no one is falling behind on required work.

- Use the overhead projector and the transparency masters included in the *Teacher's Resource Guide/Binder*. A visual presentation of concepts will increase students' ability to comprehend the material. You may want to develop your own transparencies to use in reviewing key points covered in each chapter.

If you have advanced or gifted students in your class, you will need to find ways to challenge them. These students require assignments that involve critical thinking and problem solving. Because advanced students are more capable of independent work, they can use the library and outside resources to research topics in depth. Learning experiences listed in the *Basic Skills Chart* that involve analytical skills are appropriate for gifted students. You may be able to draw on the talents of advanced students in developing case studies and learning activities to use with the entire class.

Evaluation Techniques

A variety of evaluation tools can be used to assess student achievement. Try using rating scales to observe a student's performance and rank it along a continuum. This lets students see what levels they have surpassed and what levels they can still strive to reach.

In some situations, it is worthwhile to allow students to evaluate their own work. When evaluating an independent study project, for example, students may be the best judge of whether or not they met the objectives they set for themselves. Students can think about what they have learned and see how they have improved. They can analyze their strengths and weaknesses.

You may ask students to evaluate their peers from time to time. This gives the student performing the evaluation an opportunity to practice giving constructive criticism. It also gives the student being evaluated the opportunity to accept criticism from his or her peers.

Tests and quizzes are also effective evaluation tools. These may be given in either written or oral form. In either case, however, both objective and subjective questions should be used to help you adequately assess student knowledge and understanding of class material.

Communicating with Students

Communicating with students involves not only sending clear messages, but also receiving and interpreting feedback. Following are some suggestions for productive communication with your students:

- Recognize the importance of body language and nonverbal communication in presenting material and interpreting student responses. Eye contact, relaxed but attentive body position, natural gestures, and alert facial expression all make for a presentation of material that will command attention. The same positive nonverbal cues from students are an indication of their response and reactions. Voice is also an important nonverbal communicator. Cultivating a warm, lively, enthusiastic speaking voice will make classroom presentations more interesting. By your tone, you can convey a sense of acceptance and expectation to which your students will respond.

- Use humor whenever possible. Humor is not only good medicine, it opens doors and teaches lasting lessons. Laughter and amusement will reduce tension, make points in a nonthreatening and memorable way, increase the fun and pleasure in classroom learning, and break down stubborn barriers. Relevant cartoons, quotations, jokes, and funny stories all bring a light touch to the classroom.

- Ask questions that promote recall, discussion, and thought. Good questions are tools that open the door to communication. Open-ended inquiries that ask what, where, why, when, and how will stimulate thoughtful answers. You can draw out students by asking for their opinions and conclusions. Questions with yes or no answers tend to discourage rather than promote further communication. Avoid inquiries that are too personal or that might put students on the spot.

- Rephrase students' responses to be sure both you and they understand what has been said. Paraphrasing information students give is a great way to clarify, refine, and reinforce material and ideas under discussion. For example, you might say "This is what I hear you saying . . . correct me if I'm wrong." Positive acknowledgment of student contributions, insights, and successes encourages more active participation and open communication. Comments such as "That's a very good point. I hadn't thought of it that way before" or "What a great idea" will encourage students to express themselves.

- Listen for what students say, what they mean, and what they do not say. Really listening may be the single most important step you can take to promote open communication. As students answer questions and express their ideas and concerns, try not only to hear what they say, but to understand what they mean. What is not said can also be important. Make room for silence and time to think and reflect during discussion sessions.

- Share your own feelings and experiences. The measure of what students communicate to you will depend in part on what you are willing to share with them. Express your personal experiences, ideas, and feelings when they are relevant. Don't forget to tell them about a few of your mistakes. Sharing will give students a sense of exchange and relationship.

- Lead discussion sessions to rational conclusions. Whether with an entire class or with individual students, it is important to identify and resolve conflicting thoughts and contradictions. This will help students think clearly and logically. For example, in a discussion of food choices, students may say they want to meet their nutrient needs and yet frequently eat low nutrient-density foods. Pointing out and discussing the inconsistency in these two positions will lead students to more logically consider making healthy food choices.

- Create a nonjudgmental atmosphere. Students will only communicate freely and openly in a comfortable environment. You can make them comfortable by respecting their ideas, accepting them for who they are, and honoring their confidences. It is also important to avoid criticizing a student or discussing personal matters in front of others.

- Use written communication to advantage. The more ways you approach students, the more likely you are to reach them on different levels. Very often, the written word can be an excellent way to connect. Written messages can take different forms—a notice on the chalkboard, a note attached to homework, a memo to parents (with good news as well as bad), or a letter exchange involving class members.

- Be open and available for private discussions of personal or disciplinary problems. It is important to let students know they can come to you with personal concerns as well as questions regarding course material. Be careful not to violate students' trust by discussing confidential matters outside of a professional setting.

Promoting Your Program

You can make life management one of the most important course offerings in your school. You cover material that every student and teacher can use to advantage. It pays to make the student body and faculty aware of your program. With good public relations, you can increase your enrollment, gain support from administrators and other teachers, and achieve recognition in the community. Following are some ways to promote your program:

- Create visibility. It is important to let people know what is going on in life management classes. Ways to do this include announcements of projects and activities at faculty meetings and in school bulletins or newspapers, displays in school showcases or on bulletin boards, and articles and press releases in school and community newspapers. Talk up your program with administrators, other teachers, and students. Invite them to visit your classes.

- Interact within the school. Life management is related to many fields of learning. You can strengthen your program and contribute to other disciplines by cooperating with other teachers. For example, you can work with a health teacher to present information on physical fitness and grooming, an art teacher to cover elements of design as they impact clothing and interiors, or a business teacher to discuss budgeting. The more interaction you can generate, the more you promote your life management class.

- Contribute to the educational objectives of the school. If your school follows stated educational objectives and strives to strengthen specific skills, include these overall goals in your teaching. For example, if students need special help in developing verbal or writing skills, select projects and assignments that will help them in these areas. The *Basic Skills Chart* in the *Teacher's Resource*

Guide/Binder will give you ideas for activities that strengthen specific skills. Show administrators examples of work that indicate student improvement in needed skills.

- Serve as a resource center. Life management information is of practical use and interest to almost everyone. You can sell your program by making your department a resource center of materials related to child development, nutrition, and clothing care. Invite faculty members, students, and parents to tap into the wealth of life management information available in your classroom.

- Generate involvement and activity in the community. You are teaching concepts students can apply in their everyday lives. You can involve students in community life and bring the community into your classroom through field trips, interviews with businesspeople and community leaders, surveys, and presentations from guest speakers. You may be able to set up cooperative projects between the school and community organizations around a variety of topics.

- Connect with parents. If you can get them involved, parents may be your best allies in teaching life management. Let parents know when their children have done good work. Moms and dads have had experiences related to many of the issues you discuss in class. They have managed money, found jobs, formed friendships, parented children, and handled stress. Call on them to share individually or as part of a panel addressing a specific topic. Parents can be a rich source of real-life experience. Keep them informed about classroom activities and invite them to participate as they are able.

- Establish a student sales staff. Enthusiastic students will be your best salespeople. Encourage them to tell their parents and friends what they are learning in your classes. You might create bulletin boards or write letters to parents that focus on what students are learning in your classes. Ask students to put together a newsletter highlighting their experiences in life management class. Students could write a column from your department for the school paper.

We appreciate the contributions of the following Goodheart-Willcox authors to this introduction: "Teaching Techniques" from *Changes and Choices,* by Ruth E. Bragg; and "Evaluation Techniques" from *Contemporary Living,* by Verdene Ryder.

Scope and Sequence

In planning your program, you may want to use the *Scope and Sequence Chart* below. This chart identifies the major concepts presented in each chapter of the text. Refer to the chart to find the material that meets your curriculum needs. Bold numbers indicate chapters in which concepts are found.

	Personal Development	Family Living, Relationships, and Communication
Part One: Learning About Yourself	**1:** Growth and development **2:** How personality develops **3:** Criticism; Crises	**4:** Verbal and nonverbal communication; Barriers to good communication; Communication skills **5:** Family types, functions, and roles; The family life cycle; Family relationships **6:** Forming and ending friendships; Peers and peer pressure; Dating
Part Two: Managing Your Life	**7:** Needs and wants; Values	**9:** Filing consumer complaints
Part Three: Understanding Children		**10:** Caring for and playing with infants **11:** Caring for and playing with toddlers **12:** Caring for and playing with preschoolers **14:** Caring for children as a babysitter **15:** The parent-child relationship
Part Four: Your Health and Nutrition		
Part Five: Working in the Kitchen		**31:** Influences on food customs **32:** Eating at home; Mealtime and restaurant etiquette; Having dinner guests and parties
Part Six: The Clothes You Wear	**33:** Choosing your best colors; Choosing your best lines	
Part Seven: The Place You Call Home	**40:** Homes fulfill needs **41:** Using accessories to express personality	**40:** Changing homes **41:** Sharing a room **42:** Working together to clean
Part Eight: Reaching New Heights	**45:** Interests, aptitudes, and abilities; making a career plan **47:** Work ethic; Setting priorities	**43:** Being part of a group **44:** Communication skills; The job interview **45:** Careers affect lifestyles **47:** Demands of work on families; Concerns of working parents; Caring for older relatives; Support systems

(Continued)

	Leadership and Careers	Resource Management and Decision Making
Part One: Learning About Yourself	**1:** Accepting responsibility; Becoming independent	**4:** Resolving conflicts **5:** Families face change; Technology affects family life
Part Two: Managing Your Life	**8:** Accepting responsibility for decisions	**7:** Goals and standards **8:** Types of resources; Using resources; Making decisions; Technology affects resource management **9:** Managing time, energy, and money
Part Three: Understanding Children	**14:** Finding a babysitting job; Being a responsible sitter	**15:** Impact of parenthood on resources
Part Four: Your Health and Nutrition		**19:** Making wise food choices
Part Five: Working in the Kitchen		**23:** Kitchen utensils; Cookware and bakeware; Small appliances **24:** Organizing equipment and supplies; Time-saving appliances; Convenience food products; Time-work schedules
Part Six: The Clothes You Wear		**34:** Evaluating a wardrobe inventory; Developing a clothes-buying plan **36:** Sewing equipment; Notions **37:** Planning a sewing project; Selecting a pattern
Part Seven: The Place You Call Home		**40:** Choosing a home **41:** Planning room changes **42:** Making a cleaning schedule; Organizing cleaning supplies; Reducing waste products; Conserving energy
Part Eight: Reaching New Heights	**43:** Being a good leader; Opportunities for leadership; Participating in business meetings; Being a citizen **44:** Qualities of a good employee; Employment skills; Finding a job **45:** Training and education for a career; Careers of the future; Making a career plan **46:** Family and consumer sciences careers; Entrepreneurship **47:** Reasons people work; Work ethic; Effects of personal life on work; Demands of work on families; Flextime; Job sharing; Telecommuting; Balancing family and work demands	**44:** Reading and math skills; Organizational skills;Deciding whether to take a job **45:** Choosing a career; making a career plan **47:** Delegating tasks and making schedules; Setting priorities; technology in the home

(Continued)

	Health and Safety	Parenting and Child Development
Part One: Learning About Yourself	**3:** Stress management; violence	
Part Two: Managing Your Life		
Part Three: Understanding Children	**13:** Safety of children; Health of children; Children with special needs **15:** Child abuse and neglect	**10:** How children grow and develop; Development of infants **11:** Development of toddlers **12:** Development of preschoolers **15:** Responsibilities of parenting; Parenting skills
Part Four: Your Health and Nutrition	**16:** The wellness revolution; Health risks; Treating health problems **17:** Health habits that promote good looks; Good grooming habits **20:** Factors affecting weight; Dieting dangers	
Part Five: Working in the Kitchen		
Part Six: The Clothes You Wear	**31:** Cleaning and storing clothes; Repairing and altering clothes	
Part Seven: The Place You Call Home	**40:** Protection and safety	
Part Eight: Reaching New Heights	**44:** Having good grooming habits	**47:** Concerns of working parents; Balancing work and family demands

(Continued)

	Clothing Selection and Care	Foods and Nutrition
Part One: **Learning About** **Yourself**		
Part Two: **Managing** **Your Life**		
Part Three: **Understanding** **Children**	**10:** Clothing infants **11:** Clothing toddlers **12:** Clothing preschoolers	**10:** Feeding infants **11:** Feeding toddlers **12:** Feeding preschoolers
Part Four: Your **Health and** **Nutrition**		**18:** Foods for good health; Understanding nutri- ents; Recommended Dietary Allowances **19:** Factors that influence food choices; Food Guide Pyramid; Planning meals **20:** Teenage dieting
Part Five: **Working in** **the Kitchen**		**21:** Nutrition information labels **25:** Reading and working with recipes; Measuring ingredients **26:** Storing and preparing fruits and vegetables **27:** Storing and preparing starches, cereals, and breads **28:** Storing and preparing dairy products **29:** Storing and preparing protein foods **30:** Preparing cakes, cookies, and pies **31:** Food customs of different cultures
Part Six: **The Clothes** **You Wear**	**33:** Elements and principles of design **34:** Clothing fashions; Wardrobe planning **35:** Fibers, yarns, and fabrics **36:** Preparing a pattern and fabric **38:** Machine sewing; Finishing sewing projects **39:** Cleaning and storing clothes; Repairing and altering clothes	
Part Seven: **The Place** **You Call Home**		
Part Eight: **Reaching** **New Heights**		

(Continued)

	Housing and Interior	Consumerism
Part One: **Learning About** **Yourself**		
Part Two: **Managing** **Your Life**		**9:** Consumer information; Consumer rights and responsibilities
Part Three: **Understanding** **Children**		**10:** Selecting toys for infants **11:** Selecting toys for toddlers **12:** Selecting toys for preschoolers
Part Four: Your **Health and** **Nutrition**		
Part Five: **Working in** **the Kitchen**	**23:** Large appliances **24:** Organizing kitchen space	**21:** Grocery shopping guidelines; Comparing prices; Reading labels **26:** Buying fruits and vegetables **27:** Buying cereal products **28:** Buying dairy products **29:** Buying protein foods **32:** Eating out
Part Six: **The Clothes** **You Wear**		**34:** Shopping for clothes; Buying accessories
Part Seven: **The Place** **You Call Home**	**40:** Types of homes **41:** Room design; Making a floor plan; Traffic patterns; Dividing a room **42:** Cleaning the home	**40:** Buying or renting a home **41:** Buying furniture **42:** Selecting cleaning agents and equipment
Part Eight: **Reaching** **New Heights**		

Basic Skills Chart

The chart below has been designed to identify those activities in the *Building Life Skills* text, the *Student Activity Guide*, and the *Teacher's Resource Guide/Binder* that specifically encourage the development of basic skills. The following abbreviations are used in the chart:

Apply It . . . End of the chapter activities in the text

SAG . . . Activities in the *Student Activity Guide* (designated by letters)

TRG . . . Student learning experiences described in the *Teacher's Resource Guide/Binder* (referred to by number)

Activities listed as "Verbal" include the following types: discussion, role-playing, conducting interviews, oral reports, and debates.

Activities listed as "Reading" may involve actual reading in and out of the classroom. However, many of these activities are designed to improve reading comprehension of the concepts presented in each chapter. Some are designed to improve understanding of vocabulary terms.

Activities that involve writing are listed under "Writing." The list includes activities that allow students to practice composition skills, such as letter writing, informative writing, and creative writing.

The "Math/Science" list includes activities that require students to use computation skills in solving typical problems they may encounter in their everyday living. Any activities related to the sciences are also listed.

The final category, "Analytical," lists those activities that involve the higher order thinking skills of analysis, synthesis, and evaluation. Activities that involve decision making, problem solving, and critical thinking are included in this section.

	VERBAL	READING	WRITING	MATH/SCIENCE	ANALYTICAL
Chapter 1	Apply It: 2 TRG: 2,3,7,8, 16,18,20,21	SAG: E TRG: 1,13,14	Apply It: 1 SAG: B TRG: 10,15,19		SAG: A,C,D TRG: 4,9,12
Chapter 2	Apply It: 2 TRG: 1,2,4,6,7, 13,14,15	SAG: D TRG: 8	Apply It: 1,2 SAG: C TRG: 9,12		SAG: A,B TRG: 3
Chapter 3	Apply It: 1 SAG: B TRG: 1,4,8,12, 19	TRG: 3,15	TRG: 5,6,10,14, 16,17,18		Apply It: 2 SAG: A,C TRG: 2,9,11
Chapter 4	Apply It: 1,2 TRG: 1,2,4,5,9, 10,13,15,19,23	SAG: B TRG:11,17	Apply It: 1 TRG:16,24		SAG: A TFG: 3,6,7,14, 20,21,22
Chapter 5	Apply It: 2 TRG: 1,7,9,12, 16,17,18	TRG: 5,12	TRG: 3,10,19		Apply It: 1 SAG: A,B,D TRG: 6

(Continued)

	VERBAL	READING	WRITING	MATH/SCIENCE	ANALYTICAL
Chapter 6	Apply It: 1,2 TRG: 1,3,4,9,11, 12,14,15		SAG: A,C TRG: 5,8,17		SAG: B TRG: 6,7,10
Chapter 7	TRG:1,2,9,11,13, 19	SAG: B TRG:7,12,16	SAG: A TRG: 18		Apply It: 1,2 TRG: 6,10,17,22
Chapter 8	Apply It: 2 TRG: 2,5,9,17, 19,21,22,24	SAG: A TRG: 3,26	Apply It: 3 TRG: 6,13	TRG: 7	SAG: B TRG: 11,15,16, 18,20
Chapter 9	Apply It: 2 TRG: 6,11,13,16, 17,18	SAG: C TRG: 3,12	SAG: D TRG: 4,7,19	SAG: B TRG: 10	Apply It: 1 SAG: A TRG: 3,9,14,15
Chapter 10	Apply It: 1,2 TRG: 2,7,9,12, 17,20,21	SAG: A	TRG: 10,11		SAG: B,C TRG: 3,12,19
Chapter 11	Apply It: 1 TRG: 3,4,6,8,9, 10,11,12,14,18	SAG: A TRG: 19	TRG: 6,7,17		SAG: B,C TRG: 9,18,21
Chapter 12	Apply It: 1 TRG: 2,3,4,6,11, 13, 14,15	SAG: A TRG: 12	TRG: 8,12,17		Apply It: 2 SAG: B,C TRG: 7,18
Chapter 13	SAG: B TRG: 2,4,12,16, 17,19	TRG: 18	Apply It: 1 TRG: 5,12	TRG: 13	SAG: A TRG: 1,8
Chapter 14	Apply It: 2 TRG: 1,2,3,4,8, 13,15,17		Apply It: 1 SAG: D TRG: 6,12,20,23		SAG: A,B,C TRG: 22
Chapter 15	Apply It: 2 SAG: A TRG: 1,2,3,4,7,8, 9,14,17	TRG: 5,15	TRG: 4,6	TRG: 12	SAG: B
Chapter 16	Apply It: 1 TRG: 8,10,12, 16,18	TRG: 1,2,10	Apply It: 1 SAG: A TRG: 2,3,20,21		SAG: B

(Continued)

	VERBAL	READING	WRITING	MATH/SCIENCE	ANALYTICAL
Chapter 17	Apply It: 2 SAG: B TRG: 1,2,5	TRG:3,12,15	TRG: 7,15,21	TRG: 7,8	Apply It: 1 SAG: A,C
Chapter 18	Apply It: 1 TRG: 3,15	SAG: A,B TRG: 7,11	Apply It: 1 TRG: 2,14	TRG: 6,8,12	TRG: 13
Chapter 19	Apply It: 1 TRG: 1,9,13,15	SAG: B TRG: 5	TRG: 6,13		Apply It: 2 SAG: A,C TRG: 10,12,17, 18
Chapter 20	SAG: B TRG: 1,3,7,11,18	TRG: 2	TRG: 6,15,18	TRG: 8,13,14	Apply It: 2 SAG: A TRG: 9,10,12,14, 16
Chapter 21	Apply It: 1 TRG: 4, 10	SAG: C TRG: 13	TRG: 15	SAG: B TRG: 7,8,9,14	Apply It: 2 SAG: A,D TRG: 3,7
Chapter 22	TRG: 5	TRG: 11	TRG: 17	TRG: 12	SAG: A,B TRG: 14
Chapter 23	Apply It: 2 TRG: 6	SAG: A TRG: 1	TRG: 13	TRG: 3	Apply It: 1 SAG: C TRG: 5,8
Chapter 24	TRG: 1,5,15	TRG: 2,12	TRG: 4,12,13,15	SAG: A,B TRG: 9	Apply It: 2 SAG: A,B TRG: 4,7,8,17
Chapter 25	TRG: 2	Apply It: 2 SAG: B,C TRG: 7,11,13	TRG: 5,14	Apply It: 1 TRG: 6,9,10	SAG: A
Chapter 26		SAG: A,B,C TRG: 17	TRG: 11,15	Apply It: 1 SAG: D TRG: 5,6	SAG: D TRG: 13,15,16
Chapter 27	Apply It: 2	SAG: C,D TRG: 5	TRG: 5,18	SAG: A TRG: 6	Apply It: 2 SAG: B TRG: 3,7,8,11, 13,15

(Continued)

	VERBAL	READING	WRITING	MATH/SCIENCE	ANALYTICAL
Chapter 28	Apply It: 1 TRG: 3,4,13	SAG: B TRG: 4,8,12	Apply It: 1 SAG: A TRG: 3,8,14	TRG: 7,9	Apply It: 2 SAG: C TRG: 6,13,15
Chapter 29	Apply It: 1 TRG: 5	SAG: A,B TRG: 10,11	Apply It: 2 TRG: 1	Apply It: 1 TRG: 6	SAG: C,D TRG: 14
Chapter 30	TRG: 7	SAG: A TRG: 4,11,14	TRG: 19	TRG: 6	Apply It: 2 SAG: B TRG: 5,6,13, 15, 18
Chapter 31	Apply It: 1 TRG: 4,7,11, 12, 15	Apply It: 2 SAG: A,B TRG: 4,6,7,12, 14,16	Apply It: 2 TRG: 3,6,8		TRG: 14,19
Chapter 32	Apply It: 1 TRG: 1,12,14		Apply It: 1,2 TRG: 4,6,7,8, 11, 12	SAG: B TRG: 10,15	SAG: A TRG: 10
Chapter 33	Apply It: 2 TRG: 7	SAG: B,D TRG: 19	TRG: 11		Apply It: 1 SAG: A,C TRG: 10
Chapter 34	TRG: 1,6,9	TRG: 23	TRG: 15,17,27	TRG: 7,10	Apply It: 1 SAG: A,B TRG: 18,26
Chapter 35	TRG: 20,22,24	SAG: A,D TRG: 7,18,19,21	Apply It: 2 TRG: 6		SAG: B,C TRG: 4,9,11,13
Chapter 36	Apply It: 1 TRG: 2,4,5,14,15	SAG: A,C	TRG: 8	SAG: B TRG: 16,20	
Chapter 37	Apply It: 2 TRG: 5,7	SAG: C,D,E,F TRG: 12	TRG: 17	SAG: A TRG: 8	SAG: B TRG: 3,16
Chapter 38		SAG: B,C,D,E TRG: 18	TRG: 2		SAG: A,F TRG: 7,17,19

(Continued)

	VERBAL	READING	WRITING	MATH/SCIENCE	ANALYTICAL
Chapter 39	SAG: B TRG: 3,13		TRG: 7,14	TRG: 9,11	SAG: A TRG: 9,11
Chapter 40	Apply It: 1 SAG: B TRG: 2,5,6,9,11	SAG: A,C TRG: 7	Apply It: 2 SAG: B TRG: 3,12		SAG: D,E TRG: 10,11,13
Chapter 41	TRG:2,5,15,16		Apply It: 2 TRG: 3,6,17,18	TRG: 9	Apply It: 1 SAG: A,B TRG: 4,8,9,12,19
Chapter 42	Apply It: 1 TRG: 1,4,5,10, 15,17,18,20	SAG: A TRG: 8,19	Apply It: 2 TRG: 3,7,12,17, 19		SAG: B,C TRG: 9,11,13
Chapter 43	Apply It: 1,2 TRG: 5,7,15,16, 18,19,20,22	SAG: A TRG: 2,21	TRG: 3,8,10,13, 15,17		SAG: B TRG: 5
Chapter 44	Apply It: 1 SAG: A TRG: 2,3,4,7, 10, 15		SAG: D TRG: 5,13	TRG: 6	Apply It: 2 TRG: 9,11,15
Chapter 45	Apply It: 2 TRG: 1,2,3,4, 14, 18	Apply It: 1 TRG: 7	TRG: 8		SAG: A TRG: 6,10,17,19
Chapter 46	TRG: 2,5,6,11	SAG: A TRG: 12,17	TRG: 14	Apply It: 2	SAG: B
Chapter 47	Apply It: 1,2 TRG: 1,2,4,5,8,11	TRG: 13	TRG: 3	TRG: 1	TRG: 14, 15

Part One

Learning About Yourself

Part goal: Students will learn about personal growth and development and promoting good relationships with their families and friends.

Bulletin Board

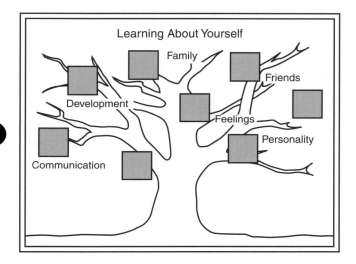

Title: "Learning About Yourself"

Place a tree made of construction paper on the bulletin board. Label various parts of the tree with the following words Personality, Family, Friends, Development, Feelings, and Communication. Have students attach photos or pictures cut from magazines that illustrate each of these words or concepts.

Teaching Materials

Text

Chapters 1–6, pages 15–82

Glossary, pages 530–540

Index, pages 551–560

Student Activity Guide

Chapters 1–6

Teacher's Resource Guide/Binder

Me, reproducible master

Introductory Activities

1. Introduce students to the glossary and index in the text. Demonstrate ways of using them by giving students words to look up and define. A game may be played by dividing the class into teams. The first team to locate all its words and define them wins.

2. *Me,* reproducible master. Have students complete this activity by sketching or mounting pictures of people, places, or things they feel describe them. They may include pictures of family members, friends, hobbies, and places they like to go. In the space provided, have them describe how the pictures relate to them. You may have students use this activity to introduce themselves to the class.

3. Ask students to write their autobiographies. It is not necessary for students to turn these in to you. This is simply an activity to enable students to get to know themselves.

Me

Name _____ **Date** _____ **Period** _____

Sketch or mount pictures of people, places, or things that describe you. You may include pictures of family, friends, hobbies, and places you like to go. In the space provided, describe how these pictures relate to you.

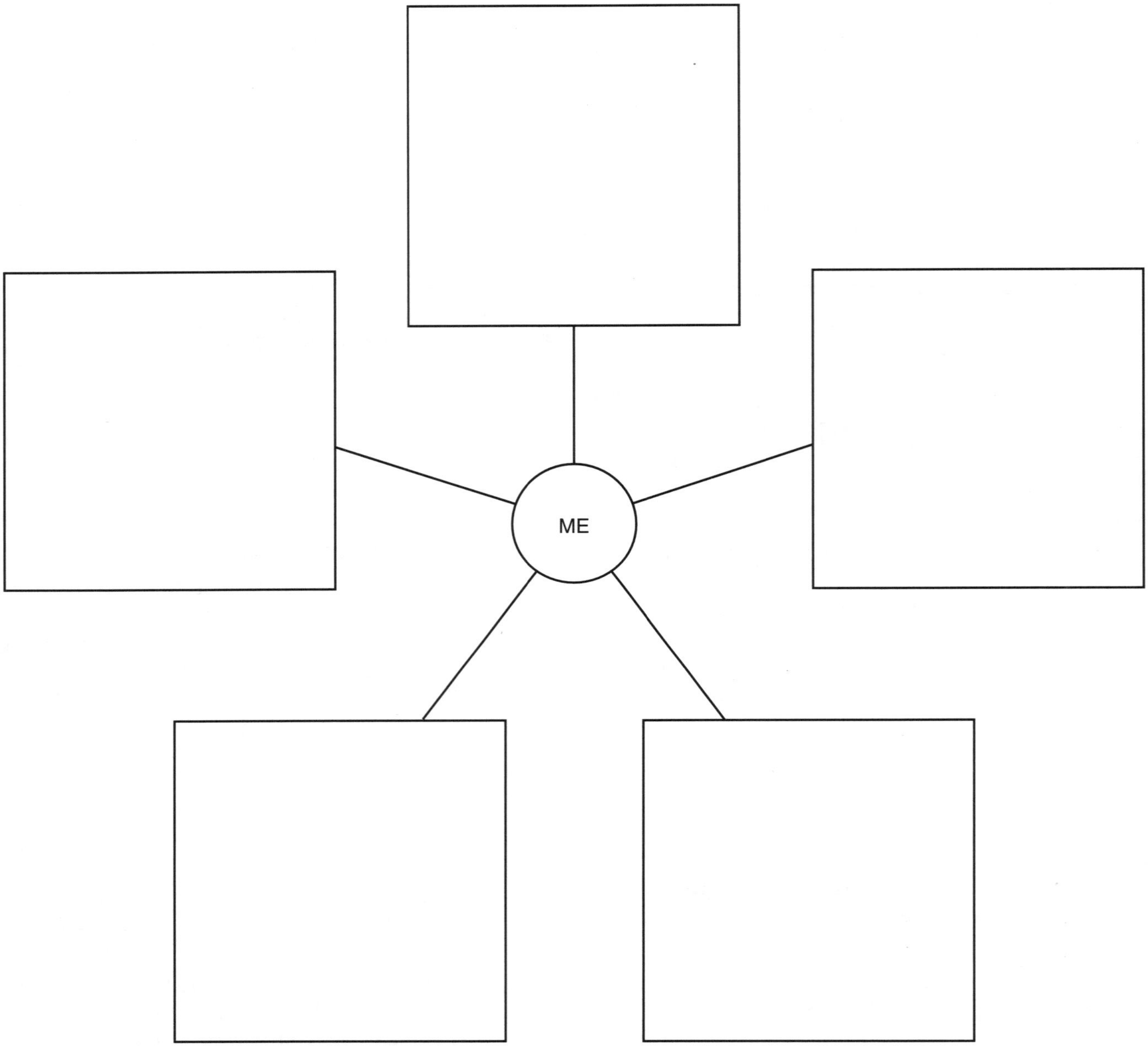

ME

_____

_____

_____

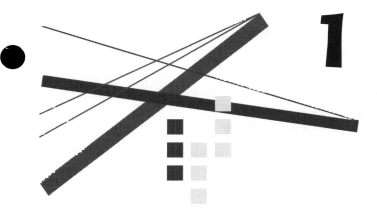

1 Growing and Changing

Objectives

After studying this chapter, students will be able to
■ describe physical, intellectual, emotional, and social changes that take place during adolescence.
■ explain ways to show responsibility as a step toward becoming independent.

Teaching Materials

Text, pages 15–24
  Words to Know
  Review It
  Apply It
  Think More About It
Student Activity Guide
  A. *Changes*
  B. *Handling Emotions*
  C. *Roles*
  D. *Responsibilities*
  E. *Growth and Change*
Teacher's Resource Guide/Binder
  Adolescence: A Time of Change, reproducible master 1-1
  Developmental Tasks of Adolescence, transparency master 1-2
  My Personal Journal, reproducible master 1-3
  Learning About Yourself, color transparency CT-1
  Chapter 1 Quiz

Introductory Activities

1. Have students define the term *adolescence.* Then have them compare their definitions with the one given in the text.
2. Have students complete the following sentence: "I show others I am responsible by . . ." Have them discuss what responsibility means to them.
3. *Learning About Yourself,* color transparency CT-1. Use this transparency to introduce the chapter.

Conduct a "whip around" in which each student makes a spontaneous contribution indicating one of his or her good qualities or assets. (Examples might include honesty, sharing a room with a sibling, and athletic team membership.) Ask a volunteer to write contributions on the transparency mirror as students "look at themselves."

Strategies to Reteach, Reinforce, Enrich, and Extend Text Concepts

■ **Growth and Development**

4. **EX** Divide into groups. Have students brainstorm ways in which people grow and develop in each of the four areas (physical, intellectual, emotional, and social) during adolescence. Ask students to compare their lists during a class discussion.
5. **RF** *Adolescence: A Time of Change,* reproducible master 1-1. Have students, individually or as a class, think about the many changes that occur during adolescence. Use this activity to stimulate student interest in the chapter.
6. **RT** *Developmental Tasks of Adolescence,* transparency master 1-2. Use this master to introduce the developmental tasks to the class.
7. **RT** *Changes,* Activity A, SAG. Various changes are described. Have students identify them as physical, intellectual, emotional, or social changes.
8. **RF** Have students discuss how adolescents are portrayed on television. On which shows do students believe they are portrayed accurately? On which shows do they feel they are misrepresented?
9. **EX** Ask students to describe six problems an immature adolescent might have. Have students suggest solutions for these problems.

10. **ER** *Handling Emotions,* Activity B, SAG. Have students pretend they are advice columnists for a teen magazine. Ask them to respond to letters suggesting ways teens might handle their emotions.

11. **ER** Ask students to list some intellectual abilities they feel they now have that they did not have a year ago.

12. **EX** *Roles,* Activity C, SAG. Have students identify roles they fill. Then have them list three of their roles and describe how they feel they are expected to act in each role. Ask students to list four roles they expect to have in the future.

13. **RT** *Growth and Change,* Activity E, SAG. Ask students to unscramble letters to form words. Then have them use the words to complete statements about growth and change.

14. **ER** Have students research adolescence in other cultures. They may use library resources or interview a foreign exchange student or someone who has grown up in another country. Ask students to present their results in class.

15. **ER** *My Personal Journal,* reproducible master 1-3. Have students make a list of their positive characteristics as well as characteristics they would like to change. Have them explain why they would like to change those characteristics. This activity should be personal. Have students turn the activity in to you without writing their names on it, or have them keep all their journal activities in a three-ring binder.

■ Accepting Responsibility

16. **RT** List some of the responsibilities teens might have on the board in columns labeled "Responsibilities to Myself," "Responsibilities at Home," and "Responsibilities at School." Ask students to add additional responsibilities. Discuss how teens can accept these responsibilities.

17. **RF** *Responsibilities,* Activity D, SAG. Ask students to complete a checklist about responsibilities. Then ask them how accepting responsibilities can help them achieve independence.

18. **EX** Have students role-play situations in which adolescents demonstrate the acceptance of responsibility for their actions. Also have them role-play situations in which adolescents do not act responsibly. Have the rest of the class determine which situations were handled responsibly and which were not.

■ Becoming Independent

19. **ER** Have students write a "Declaration of Independence" for themselves. In the declaration, ask them to describe the types of independence they want along with the responsibilities that will go along with them.

20. **ER** Have students survey three teens and three adults about what independence means to them. Ask students to share their findings in class.

21. **RF** Have students distinguish between independence and dependence by looking the words up in the dictionary and discussing them in class.

Answer Key

■ Text

Review It, page 24
1. adolescence
2. C
3. Physical changes occur as the body matures, intellectual changes occur as you learn more about the world around you, emotional changes affect how you feel about situations and how you express those feelings, social changes occur as you meet more people and learn how to get along with them.
4. (List five:) All teens: develop an adult figure or physique, grow rapidly, develop larger muscles, gain improved ability to use muscles (better eye-hand coordination), become able to be parents; Guys: necks get thicker, shoulders broaden, facial hair appears, voices deepen; Girls: hips widen, breasts enlarge
5. selecting and preparing for a career
6. (Give one example of each.) positive—love, affection, joy; negative—anger, jealousy, envy, fear (Students may justify other responses.)
7. because teens are no longer children, yet adults may not yet treat them as equals
8. true
9. (Give one example.) attend regularly, arrive on time, complete assignments, participate in class, bring necessary supplies, obey rules (Students may justify other responses.)
10. (List three:) responsible for his or her actions, provide for his or her own needs and wants, in control of his or her own life, have his or her own identity, prepare for a career, use socially acceptable behavior (Students may justify other responses.)

■ Student Activity Guide

Changes, Activity A

1. E	4. S	7. E	10. S
2. P	5. P	8. I	11. E
3. I	6. S	9. P	12. I

Growth and Change, Activity E

1. adolescence	8. hormones
2. developmental tasks	9. emotions
3. physical changes	10. peers
4. intellectual changes	11. role
5. emotional changes	12. responsibilities
6. social changes	13. independence
7. growth spurts	

■ Teacher's Resource Guide/Binder

Chapter 1 Quiz

1.	T	10.	T
2.	T	11.	T
3.	F	12.	F
4.	T	13.	F
5.	T	14.	B
6.	F	15.	A
7.	T	16.	C
8.	T	17.	E
9.	F	18.	D

19. (Student response.)
20. Becoming independent involves forming your own identity. It means becoming responsible for your own decisions and developing socially acceptable behavior.

Adolescence: A Time of Change

Name _____ **Date** _____ **Period** _____

During adolescence, you will experience four major types of changes as you grow and develop. These changes are listed in the left-hand column below. Describe each change and give examples of each.

Changes	Description	Examples
Physical		
Intellectual		
Emotional		
Social		

Developmental Tasks of Adolescence

Learn to accept changes in body

Select and prepare for a career

Achieve emotional independence

Learn to get along with peers

Acquire a set of standards that guide your behavior

Learn what behavior will be expected in adult roles

Accept responsibility

Become independent of adults

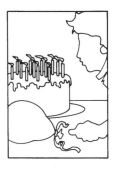

My Personal Journal

Think of some characteristics that describe you. Which of your characteristics are positive? Which ones might you like to change? Why would you like to change these characteristics?

_____

_____

_____

_____

_____

_____

_____

_____

_____

_____

_____

_____

_____

_____

_____

_____

_____

_____

_____

_____

_____

_____

_____

_____

_____

Growing and Changing

Name _____

Date _____ Period _____ Score _____

CHAPTER 1 QUIZ

☐ True/False: Circle *T* if the statement is true or *F* if the statement is false.

T F 1. Adolescence usually lasts from about age 11 to age 17.

T F 2. The ability to reason and solve problems generally develops between the ages of 13 and 15.

T F 3. During adolescence, your emotions may become less intense than they've ever been before.

T F 4. During adolescence, interest in members of the opposite sex takes on new importance.

T F 5. Everyone grows and develops at an individual rate.

T F 6. Most adolescents do not want anything to do with their peers.

T F 7. Talking about your feelings is a good way of dealing with negative emotions.

T F 8. Being responsible means you can be trusted to carry through a duty or a job.

T F 9. Failing to fulfill some of your school responsibilities does not matter much.

T F 10. People who have achieved independence are those who are responsible for their own actions.

T F 11. One of the goals of adolescence is to start becoming independent of adults.

T F 12. Independence is achieved all at once.

T F 13. Becoming independent gives you less freedom.

☐ Matching: Match the following terms with their definitions.

_____ 14. Certain skills and behavior patterns that normally develop.

_____ 15. These occur as your body grows and matures.

_____ 16. These take place as you learn more about the world around you.

_____ 17. These affect how you feel about situations and how you express those feelings.

_____ 18. These occur as you meet more people and learn how to get along with them.

A. physical changes
B. developmental tasks
C. intellectual changes
D. social changes
E. emotional changes

☐ Essay Questions: Provide the answers you feel best show your understanding of the subject matter.

19. Give three examples of ways you can show you are becoming a responsible person.

20. What does becoming independent involve?

Reproducible Quiz

2 Your Personality

Objectives

After studying this chapter, students will be able to
- explain how heredity and environment affect personality development.
- define *self-concept*.
- list suggestions for improving self-concept.

Teaching Materials

Text, pages 25–34
  Words to Know
  Review It
  Apply It
  Think More About It
Student Activity Guide
  A. *Personality Traits*
  B. *Heredity and Environment*
  C. *Your Self-Concept*
  D. *Personality*
Teacher's Resource Guide/Binder
  Birth Order, transparency master 2-1
  My Personal Journal, reproducible master 2-2
  Think Positively—Stay Happy! transparency master 2-3
  Developing a Shining Personality, color transparency CT-2
  Chapter 2 Quiz

Introductory Activities

1. Ask students what factors they think affect their personalities.
2. *Developing a Shining Personality,* color transparency CT-2. Use this transparency as the basis for discussion noting how each of the identified "rays" contributes to a shining personality. Have students add their own ideas to fill in the blank rays.

Strategies to Reteach, Reinforce, Enrich, and Extend Text Concepts

■ How Personality Develops

3. **ER** *Personality Traits,* Activity A, SAG. Have students check all the personality traits on the illustration they think describe them. Then have them answer questions about personality traits they consider to be desirable and list personality traits they would like to change or overcome. They are also asked whether their best friend would check the same traits they checked.
4. **EX** In small groups or as a class, ask students to write the name of a famous person on a card and turn it face down. Ask each student to describe the personality traits of this person. The rest of the class will try to guess who the person is. Discuss how personality traits make a person unique. Have students identify factors that shape their personalities.
5. **RF** *Heredity and Environment,* Activity B, SAG. Students are asked to list their inherited traits and their acquired traits. They are then asked to answer questions related to these lists.
6. **ER** Have students interview employers about personality traits they look for as they hire employees. Ask them to give examples of how personality can affect job success.
7. **ER** *Birth Order,* transparency master 2-1. Use this master to introduce a discussion on how birth order affects personality development. Group students into four groups according to their birth order in their families: first, middle, youngest, and only. Have students discuss how their birth order relates to their personality development. Ask if they agree

with the characteristics listed on the transparency. Then have each group present its ideas to the class.

8. **RF** *Personality*, Activity D, SAG. Students are asked to complete a word puzzle using words that relate to personality.

■ Self -Concept

9. **EX** *Your Self-Concept*, Activity C, SAG. Students are asked to write a letter to themselves. In the letter, students should write about their strengths, weaknesses and goals.

10. **RF** Ask students to draw self-portraits. If they wish, they may share them with the class or class members may want to guess which person created each portrait.

11. **RT** Have students draw or bring to class cartoons illustrating people with poor self-concepts and people with good self-concepts. Display them on the bulletin board.

12. **ER** *My Private Journal,* reproducible master 2-2. Have students write a personal letter to help build a friend's self-concept. They should list the friend's good qualities and reasons they like being friends with this person.

■ Improving Self-Concept

13. **RF** Have students give "compliment notes" to each other on which they have written something nice about the other person. (For instance, "You look great today" or "I thought your report was really interesting"). Arrange it so each student in the class gets at least one note. Then have students discuss how receiving the notes affected their self-concepts.

14. **EX** Have students role-play situations in which they react as a pessimist would and then as an optimist would.

15. **RT** *Think Positively—Stay Happy!* transparency master 2-3. Use this activity as a basis for a discussion about developing a positive attitude. Present each situation. Ask students to discuss how a pessimist might view the situation compared to how an optimist might view the same situation.

Answer Key

■ Text

Review It, page 34

1. D
2. inherited
3. false
4. (List five:) family, friends, classmates, teachers, home, school, neighborhood, community (Students may justify other responses.)

5. Select one area for improvement. Write down a specific plan of what you will do to change the trait. Set a realistic goal. Plan a reward for yourself. Put your plan into action.

6. self-concept

7. (List three:) feel good about themselves; accept the things about themselves they can't change, are confident they can change things about themselves that need to be changed, have a happy outlook on life, don't let things get them down, don't worry about what other people say, can help other people have positive self-concepts (Students may justify other responses.)

8. He or she may compare his or her weaknesses with another person's strengths. This is not a fair comparison.

9. true

10. Optimists have positive attitudes. They look on the bright side of situations and have a "can-do" approach to problems. Pessimists have negative attitudes. They find something wrong with every situation and have a "can't-do" approach to problems.

■ Student Activity Guide

Personality, Activity D

1							O	P	T	I	M	I	S	T		
2						I	N	H	E	R	I	T	E	D		
3			A	C	Q	U	I	R	E	D						
4				P	E	S	S	I	M	I	S	T				
5		E	N	V	I	R	O	N	M	E	N	T				
6					C	O	N	C	E	P	T					
7				T	R	A	I	T	S							
8	P	E	R	S	O	N	A	L	I	T	Y					
9			C	O	N	F	I	D	E	N	C	E				
10				A	T	T	I	T	U	D	E	S				
11	H	E	R	E	D	I	T	Y								

■ Teacher's Resource Guide/Binder

Chapter 2 Quiz

1. T	5. F	9. F	13. A
2. F	6. T	10. F	
3. T	7. T	11. C	
4. F	8. T	12. B	

14. Inherited traits are traits you received from your parents and ancestors when you were born. Acquired traits develop as a result of your environment. (Examples are student response.)

15. Take a look at his or her good qualities. Try not to compare himself or herself with others. Learn to give and accept compliments. Develop new interests. Develop a positive attitude. Learn to smile and laugh.

Birth Order

The oldest child

- ■ has leadership ability and is very responsible

- ■ is independent and self-confident

The middle child

- ■ often puts extra effort into special skills such as sports or the arts

- ■ is often the peacemaker

The youngest child

- ■ is relaxed and secure

- ■ is cheerful and outgoing

The only child

- ■ is an achiever and a perfectionist

- ■ is unselfish and has a good self-concept

My Personal Journal

Write a letter to a friend that will help build his or her self-concept. Tell the friend how you feel about him or her. What are your friend's best qualities? Why do you like being that person's friend? How do others view your friend?

_____

_____

_____

_____

_____

_____

_____

_____

_____

_____

_____

_____

_____

_____

_____

_____

_____

_____

_____

_____

_____

_____

_____

_____

Think Positively—Stay Happy!

Situation: A final exam is approaching.

 Pessimist: "I'm sure I'll blow it, even though I've studied hard."

 Optimist: "I can hardly wait to take this exam. With all my studying, I'll get an A+."

Situation: You are invited to a party where you do not know anyone.

Pessimist: "Being a total stranger, no one will want to talk to me."

 Optimist: "Here's my chance to meet new people and make new friends."

Situation: You have to give a speech.

Pessimist: "I'll forget what I have planned to say. Nobody will listen anyway."

 Optimist: "I know just what I'm going to say so I'll relax and give an interesting speech."

Situation: You have been selected to play first base in softball.

Pessimist: "I bet I'll miss every ball thrown to me. I'll never put anyone out."

Optimist: "I can hardly wait to show everyone what a good player I am."

Your Personality

Name _____

Date _____ **Period** _____ **Score** _____

CHAPTER 2 QUIZ

☐ True/False: Circle *T* if the statement is true or *F* if the statement is false.

T F 1. There is no other person in the world exactly like you.

T F 2. Heredity refers to those traits you receive from your friends.

T F 3. Your acquired traits develop as a result of your environment.

T F 4. When thinking about changing your personality, it is best to try to change everything about yourself at once.

T F 5. People with positive self-concepts worry about their failures and dwell on their past mistakes.

T F 6. Self-confidence is the courage to deal with new things and people in a positive way.

T F 7. Giving people compliments builds their self-concepts.

T F 8. You can improve your self-concept by getting involved in activities you do well.

T F 9. You were born with your attitudes.

T F 10. People who have negative attitudes are called optimists.

☐ Multiple Choice: Choose the best answer and write the corresponding letter in the blank.

_____ 11. The traits you received from your parents and ancestors when you were born are your _____.

    A. positive traits
    B. acquired traits
    C. inherited traits
    D. negative traits

_____ 12. The most important environmental force in shaping your personality is your _____.

    A. school
    B. family
    C. peer group
    D. community

_____ 13. To help improve your self-concept, you can _____.

    A. take a look at your good qualities
    B. compare yourself with others
    C. shy away from new interests
    D. be a pessimist

☐ Essay Questions: Provide the answers you feel best show your understanding of the subject matter.

14. Explain the difference between inherited traits and acquired traits and give two examples of each.

15. List six ways a person can improve his or her self-concept.

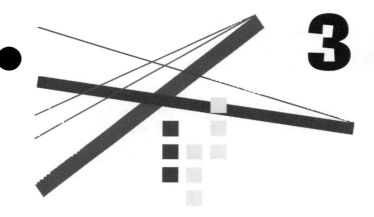

3 Challenges You Face

Objectives

After studying this chapter, students will be able to
■ explain how feelings develop and change.
■ discuss how to give and receive criticism.
■ describe how to manage the stress of everyday living.
■ analyze changes that crisis events can create and list resources for handling crises.

Teaching Materials

Text, pages 35–45
Words to Know
Review It
Apply It
Think More About It
Student Activity Guide
A. *Criticism*
B. *Handling Stress*
C. *Sources of Help*
Teacher's Resource Guide/Binder
Offering Constructive Criticism, reproducible master 3-1
My Personal Journal, reproducible master 3-2
Coping with Crisis, transparency master 3-3
Chapter 3 Quiz

Introductory Activities

1. Have students complete the following statement using a variety of feelings such as happy, sad, angry, proud, bored, etc.: "When I feel _____, I . . ."
2. Ask students to think of a crisis they have faced. How did they handle the crisis? How did it make them feel?

Strategies to Reteach, Reinforce, Enrich, and Extend Text Concepts

■ Criticism

3. **RF** *Criticism,* Activity A, SAG. Have students define *destructive criticism* and *constructive criticism.* Then have them read about various situations and determine what type of criticism was given and how they would handle it.
4. **RT** In a class discussion, have students relate instances when they received destructive criticism and how it made them feel. Then have them relate instances of when they received constructive criticism and how it helped them improve.
5. **RF** *Offering Constructive Criticism,* reproducible master 3-1. Have students read each example of destructive criticism and rewrite it as constructive criticism.
6. **ER** *My Personal Journal,* reproducible master 3-2. Have students write about a time they hurt someone's feelings with destructive criticism.
7. **ER** Have students list a variety of feelings on the chalkboard. Then have each student select one and pantomime it in front of the class. Let the other students try to guess the feeling.
8. **ER** Have students interview three adults and three students. Ask them to survey these people on their definitions of the following words: love, jealousy, anger, happiness, disappointment, and joy. Have students record the responses and compare them.
9. **RT** Have students keep track of their feelings for a day. Have them describe the various feelings they experienced during the day. Then ask them to describe the good feelings and how they dealt with the bad feelings.

10. **RF** Ask students to write a letter to an imaginary friend. In the letter, ask them to write about how they feel.

■ Stress

11. **RT** *Handling Stress*, Activity B, SAG. Have students define *stress*. Then have them describe a stressful situation and how they would handle it. Discuss the various types of stress in class.
12. **RT** Discuss the statement "Adolescence is a period of storm and stress."
13. **ER** Ask a counselor or a doctor to speak to the class about effective techniques for managing stress. Have students prepare a list of questions in advance.
14. **EX** Have students write a "Dear Ann" letter describing a problem of an imaginary teen. Ask them to exchange their letters with a classmate and respond to the letters they receive. Discuss the letters and responses in class.

■ Crises

15. **ER** *Sources of Help*, Activity C, SAG. Students are asked to rank a list of crises from most stressful to least stressful. They are then asked to list a source or sources of help in dealing with each crisis. Parents, a guidance counselor, a teacher, a family doctor, a religious leader, and hotlines (often found in the Yellow Pages of the phone directory) are possible sources of help.
16. **EX** Ask students to write a short story about an imaginary person facing a crisis. Have them suggest ways the person in the story can try to deal with the crisis. Discuss the stories in class.
17. **ER** Using the telephone directory or resources from the library, have students make a pamphlet of the various community agencies and organizations that help teens in crisis. The pamphlet should include a description of the services offered, any cost, phone number, and any other facts. You may want to invite someone from one of the organizations to speak to the class.
18. **ER** Take the class on a field trip to a funeral home. Have each student prepare two or more questions to ask the funeral director. Ask students to write a report about their experience.
19. **RT** *Coping with Crisis*, transparency master 3-3. Use this transparency master to discuss feelings that might result during various crises. Then discuss and list ways of coping with these crises.

Answer Key

■ Text

Review It, page 45
1. Someone might give destructive criticism because of jealousy or resentment.

2. (Student response.)
3. (Name four:) Your heart may beat faster. You may breathe faster and perspire more. Your muscles may tense. Your mouth may feel dry. Your stomach may feel like it's in knots.
4. Learn to identify the events in your life that cause stress. Some stress can be prevented by planning. Keep your body healthy and fit.
5. (List three:) Keep a positive attitude. Add to the family income by doing odd jobs. Walk or ride their bikes whenever possible so their parents wouldn't have to use the family car. They could use their cooking skills instead of buying prepared foods. Fun evenings could be planned at home instead of going to the movies.
6. false
7. false
8. sadness, loss, anger, guilt (Students may justify other responses.)
9. true
10. true

■ Student Activity Guide

Criticism, Activity A
Destructive criticism: Criticism that uses negative comments to tear a person down.
Constructive criticism: Criticism that tells where or how a person could improve.
1. destructive criticism
2. constructive criticism
3. destructive criticism
4. constructive criticism
5. constructive criticism
(Descriptions are student response.)
Handling Stress, Activity B
Stress: The mental or physical tension you feel when faced with change.

■ Teacher's Resource Guide/Binder

Chapter 3 Quiz

1.	F	8.	F
2.	T	9.	T
3.	T	10.	T
4.	F	11.	D
5.	T	12.	D
6.	T	13.	B
7.	T		

14. anxiety, fear, conflict, worry (Students may justify other responses.)
15. Don't ignore the person's remarks. Let him or her know you care. Suggest the person talk with his or her parents or other concerned adults. Many communities have suicide hotline numbers the person can call for counseling.

Offering Constructive Criticism

Name _____ **Date** _____ **Period** _____

Read each example of destructive criticism and rewrite it as constructive criticism.

You never catch the ball! Why do we even let you play?

_____

_____

That outfit is ugly! Those colors don't match!

_____

_____

You got the worst grade in the class! Don't you ever study?

_____

_____

What did you do to your hair?

_____

_____

You're so moody I don't even want to hang around with you.

_____

_____

I can't believe you actually listen to that kind of music.

_____

_____

You're so unorganized, you'll never get to be team leader!

_____

_____

That was a really stupid decision.

_____

_____

My Personal Journal

Think of a time when you used destructive criticism and hurt someone's feelings. What did you say? How did it make that person feel? How did it make you feel? What could you have said differently?

_____

_____

_____

_____

_____

_____

_____

_____

_____

_____

_____

_____

_____

_____

_____

_____

_____

_____

_____

_____

_____

Coping with Crisis

Crisis	Feelings	Ways to Cope
Failure in school		
Moving		
Loss of a job		
Suicide of a friend		
Breaking up with a dating partner		
Death of a family member		
Divorce of parents		
Others:		

Challenges You Face

Name _____

Date _____ Period _____ Score _____

CHAPTER 3 QUIZ

☐ True/False: Circle *T* if the statement is true or *F* if the statement is false.

T   F   1. Criticism that uses negative comments to tear a person down is called constructive criticism.

T   F   2. Learning to handle criticism can help you manage hurt feelings and benefit from the criticism.

T   F   3. Stress is the mental or physical tension you feel when you are faced with change.

T   F   4. Everyone reacts to stress in the same way.

T   F   5. To avoid too much stress, it is helpful to know your limits.

T   F   6. When family members solve a problem together, a new closeness can develop.

T   F   7. When a couple decide to divorce, all family members are affected.

T   F   8. When trying to ease the pain of a loved one's death, it's not a good idea to cry or talk about the deceased person.

T   F   9. Among young people, suicide is the third leading cause of death.

T   F   10. No matter how difficult a teen's problems are, there is a solution.

☐ Multiple Choice: Choose the best answer and write the corresponding letter in the blank.

_____ 11. Destructive criticism may be motivated by _____.

A. a desire to help another person
B. jealousy
C. resentment
D. Both B and C.

_____ 12. Which of the following can be a good way of handling stress?

A. Talking to someone about your problems.
B. Working off your tension through exercise.
C. Learning to relax.
D. All of the above.

_____ 13. When faced with a serious personal crisis, the best way to solve the problem is to _____.

A. run away
B. talk to your parents or other adults, such as a teacher, counselor, family doctor, or religious leader
C. turn to drugs or alcohol
D. become involved with a dating partner

☐ Essay Questions: Provide the answers you feel best show your understanding of the subject matter.

14. List four signs of stress.

15. What is the best thing to do if someone you know talks about committing suicide?

Reproducible Quiz

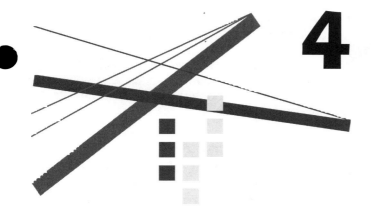

4 Communicating with Others

Objectives

After studying this chapter, students will be able to
- discuss the various forms of verbal and nonverbal communication.
- describe how to avoid communication barriers.
- identify techniques for improving communication skills.
- explain how communication skills can be used to help resolve conflicts.

Teaching Materials

Text, pages 46–57
  Words to Know
  Review It
  Apply It
  Think More About It
Student Activity Guide
  A. *Communication Skills*
  B. *Communication Terms*
Teacher's Resource Guide/Binder
  Emphasis Can Change the Meaning, transparency master 4-1
  Nonverbal Communication, reproducible master 4-2
  My Personal Journal, reproducible master 4-3
  Sex Stereotyping, color transparency CT-4
  Chapter 4 Quiz

Introductory Activities

1. *Emphasis Can Change the Meaning,* transparency master 4-1. Have students read each of the sentences aloud, emphasizing the underlined words. Discuss how the message varies.
2. Come into the classroom and communicate a message using only body language. Use this as a basis for discussion about nonverbal communication.

Strategies to Reteach, Reinforce, Enrich, and Extend Text Concepts

■ Verbal Communication

3. **EX** Have students listen to a television or radio announcer and evaluate that person's ability to communicate.
4. **RF** Have students discuss the importance of speaking clearly on the telephone. Ask them to prepare a list of do's and don'ts when talking on the telephone.
5. **EX** Have students pretend a group is touring their school. Have students prepare a short speech about the school. Allow a set time for each speech. Ask students to evaluate each speech in terms of the speaker's verbal communication skills. Have students list good points about the speeches and suggestions for improvement. Have students discuss the importance of each of the following: writing legibly, using correct English, and keeping it simple.

■ Nonverbal Communication

6. **RF** Ask four students to sit facing the class. Let the class study the body language of each student. Who looks uncomfortable? Who appears relaxed? Discuss types of body language that are being demonstrated.
7. **RF** *Nonverbal Communication,* reproducible master 4-2. Have students read each example and explain the impression each person gives.
8. **ER** Have students plan a skit in which they show many emotions through body language. Have other class members guess which emotions are being expressed.

9. **RF** Have students watch a television program with the sound turned off. Ask them to observe the nonverbal communication and discuss what they think the storyline of the program was.

■ Barriers to Good Communication

10. **EX** Role-play situations where good and poor communication skills altered the outcome of situations. Use examples of situations at school, home, or work.

11. **RT** Ask students to brainstorm about slang terms that are popular. List the terms on the board. Have students define the terms and discuss how use of the terms may create barriers to communication with older people, people from other countries, etc.

12. **ER** *Sex Stereotyping,* color transparency CT-4. Cover the title on the transparency. Have students copy the remainder on a sheet of paper. Ask them to draw stick figures, including the face and hair, illustrating each of the topics. Tabulate the number who drew females and males for each. On the transparency, have a volunteer draw what the majority of the class thought was the appropriate sex for each. Uncover the title and discuss sex stereotyping.

13. **RF** Have students list common stereotypes on the board. Discuss how these stereotypes are damaging to people and how stereotypes can be barriers to communication.

14. **RF** Have students list common prejudices. How do these prejudices affect the communication process? How can this barrier to communication be eliminated?

■ Improving Your Communication Skills

15. **EX** Role-play situations involving communication problems between teens and parents and teens and teachers. Discuss how the problems can be solved by improving communication skills.

16. **RF** *Communication Skills,* Activity A, SAG. Have students read statements about communication. Ask them to indicate whether the people described in the activity are demonstrating good communication skills and to explain why. Then have them think about their own communication skills. Ask them how they think their parents, teachers, and friends would rate their communication skills.

17. **RF** *Communication Terms,* Activity B, SAG. Have students complete a phone puzzle using terms related to communication.

18. **RT** Ask students to list 10 ways they can improve their communication skills.

19. **ER** Read the day's announcements. Have students practice active listening by restating what was said.

20. **EX** Have students analyze the importance of improving their communication skills. How could improving their communication skills help them now and in the future?

■ Resolving Conflicts

21. **ER** Ask students to collect articles about current world and national conflicts. Have students identify the barriers to communication that exist and how they feel these conflicts could be solved through communication.

22. **ER** Have students list various conflicts teens face with parents, friends, and teachers. Then have the students list at least three ways these conflicts could be resolved through effective communication and compromise.

23. **EX** Arrange for a panel of students from a rival school to come to class. Have students list differences between the two schools and their similarities. Have them discuss ways communication could be improved between the two schools.

24. **ER** *My Personal Journal,* reproducible master 4-3. Have students write about a time a barrier in communication caused a conflict with another person. Have them explain how they resolved the conflict.

Answer Key

■ Text

Review It, page 57

1. communication
2. (List four:) Use language that listeners understand, use clear pronunciations, use words with familiar meanings, use the voice to emphasize the message, don't mumble, speak in a voice that is neither too loud nor too soft, avoid speaking too slowly or too quickly.
3. (List three:) use readable handwriting, use correct grammar, use correct spelling, prepare an outline before writing
4. A
5. how well you know the person and the situation you are in
6. not saying what you mean and sending one message with your words and another message with your actions
7. A stereotype is a fixed belief that all members of a group are the same. A prejudice is an opinion that is formed without complete knowledge.
8. true

9. An active listener uses feedback to let the speaker know whether or not the message was received correctly.
10. In a compromise, everyone involved in a conflict has to give in a little bit to find a solution that is fair and agreeable to all.

■ Student Activity Guide

Communication Skills, Activity A
1. bad
2. bad
3. good
4. bad
5. good
6. bad
7. good
8. bad

(Reasons are student response.)

Communication Terms, Activity B
1. communication
2. verbal
3. nonverbal
6. mixed messages
7. stereotype
8. prejudices

4. body language
5. personal space
9. active listening
10. feedback

■ Teacher's Resource Guide/Binder

Chapter 4 Quiz
1. T
2. F
3. T
4. T
5. C
6. N
7. L
8. I
9. B
10. J
11. H
12. M
13. K
14. G
15. A
16. F
17. E
18. D

19. All jobs require some communication skills. Using good communication skills can help you get along with others. Success at a job is more likely to occur if you get along well with your coworkers. (Example is student response.)
20. (Student response.)

Emphasis Can Change the Meaning!

<u>What</u> do you want me to do? (Anger)

What <u>do</u> you want me to do? (Complaining)

What do <u>you</u> want me to do? (Accusation)

What do you <u>want</u> me to do? (What do you really want?)

What do you want <u>me</u> to do? (As opposed to him or her)

What do you want me to <u>do</u>? (Plaintive plea)

Nonverbal Communication

Name _____ **Date** _____ **Period** _____

Read each of the following examples. Then explain what impression each person's appearance gives and why.

Toby sits slumped in his seat.

_____

_____

Ruby wears a bright sweater and clean slacks.

_____

_____

Cary smiles when people ask him questions.

_____

_____

Raul looks people straight in the eye when speaking to them.

_____

_____

Laurie sits by herself at lunch and doesn't talk to anyone.

_____

_____

Erik's hair is uncombed and his fingernails are dirty.

_____

_____

Josie holds her head high when she walks down the hall.

_____

_____

Matthew scowls at everyone he sees.

_____

_____

Ronna's dress is wrinkled.

_____

_____

My Personal Journal

Write about a time a barrier in communication caused a conflict with another person. How was the conflict resolved?

_____

_____

_____

_____

_____

_____

_____

_____

_____

_____

_____

_____

_____

_____

_____

_____

_____

_____

_____

_____

_____

_____

_____

_____

_____

Communicating with Others

Name _____

Date _____ **Period** _____ **Score** _____

CHAPTER 4 QUIZ

☐ True/False: Circle *T* if the statement is true or *F* if the statement is false.

T   F   1. Research shows that people spend 70 percent of each day communicating in some way.

T   F   2. Communication is a one-way process.

T   F   3. All forms of communication can be grouped as being either verbal or nonverbal.

T   F   4. Improving your communication skills can help you resolve conflicts.

☐ Matching: Match the following terms with their definitions.

_____ 5. The process of sending or receiving information.

_____ 6. Involves the use of words to send information.

_____ 7. Words used by a particular group of people that have meanings that are different from the usual meanings.

_____ 8. Includes any means of sending a message that does not use words.

_____ 9. The sending of messages through body movements.

_____ 10. The area around you.

_____ 11. This results when people don't say what they mean or their actions send one message and their words say something else.

_____ 12. A fixed belief that all members of a group are the same.

_____ 13. Opinions that are formed without complete knowledge.

_____ 14. Rules for proper conduct.

_____ 15. A practice that involves the listener in the communication process.

_____ 16. It lets the speaker know whether or not the message was received correctly.

_____ 17. Disagreements or problems in a relationship.

_____ 18. Both sides give up some of what they wanted in order to settle a conflict.

A. active listening
B. body language
C. communication
D. compromise
E. conflicts
F. feedback
G. manners
H. mixed messages
I. nonverbal communication
J. personal space
K. prejudice
L. slang
M. stereotype
N. verbal communication

☐ Essay Questions: Provide answers you feel best show your understanding of the subject matter.

19. Explain how your future success might depend upon your ability to communicate. Give an example.

20. List 10 examples of how you have used communication today.

5 Your Family

Objectives

After studying this chapter, students will be able to
- describe the four main types of families.
- explain functions served by the family and roles and responsibilities filled by family members.
- discuss the stages of the family life cycle and changes that may occur within each stage.
- list techniques that can be used to help improve relationships with family members.

Teaching Materials

Text, pages 58–70
Words to Know
Review It
Apply It
Think More About It
Student Activity Guide
  A. *Families*
  B. *The Family Life Cycle*
  C. *Families Coping with Crisis*
  D. *Family Relationships*
Teacher's Resource Guide/Binder
My Personal Journal, reproducible master 5-1
Types of Families, transparency master 5-2
The Circle of Life, transparency master 5-3
Chapter 5 Quiz

Introductory Activities

1. Initiate a discussion on family by having each student finish the following sentence: "A family is . . ."
2. Have students make a family tree. Have them include parents, grandparents, and siblings.

Strategies to Reteach, Reinforce, Enrich, and Extend Text Concepts

■ Your Cultural Heritage

3. **RF**   Ask family members of various cultural or ethnic groups to describe the traditions they observe, foods they eat, and holidays they celebrate.
4. **ER**   *My Personal Journal,* reproducible master 5-1. Have students think about a family member who has helped shape the traditions of their family. Have them write a thank-you letter to that person to express their gratitude. They should include in their letter some of their family traditions they most enjoy.

■ Types of Families

5. **RT**   *Families*, Activity A, SAG. Ask students to define the term *family*. Then have them identify the various types of families described, and ask them to list the functions served by a family.
6. **ER**   Divide the class into three groups. Ask them to identify the types of families shown in television programs. Have the groups compare their answers. Which types of families are most common? Why?
7. **RF**   *Types of Families,* transparency master 5-2. Define each of the following types of families: A. Nuclear family B. One-parent family C. Blended family D. Extended family. Then have students discuss what advantages and challenges of living in each of the types of families might be.

■ Functions of the Family

8. **ER** Have students create a bulletin board entitled "How the Family Helps." The bulletin board should show various ways the family supports its members.
9. **ER** Have students interview senior citizens about their parents and families. If possible, tape the interviews. Discuss how, in their opinions, the functions of the family have changed.

■ Family Roles and Responsibilities

10. **ER** Have students write a story about an imaginary family. Ask them to include details about the roles and responsibilities of each family member in the story.
11. **ER** Invite elderly members of the community as guest speakers to speak about roles and responsibilities of family members in past generations.

■ The Family Life Cycle

12. **RT** *The Circle of Life*, transparency master 5-3. Use this transparency to introduce a discussion on the family life cycle.
13. **RF** *The Family Life Cycle*, Activity B, SAG. Have students read statements about a family and identify the stages in the family life cycle being described. Then have students describe what usually happens during each stage.
14. **ER** Invite a panel of adults whose families are at various stages of the family life cycle. For instance, you may wish to invite a newly married person, a parent of a baby, a parent of school-age children, a parent with children in college or the military, and a grandparent to class. Ask these people to describe family life at the various stages of the life cycle. What are their concerns? What are their goals?

■ Families Face Change

15. **ER** *Families Coping with Crisis*, Activity C, SAG. Invite a family counselor to speak to the class about how families can cope with the following crises: A. a family member dies B. a family member has a serious illness or disability C. a family member has a substance abuse problem D. a family faces domestic violence E. a family has financial problems.
16. **EX** Have students write and present skits entitled "How the Family Handles (a problem or crisis)." Have the class discuss how the "family" handled its problems or crises. Did the "family" handle each problem of crises effectively?

■ Family Relationships

17. **RF** Have students compile a list of problems typical of teens, such as sharing family possessions, sibling rivalry, coping with increased responsibility, and peer relationships. Discuss effective ways of handling these problems.
18. **EX** Have students debate the topic "The Advantages Versus the Disadvantages of Growing Old."
19. **RF** *Family Relationships*, Activity D, SAG. Have students name ways teens might strengthen relationships between themselves and their parents, siblings, and grandparents. Students are asked to write their responses on a diagram of chain links representing bonds between people.

Answer Key

■ Text

Review It, page 70
1. blood (birth), marriage, adoption
2. A nuclear family is made up of a couple and any children they have or adopt together. A one-parent family is made up of one parent and a child or children. A blended family is formed when a single parent marries. An extended family includes relatives other than parents and their children living together in one home.
3. In the past, families had to grow their own food and make their own clothes and houses. Today, family members work to earn money to buy food, clothing, and shelter.
4. false
5. C
6. (List three. Student response.)
7. social service organization or crisis intervention numbers in the Yellow Pages; Department of Human Services, Social Service, or Public Welfare numbers in the white pages; local police department; religious organizations (Students may justify other responses.)
8. (List two:) accept the change, prepare for the change, support the change
9. Teens are maturing and want to be more independent. Parents may not yet be ready to give their children the freedom they want.
10. sibling rivalry

■ Student Activity Guide

Families, Activity A
  Family: A group of people who are related to each other by blood, marriage, or adoption.
1. nuclear
2. one-parent
3. blended
4. extended or extended nuclear
5. foster

The Family Life Cycle, Activity B
1. beginning
2. expanding
3. developing

4. launching
5. aging
(Descriptions are student response.)

■ Teacher's Resource Guide/Binder

Chapter 5 Quiz

1. T	10. T
2. T	11. T
3. F	12. F
4. T	13. F
5. F	14. D
6. T	15. A
7. F	16. E
8. T	17. B
9. T	18. C

19. beginning stage, expanding stage, developing stage, launching stage, aging stage (Examples are student response.)
20. (List four:) share concerns, show they care, show they are responsible, show they can be trusted (Other appropriate responses may be accepted.)

My Personal Journal

Think of a family member who has had a major role in shaping your family's traditions. Write a thank-you letter to this person. Include some of your family's traditions you particularly enjoy.

_____

_____

_____

_____

_____

_____

_____

_____

_____

_____

_____

_____

_____

_____

_____

_____

_____

_____

_____

_____

_____

_____

_____

_____

_____

Types of Families

Nuclear Family	
Advantages:	Challenges:

One-parent Family	
Advantages:	Challenges:

Blended Family	
Advantages:	Challenges:

Extended Family	
Advantages:	Challenges:

The Circle of Life

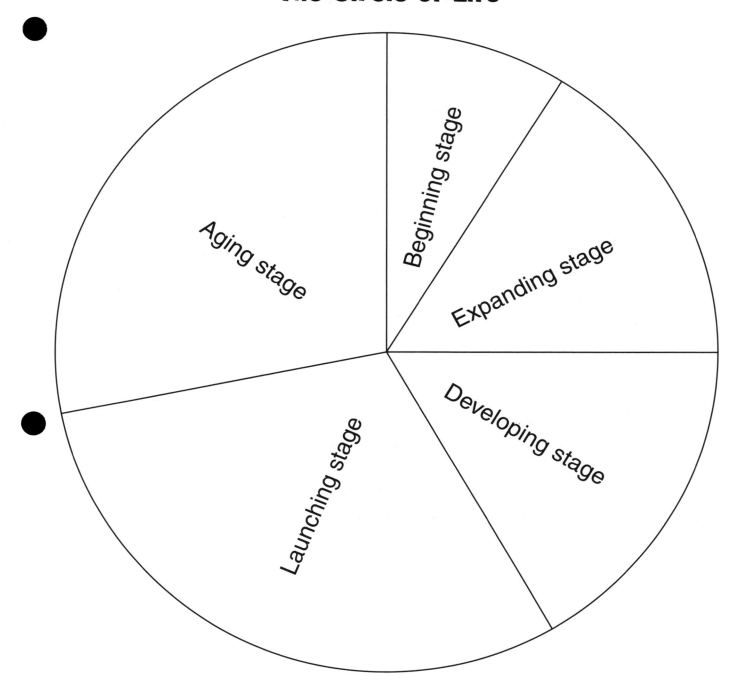

Your Family

Name _____

Date _____ **Period** _____ **Score** _____

CHAPTER 5 QUIZ

☐ True/False: Circle *T* if the statement is true or *F* if the statement is false.

T	F	1.	Ethnic groups help preserve the cultural heritage of a family.
T	F	2.	Family members may be related by blood (birth), marriage, or adoption.
T	F	3.	The first stage in the family life cycle is the aging stage.
T	F	4.	Throughout the family life cycle, stages may overlap.
T	F	5.	Changes in the family structure require family members to make few, if any, adjustments.
T	F	6.	Substance abuse involves misusing drugs, alcohol, or some other chemical to a potentially harmful level.
T	F	7.	If a family member develops a drug or drinking problem, family members should ignore the problem or try to cover it up.
T	F	8.	The first relationship most people have is with their parents.
T	F	9.	Relationships with family members are likely to continue throughout life.
T	F	10.	During the teen years, relationships with parents may become strained.
T	F	11.	Sibling rivalry is competition between brothers and sisters.
T	F	12.	Cooperation means everyone works toward his or her own individual goals.
T	F	13.	Relationships with grandparents are unimportant.

☐ Matching: Match the following types of families with their descriptions.

_____ 14. In this type of family, at least one of the parents is a stepparent.

_____ 15. A group of people who are related to each other.

_____ 16. In this type of family, relatives other than the parents (or stepparents) and children live together in one home.

_____ 17. This type of family is formed when a couple marries.

_____ 18. This type of family includes one parent and one or more children.

    A. family
    B. nuclear family
    C. one-parent family
    D. blended family
    E. extended family

☐ Essay Questions: Provide the answers you feel best show your understanding of the subject matter.

19. Name the five stages of the family life cycle. Give an example of a change that may occur within each stage.

20. List four suggestions that may help teens to improve their relationships with their parents.

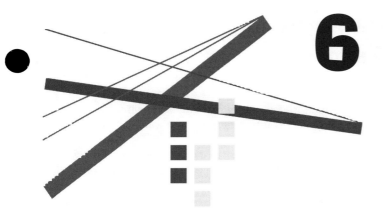

6 Your Friends

Objectives

After studying this chapter, students will be able to
- describe types of friendships and qualities people seek in their friends.
- give suggestions for forming and ending friendships, handling negative peer pressure, and using positive peer pressure.
- discuss the stages of dating and the types of activities and emotions that may be involved at each stage.

Teaching Materials

Text, pages 71–82
  Words to Know
  Review It
  Apply It
  Think More About It
Student Activity Guide
  A. *Friends*
  B. *Handling Peer Pressure*
  C. *Friendship and Dating*
Teacher's Resource Guide/Binder
  Ending a Friendship, reproducible master 6-1
  Dating Tips, transparency master 6-2
  My Personal Journal, reproducible master 6-3
  Chapter 6 Quiz

Introductory Activities

1. Have students complete the following statement, "A real friend is someone who . . ."
2. Have students design a bulletin board entitled, "A Good Friend Is . . ."

Strategies to Reteach, Reinforce, Enrich, and Extend Text Concepts

■ What Is a Friend?

3. **ER** Ask students to interview three other teens having them list five qualities of a true friend. Students can compare their lists with others in the class.
4. **RF** Ask students to answer the following question: What does being "as good as your word" mean?
5. **ER** Have students write a paper describing a real or imaginary friend. Ask them to include descriptions of the person's good qualities, faults, interests, and opinions.
6. **ER** *Friends,* Activity A, SAG. Students are asked to pretend they are advice columnists for a teen magazine and respond to letters about situations related to friendships.

■ Making Friends

7. **RT** Have students list some characteristics of people that make it easy to like them. Make another list of characteristics that can hurt friendships.
8. **RF** Ask students to write "recipes" entitled "How to Make and Keep a Friend." This may be done on recipe cards.

■ Ending a Friendship

9. **EX** Have students role-play situations about how to end a friendship. Discuss how each situation was handled.

10. **RF** *Ending a Friendship,* reproducible master 6-1. Have students read each example and explain how they would handle each situation. (This activity should not be collected.)
11. **RF** Have students discuss situations in which it might be necessary to end a friendship. Discuss other situations when a friendship might be saved.

■ Peers and Peer Pressure

12. **RF** Have students identify various types of peer pressure they face every day. As a group discuss ways they can handle the situation.
13. **ER** Ask students to design posters giving hints on how to say no to peer pressure. Display the posters in the classroom or, with permission, display them throughout the school.
14. **RF** *Handling Peer Pressure,* Activity B, SAG. Students are asked to describe four examples of peer pressure. They are then asked to explain how they have handled or would handle each situation. Responses can be discussed in class.

■ Dating

15. **RF** *Dating Tips,* transparency master 6-2. Use this transparency master as a basis of discussion about dating. Ask students to suggest other dating tips in addition to the ones given.
16. **ER** *Friendship and Dating,* Activity C, SAG. Students are asked to complete statements related to friendship and dating. Responses can be discussed in class.
17. **ER** *My Personal Journal,* reproducible master 6-3. Have students think about a person they have dated or wanted to date and write a letter to that person. Have them answer some of the included questions in their letters.

Answer Key

■ Text

Review It, page 82
1. B
2. (List three:) loyalty, caring, reliability, trustworthiness (Students may justify other responses.)
3. jealousy
4. (List three:) school, work, religious groups, sports teams, clubs, activity groups (Students may justify other responses.)
5. A strong self-concept helps a person feel good about himself or herself. This, in turn, allows others to feel good about the person and enjoy being his or her friend.
6. (Student response.)
7. true
8. (Student response.)
9. (Student response.)
10. group dating, casual dating, and steady dating

■ Teacher's Resource Guide/Binder

Chapter 6 Quiz
1.	F	6.	C
2.	T	7.	B
3.	T	8.	A
4.	T	9.	B
5.	T	10.	D

11. (Student response.)
12. Love is a strong feeling of affection between two people. It grows stronger with time. Love is unselfish. It is based on the total person, not just the outward appearance. It is based on trust and openness. Love is not jealous or possessive. Infatuation is an intense feeling of attraction that begins and ends quickly. The attraction is usually based on physical appearance and popularity. Infatuation is unlike love because love is a shared feeling.

Ending a Friendship

Name _____**Date** _____ **Period** _____

Read each example and explain how you would handle the situation.

Your friend moves away. After a few months, your friend stops responding to your letters.

_____

_____

_____

You and your friend have a disagreement.

_____

_____

_____

Your friend is involved with a new group of friends and doesn't spend much time with you.

_____

_____

_____

Your friend suddenly stops talking to you, and you don't know why.

_____

_____

_____

You find out your friend is spreading rumors about you.

_____

_____

_____

Dating Tips

- Be yourself. Your date was attracted to you—not someone else.

- Choose a type of entertainment both of you will enjoy, such as a movie or an athletic event. Having something to watch will help calm your nerves during the first part of the date. After the event, you will have something to talk about.

- Before you go out, think about topics your date might enjoy discussing. You might talk about moves, TV programs, school events, or news items. Let your date do as much talking as you do.

- Take time to really learn about your date. Ask about his or her thoughts and opinions using questions that require more than a "yes" or "no" answer.

- If you have a mishap, such as tripping or spilling food, try to laugh it off. If your date has a mishap, try to make him or her feel at ease. In either case, try to forget the incident as quickly as possible.

- Don't cancel a date unless it's absolutely necessary. Be honest with your excuse.

- Be ready at the agreed time, or call if you must be late.

- Be in a good frame of mind. Do not tell your date all your problems and troubles.

- After the date, keep the details of your date to yourself. A date is a personal experience.

My Personal Journal

Think about a person you have dated or wanted to date. Write a letter to that person. Are you friends with the person? What good qualities does he or she have? What do you like and dislike about your relationship?

_____

_____

_____

_____

_____

_____

_____

_____

_____

_____

_____

_____

_____

_____

_____

_____

_____

_____

_____

_____

_____

_____

_____

_____

_____

Your Friends

Name _____

Date _____ **Period** _____ **Score** _____

CHAPTER 6 QUIZ

☐ True/False: Circle *T* if the statement is true or *F* if the statement is false.

T F 1. Friends with whom you share your deepest thoughts and secrets are called acquaintances.

T F 2. You'll find making new friends easier if you have a positive attitude.

T F 3. Most adult friendships are formed during adulthood.

T F 4. Your peers are people who are about the same age as you.

T F 5. Most teens are nervous on their first real date.

☐ Multiple Choice: Choose the best answer and write the corresponding letter in the blank.

_____ 6. A true friend sticks with you _____.
   A. only when it's convenient
   B. in bad times
   C. in good times and bad times
   D. in good times

_____ 7. Knowing how to make friends is a skill you will _____.
   A. never use
   B. use throughout your life
   C. find useful only as a teen
   D. probably use only when you are older

_____ 8. Before ending a close friendship, it is best to _____.
   A. talk to the other person
   B. ignore the other person
   C. tell everyone except the other person that the friendship is over
   D. None of the above.

_____ 9. When faced with negative peer pressure, _____.
   A. conform
   B. say no
   C. argue
   D. give in to the pressure

_____ 10. Usually, a person you date is someone _____.
   A. to whom you are attracted
   B. close to your own age
   C. who has a family background similar to yours
   D. All of the above.

☐ Essay Questions: Provide the answers you feel best show your understanding of the subject matter.

11. Explain why friendships are important to you.

12. Describe the difference between love and infatuation.

Part Two

Managing Your Life

Part goal: Students will learn how to set goals, make decisions, and manage their time, energy, and money.

Bulletin Board

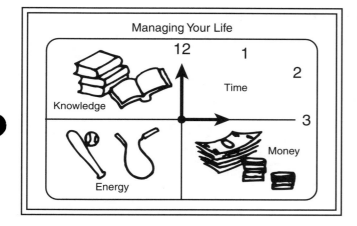

Title: "Managing Your Life"

Use construction paper or other material to make four sections of the bulletin board as shown above. Label each section with major concepts presented in this part—Knowledge, Time, Energy, and Money. Make drawings or cutouts of books, numbers and hands of a clock, money, and sports equipment to illustrate each concept.

Teaching Materials

Text

Chapters 7–9, pages 83–118

Student Activity Guide

Chapters 7–9

Teacher's Resource Guide/Binder

Your Management Profile, reproducible master
Managing Provides a Good Foundation for Life, color transparency CT-7

Introductory Activities

1. Have students look up the definition of *management* in a dictionary. Ask them how they think this concept would apply to managing their lives.
2. *Your Management Profile*, reproducible master. Students are asked to respond to questions to reveal their understanding of management concepts. The responses will help you to determine your students' interests and educational needs.
3. Have students complete the following phrases: "Good management means . . ." and "Poor management means . . ." Without writing their names, have students turn in their responses. Read and discuss some of the responses in class.
4. Ask a business owner or manager to speak to the class about management techniques. Have students prepare a list of questions in advance. The following day, ask students to list business management techniques that they could apply to the management of their own lives.
5. *Managing Provides a Good Foundation for Life,* color transparency CT-7. Use this transparency to illustrate some basic management techniques. Ask students to give examples of how they can apply these management steps in their everyday lives.

Your Management Profile

Name _____ **Date** _____ **Period** _____

Respond to the following statements by placing a check beside the phrases or statements that express your interests or opinions. There are no wrong or right answers.

1. After I graduate from high school, I plan to
   _____ attend college
   _____ attend a vocational school
   _____ join the military
   _____ get a job as a(n): _____
   _____ get married
   _____ Other: _____

2. In this class, I would like to learn more about the following topics:
   _____ setting and reaching goals
   _____ identifying and using my resources
   _____ how to get the most for my money
   _____ how to improve my study habits
   _____ using the computer as a resource
   _____ managing time
   _____ managing energy
   _____ managing money
   _____ making good decisions
   _____ using credit
   _____ using banks
   _____ budgeting
   _____ where to shop
   _____ advertising
   _____ Other: _____
   _____ Other: _____

3. The following statements describe me:
   _____ I set goals and often reach them.
   _____ I live for today and let tomorrow take care of itself.
   _____ I get an allowance.
   _____ I have a job.
   _____ My parents give me money.
   _____ Advertisements have a lot of influence on what I buy.
   _____ I compare prices and brands before I buy.
   _____ I buy the first thing I see.
   _____ I feel satisfied about most of my purchases.
   _____ I feel cheated about most of my purchases.
   _____ I have a checking account
   _____ I have a savings account.
   _____ I use credit cards.
   _____ When I have a complaint about a product or service, I complain to the appropriate person.
   _____ When I have a complaint about a product or services, I just live with it.
   _____ I can't make a decision.
   _____ My decisions are always the "wrong" ones.
   _____ I make decisions, and I am usually happy with the results.

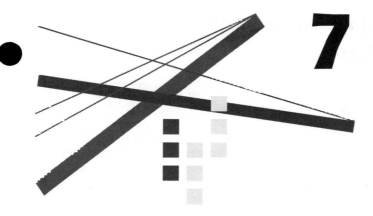

7 Getting Ready to Manage

Objectives

After studying this chapter, students will be able to
- identify their physical and psychological needs.
- describe how wants differ from needs.
- explain how their values and goals affect their standards.

Teaching Materials

Text, pages 84–93
  Words to Know
  Review It
  Apply It
  Think More About It
Student Activity Guide
  A. *Values*
  B. *Setting and Reaching Goals*
Teacher's Resource Guide/Binder
  Needs or Wants? reproducible master 7-1
  Goals, transparency master 7-2
  My Personal Journal, reproducible master 7-3
  Chapter 7 Quiz

Introductory Activities

1. Have students list their wants. Ask them to rank them from most important to least important. Have students compare their lists and discuss differences and similarities.
2. Ask students to list five goals they have for the day. Then ask them to list five goals they have for the next 10 years. Use this as the basis for a discussion on short-term goals and long-term goals.

Strategies to Reteach, Reinforce, Enrich, and Extend Text Concepts

■ Needs and Wants

3. **RT** Ask students to distinguish between needs and wants.
4. **RF** *Needs or Wants?* reproducible master 7-1. Have students decide whether each item listed is a need or want and answer the questions that follow.
5. **RT** Ask students to list physical needs and psychological needs.
6. **EX** Have students analyze their lists of wants. Ask them what influenced them to want these items.

■ Values

7. **RT** Have students define *values* and give examples of values.
8. **RF** *Values*, Activity A, SAG. Students are asked to look at a list of values and to place a check next to those they feel are important. They are then asked to complete statements about values.
9. **RF** Ask students to discuss how the following can influence a person's values: A. family B. religion C. school D. friends E. community F. mass media G. personal experiences
10. **ER** Have students make a list of six values. Ask them to rank them in order of importance to them.
11. **ER** Have students role-play situations in which the values of one person clash with those of another person.

■ Goals

12. **ER** *Setting and Reaching Goals*, Activity B, SAG. Students are asked to define terms related to setting and reaching goals. They are then asked to give examples of short-term and long-term goals and describe how they would meet the goals. Also have them describe their priorities and the standards they would set.

13. **RF** *Goals*, transparency master 7-2. In a discussion about goals, compare setting and reaching goals to a football game. Ask students why people set goals. Then ask them to identify typical goals teens have and discuss standards for reaching these goals.

14. **RF** Have students distinguish between long-term and short-term goals.

15. **RT** Ask students to give examples of how short-term goals can influence attaining long-term goals.

16. **ER** Ask students to read a biography of a famous person. Have students try to identify what that person's goals in life probably were.

17. **ER** Ask students to describe their career goals. Have them explain how these goals are related to their values.

18. **ER** *My Personal Journal*, reproducible master 7-3. Have students write about a goal they have accomplished.

■ Standards

19. **RF** Have students discuss how standards are related to goals.

20. **RT** Discuss with students standards that must be met to pass this class.

21. **RT** Have students list examples of standards they must meet at home, school, and work.

22. **RT** Ask students to cite examples of how people sometimes set their standards at different levels.

Answer Key

■ Text

Review It, page 93

1. true
2. (Student response.)
3. physical
4. the need to feel secure; the need to feel accepted and loved; the need to have self-respect and the respect of others (Student response for descriptions.)
5. (Student response.)
6. (List three. Student response.)
7. false
8. You need goals to provide direction in your life.
9. A. short-term
   B. short-term
   C. long-term
   D. long-term
10. C

■ Student Activity Guide

Setting and Reaching Goals, Activity B

Goal: What you are trying to achieve or the aims you are trying to reach.

Short-term goal: A goal that can be met in a short period of time.

Long-term goal: A goal that takes many months, a year, or many years to reach.

Priorities: What is considered most important based on values.

Standards: The way you measure what you have done.

■ Teacher's Resource Guide/Binder

Chapter 7 Quiz

1. F	5. T	9. F	13. D
2. T	6. F	10. C	
3. T	7. T	11. A	
4. T	8. F	12. B	

14. (Student response.)
15. (Student response.)

Needs or Wants?

Name _____ **Date** _____ **Period** _____

Determine if each item is a need or a want. If the item is a need, place an *N* on the line. If the item is a want, place a *W* on the line. Then answer the questions that follow.

_____ 1. air

_____ 2. a new compact disc

_____ 3. shelter

_____ 4. a steak dinner

_____ 5. shoes

_____ 6. love

_____ 7. air conditioning

_____ 8. a computer

_____ 9. a candy bar

_____ 10. sleep

_____ 11. a new pair of jeans

_____ 12. breakfast

_____ 13. water

_____ 14. security

_____ 15. toothpaste

_____ 16. self-respect

_____ 17. good grades

_____ 18. a blanket

_____ 19. an entertainment center

_____ 20. tickets to a sports event

Which items did you think could be a need *or* a want? Why?

_____

Which of your answers would your parents disagree with? Why?

_____

_____

Goals

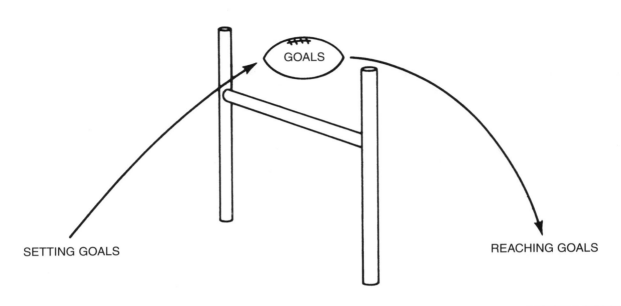

SETTING GOALS

REACHING GOALS

Reasons people set goals:

Typical goals:

Standards for reaching goals:

My Personal Journal

Write about a time you accomplished a goal you set. How did you decide to set the goal? Did anyone influence you to set the goal? How did you feel when you accomplished your goal? How has this accomplishment helped you?

_____

_____

_____

_____

_____

_____

_____

_____

_____

_____

_____

_____

_____

_____

_____

_____

_____

_____

_____

_____

_____

_____

_____

Getting Ready to Manage

Name _____

Date _____ Period _____ Score _____

CHAPTER 7 QUIZ

☐ True/False: Circle *T* if the statement is true or *F* if the statement is false.

T F 1. Needs and wants are the same.

T F 2. People of all ages need to feel love and to feel that they are loved.

T F 3. When you have self-respect, other people tend to think of you more highly.

T F 4. Factors such as friends and advertisements can cause you to become confused about what your needs and wants really are.

T F 5. Everything you think, do, or say is affected by your values.

T F 6. In order for a friendship to exist, you must always agree with your friend's values.

T F 7. Your goals are closely based on your values.

T F 8. An example of a long-term goal would be to get an "A" on a test next week.

T F 9. If you set challenging goals for yourself, you will probably become bored in the future.

☐ Multiple Choice: Select the best answer and write the letter in the blank.

_____ 10. Which of the following is a psychological need?
   A. Water.
   B. Shelter.
   C. Self-respect.
   D. Sleep.

_____ 11. Many of the values you learned as a child will _____.
   A. stay with you throughout life
   B. change during your teen years
   C. become unimportant
   D. None of the above.

_____ 12. People without goals _____.
   A. are happier
   B. are on an aimless trip through life
   C. often succeed in life
   D. None of the above.

_____ 13. Which of the following statements is *not* true about standards?
   A. They are a way to measure what you have done.
   B. Others may set them for you.
   C. You can set them for yourself.
   D. People always have the same level of standards.

☐ Essay Questions: Provide the answers you feel best show your understanding of the subject matter.

14. List two examples of short-term goals and two examples of long-term goals.

15. Describe three ways in which standards are a part of your daily life.

Reproducible Quiz

8 Managing Your Resources

Objectives

After studying this chapter, students will be able to
■ identify their personal and material resources.
■ describe the ways they can use their resources.
■ apply the decision-making process in their daily lives.

Teaching Materials

Text, pages 94–104
 Words to Know
 Review It
 Apply It
 Think More About It
Student Activity Guide
 A. *Your Resources*
 B. *It's Your Decision*
Teacher's Resource Guide/Binder
 My Personal Journal, reproducible master 8-1
 The Management Process, reproducible master 8-2
 The Decision-Making Process, transparency master 8-3
 Recycling Depends on You, color transparency CT-8
 Chapter 8 Quiz

Introductory Activities

1. Ask students to list some resources they use every day.
2. Have students finish the following sentence: "Some of the ways I use computers to help me manage my resources are . . ."

Strategies to Reteach, Reinforce, Enrich, and Extend Text Concepts

■ Your Resources

3. **RT** *Your Resources*, Activity A, SAG. Students are asked to define words related to resources. They are then asked to identify resources as personal or material resources and identify resources that are available to them.
4. **RT** Ask students to distinguish between personal and material resources.
5. **RF** Discuss how resources can be used in meeting goals. Have students give examples that illustrate this.
6. **ER** *My Personal Journal,* reproducible master 8-1. Ask students to describe their most valuable personal resources and answer the questions that follow.
7. **ER** Have students make a map of the community. On the map, have students locate all the community resources that are available, such as schools, libraries, stores, theaters, parks, zoos, and museums.
8. **ER** Ask a representative from a computer company to demonstrate how the newest computer software can be a valuable resource in meeting goals. Ask students to prepare a list of questions in advance.

9. **RF** Ask students to describe recycling efforts that are being, or could be, carried out in their school.

10. **RF** *Recycling Depends on You,* color transparency CT-8. Use this transparency to illustrate the recycling process and discuss the part students play in recycling. Have students identify various items that can be recycled and items that can be made from recycled items.

■ How Resources Can Be Used

11. **ER** Ask students to list three goals. Then have them list the resources they could use in meeting those goals.

12. **RT** Have students list examples of resources they share with family members.

13. **ER** Ask students to write reports on how natural resources such as air, water, and land can be protected.

14. **RT** Ask students to give four examples of how resources can be exchanged.

15. **RT** Ask students to list three ways they can substitute one resource for another.

16. **RF** Have students describe how they can use resources they already have to provide other resources.

■ Using the Management Process

17. **RT** Discuss the steps of the management process with the class.

18. **RF** *The Management Process,* reproducible master 8-2. Have students identify one of their goals. They should then list the steps of the management process and apply the steps to show how they might reach their goals.

■ Making Decisions

19. **RT** *The Decision-Making Process,* transparency master 8-3. Use this transparency master as a basis of discussion about the steps of the decision-making process.

20. **RF** *It's Your Decision,* Activity B, SAG. Students are asked to make a decision using the decision-making steps outlined. Decisions can be discussed in class.

21. **ER** Have students survey three adults about how they arrive at decisions. Discuss the responses in class.

22. **EX** Have students role-play situations in which they must make a decision. Ask them to use the decision-making steps outlined in the chapter.

23. **RT** Ask students to distinguish between simple and complex decisions. Ask them to give examples of each.

24. **EX** Ask students to role-play situations in which a wrong decision was made. Have them discuss the consequences.

25. **RT** Discuss the importance of establishing goals in the decision-making process.

26. **ER** Have students bring to class newspaper clippings about current events in which decisions have to be made by local, national, and world leaders. Have students pretend they must make the decisions. Have them use the decision-making process. Ask them to describe what the consequences of their decisions might be.

Answer Key

■ Text

Review It, page 104
1. false
2. (List four of each. Student response.)
3. positive
4. false
5. B, A, D, C
6. B
7. (List four. Student response.)
8. personal priorities, goals, standards, needs, wants
9. goal
10. Step 1 State the problem to be solved or decision to be made.
    Step 2 List all possible alternatives.
    Step 3 Think about your alternatives.
    Step 4 Choose the best alternative.
    Step 5 Act on your decision.
    Step 6 Evaluate your decision.

■ Student Activity Guide

Your Resources, Activity A
Resources: Anything that can help you reach a goal.
Personal resources: Resources that come from within yourself or from your relationships with other people.
Material resources: Money, community resources, possessions, and natural resources.

1. P	6. P	11. M	16. M
2. M	7. M	12. P	17. M
3. P	8. M	13. P	18. M
4. M	9. M	14. M	19. M
5. M	10. P	15. P	20. P

(Student response.)

■ Teacher's Resource Guide/Binder

Chapter 8 Quiz

1. T	5. F	9. F	13. A
2. F	6. T	10. D	
3. F	7. F	11. C	
4. T	8. T	12. D	

14. (Student response.)
15. (Student response.)

My Personal Journal

Think about your most valuable personal resource. What makes this resource valuable to you? Why is it important that you have this resource? Will this resource be important to you in five years? in ten years?

_____

_____

_____

_____

_____

_____

_____

_____

_____

_____

_____

_____

_____

_____

_____

_____

_____

_____

_____

_____

_____

_____

_____

_____

_____

The Management Process

Name _____**Date** _____ **Period** _____

List one of your goals. Then list the steps of the management process. Finally, apply the steps of the management process to reaching your goal.

Goal:_____

Steps of the management process:

_____

_____

_____

_____

_____

_____

How to use the management process to meet my goal:

_____

_____

_____

_____

_____

_____

_____

_____

_____

_____

_____

_____

_____

_____

_____

The Decision-Making Process

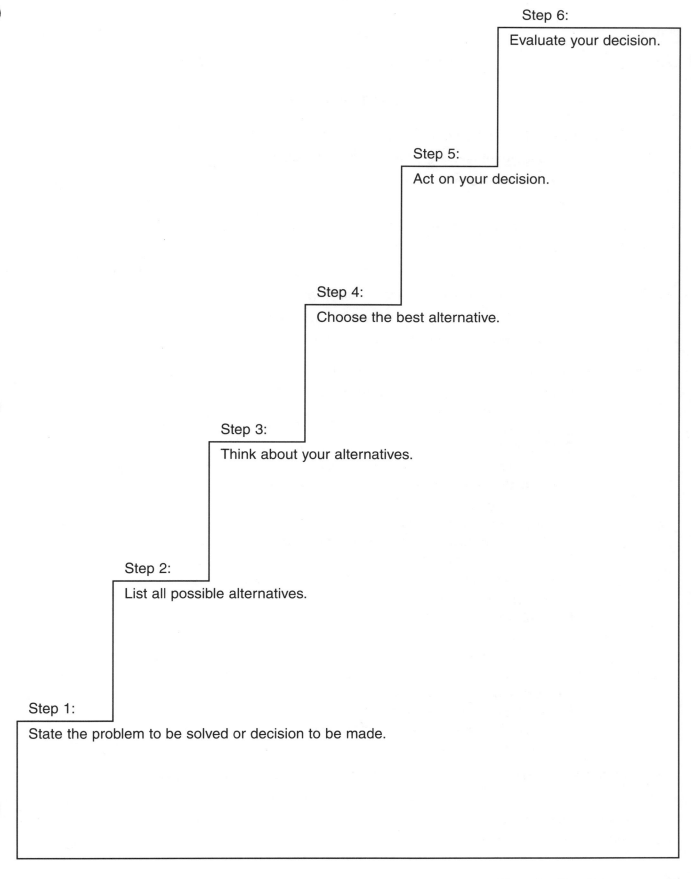

Step 6:
Evaluate your decision.

Step 5:
Act on your decision.

Step 4:
Choose the best alternative.

Step 3:
Think about your alternatives.

Step 2:
List all possible alternatives.

Step 1:
State the problem to be solved or decision to be made.

Managing Your Resources

Name _____

Date _____ **Period** _____ **Score** _____

CHAPTER 8 QUIZ

☐ True/False: Circle *T* if the statement is true or *F* if the statement is false.

T F 1. Management is using your resources to reach a goal.

T F 2. Time is a material resource.

T F 3. A computer is a personal resource.

T F 4. The types of information you can store in a computer are unlimited.

T F 5. Most resources are unlimited.

T F 6. Natural resources and community resources are shared resources.

T F 7. The decision-making process should only be used when making a complex decision.

T F 8. For most decisions, you will have more than one option.

T F 9. A negative approach to making decisions is to state your decision or problem as a goal.

☐ Multiple Choice: Select the best answer and write the letter in the blank.

_____ 10. Which of the following is a personal resource?

    A. Your attitude.
    B. Your abilities.
    C. Your energy.
    D. All of the above.

_____ 11. The first step in the decision-making process is to _____.

    A. evaluate your decision
    B. list all possible alternatives
    C. state the problem to be solved or the decision to be made
    D. act on your decision

_____ 12. Which of the following affects decisions you make?

    A. Personal priorities.
    B. Goals and standards.
    C. Needs and wants.
    D. All of the above.

_____ 13. If you make the wrong choice when making a decision, you _____.

    A. must accept the consequences
    B. can blame someone else
    C. should refuse to accept responsibility
    D. None of the above.

☐ Essay Questions: Provide the answers you feel best show your understanding of the subject matter.

14. Give four examples of how you could use a computer as a resource to meet your goals.

15. Describe a typical decision a teen might have to make. Then, using the steps in the decision-making process, arrive at a decision.

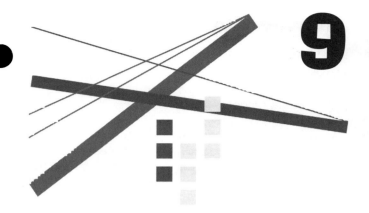

9 Managing Time, Energy, and Money

Objectives

After studying this chapter, students will be able to
- discuss ways to manage their time wisely.
- describe factors that affect their energy levels.
- develop a budget and a savings plan for managing their money.
- relate knowledge of basic consumer information to their own lives.

Teaching Materials

Text, pages 105–118
Words to Know
Review It
Apply It
Think More About It
Student Activity Guide
A. *Your Schedule*
B. *Budget Basics*
C. *Money Matters*
D. *Consumer Complaint*
Teacher's Resource Guide/Binder
My Personal Journal, reproducible master 9-1
Flexible Versus Fixed Expenses, reproducible master 9-2
Management Tips for Teens, transparency master 9-3
Advertising Analysis, color transparency CT-9
Chapter 9 Quiz

Introductory Activities

1. Ask students to make up two lists—"Time Wasters" and "Time Savers." Ask students to share their lists with the class.
2. Ask students how many of them have a budget. Ask them to describe how the budget has helped them manage their money.

Strategies to Reteach, Reinforce, Enrich, and Extend Text Concepts

■ Managing Time

3. **RF** *Your Schedule*, Activity A, SAG. Students are asked to define *schedule* and *procrastination*. Then they are asked to compile a "to do" list and make a personal schedule. They are to follow the schedule for a day and evaluate it by answering questions about it.
4. **ER** Ask students to write articles on improving study habits. Students may want to submit their articles to the school newspaper for publication.

■ Managing Your Energy

5. **ER** Ask a dietitian to speak to the class about how food affects energy levels. Have students prepare a list of questions in advance.
6. **ER** Have students interview local athletes about how they manage their energy. Have students ask the athletes how food, sleep, and exercise affect energy levels.
7. **ER** *My Personal Journal*, reproducible master 9-1. Students should write about how they manage their energy levels. They should include information about how tenergy relates to food, sleep, and exercise.

■ Managing Money

8. **ER** Ask a financial counselor from a bank to speak to the class about effective methods of managing money that teens can use now and in the future.
9. **RT** *Flexible Versus Fixed Expenses*, reproducible master 9-2. Have students determine

which of the listed expenses are flexible and which are fixed.

10. **EX** *Budget Basics*, Activity B, SAG. Students are to complete a monthly budget and evaluate it by answering questions about it.

11. **EX** Have students debate the advantages versus the disadvantages of using credit.

12. **RF** *Money Matters*, Activity C, SAG. Students are asked to complete statements by filling the blanks with words related to money management.

13. **RT** *Management Tips for Teens*, transparency master 9-3. Using an overhead projector, write down management tips students have for managing time, energy, and money. Then discuss the effectiveness of the tips in class.

■ Consumer Basics

14. **EX** Ask students to bring various types of advertisements to class. Ask them to analyze the advertisements in terms of accuracy and whether or not the information was helpful.

15. **RF** *Advertising Analysis,* color transparency CT-9. Divide the class into buzz groups. Analyze the advertisement by
   A. Identifying the attention-getter
   B. Listing the useful information
   C. Listing information that is not useful
   D. Listing reasons the advertisement would or would not encourage you to purchase the product

16. **RF** Ask students to prepare a list of the "Top 10 Places to Shop." Ask students to defend why they chose these places as the best. Discuss reasons why other stores didn't make the list.

17. **RF** Ask students to discuss comparison shopping versus impulse buying. Ask them to cite examples of each and describe the results.

18. **RF** *Consumer Complaint*, Activity D, SAG. Students are asked to describe a consumer problem they have had with a product or service. They are then asked to answer questions about it. Responses can be discussed in class.

19. **EX** Ask students to write a letter of complaint regarding a (real or imaginary) problem with goods or services they have purchased. Read and analyze the letters in class.

Answer Key

■ Text

Review It, page 118
1. schedule
2. (Student response.)
3. false
4. food, sleep, and exercise
5. income, fixed expenses, flexible expenses
6. Fixed expenses are regular expenses and do not vary from time to time. Flexible expenses do not occur regularly, and they may vary in amount. (Student response for examples.)
7. C, E, D, A, B
8. the right to safety, the right to be informed, the right to choose, the right to be heard
9. false

■ Student Activity Guide

Your Schedule, Activity A
Schedule: A written plan for reaching your goals within a certain period of time.
Procrastination: Putting off difficult or unpleasant tasks until later.
Money Matters, Activity C

1. money	11. discount
2. budget	12. factory outlet
3. fixed	13. comparison
4. flexible	14. specialty
5. savings	15. income
6. checking	16. expenses
7. credit card	17. interest
8. automatic teller	18. credit
9. consumer	19. advertisement
10. department	20. impulse

■ Teacher's Resource Guide/Binder

Chapter 9 Quiz

1. T	6. F	11. F	16. A
2. F	7. F	12. T	17. F
3. T	8. F	13. E	18. B
4. F	9. T	14. C	
5. T	10. F	15. D	

19. (Student response.)
20. the right to safety, the right to be informed, the right to choose, the right to be heard

My Personal Journal

How do you manage your personal energy? How is your energy level affected by the food you eat? Do you think you get enough or too much sleep? Do you get an appropriate amount of exercise? Where do you need improvements?

_____

_____

_____

_____

_____

_____

_____

_____

_____

_____

_____

_____

_____

_____

_____

_____

_____

_____

_____

_____

_____

_____

_____

_____

Flexible Versus Fixed Expenses

Name _____ **Date** _____ **Period** _____

Review the following list of expenses. Write *flexible* if the item is a flexible expense or *fixed* if the item is a fixed expense.

_____ 1. Monthly savings

_____ 2. A new computer game

_____ 3. A new sweater

_____ 4. Club dues

_____ 5. Movie tickets

_____ 6. The phone bill

_____ 7. A car payment

_____ 8. School pictures

_____ 9. Lunch money

_____ 10. A birthday gift for your friend

_____ 11. Online services

_____ 12. Dinner with friends

_____ 13. Bus money

_____ 14. School supplies

_____ 15. Haircut and style

Management Tips for Teens

Time:

Energy:

Money:

Managing Time, Energy, and Money

Name _____

Date _____ **Period** _____ **Score** _____

CHAPTER 9 QUIZ

☐ True/False: Circle *T* if the statement is true or *F* if the statement is false.

T F 1. The most efficient way to plan the use of your time is to use a schedule.

T F 2. Procrastination helps you make the most of the time you have.

T F 3. You need to schedule your study time just as you schedule other activities in your life.

T F 4. When working on a long project or report, do it all in one day.

T F 5. What you eat and how much sleep you get affect the amount of energy you have.

T F 6. Exercising takes away your energy.

T F 7. A savings account allows you to write checks when you purchase items at stores.

T F 8. If a product is endorsed by a famous person, you can be sure it is a good product.

T F 9. Discount stores often have lower prices and fewer services than department stores.

T F 10. Impulse buying is a smart way to shop.

T F 11. As a consumer, if you have a problem with a product or service, it is best to ignore it.

T F 12. Complaint letters follow the form of other business letters.

☐ Matching: Match the following terms with their descriptions.

_____ 13. The money you earn.

_____ 14. Regular expenses you cannot avoid such as dues to a club.

_____ 15. Expenses that can vary from time to time, such as snacks or gifts.

_____ 16. A written plan for spending money. It helps you see how much money you have and how you spend it.

_____ 17. An amount of money paid to you for the use of your money.

_____ 18. Funds allowed for purchases you make now and promise to pay for at a later date.

    A. budget
    B. credit
    C. fixed expenses
    D. flexible expenses
    E. income
    F. interest

☐ Essay Questions: Provide the answers you feel best show your understanding of the subject matter.

19. List two tips each for managing your time, energy, and money.

20. List the four rights of the consumer as defined by President Kennedy.

Part Three — Understanding Children

Part goal: Students will learn how children grow and develop and how to care for infants, toddlers, and preschoolers.

Bulletin Board

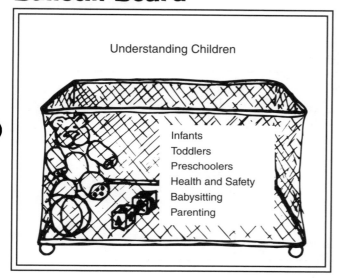

Understanding Children

Infants
Toddlers
Preschoolers
Health and Safety
Babysitting
Parenting

Title: "Understanding Children"

Draw the frame of a playpen on the bulletin board. Attach a portion of netting to the board to give the appearance of a playpen. Place a few lightweight toys behind the netting. Attach to the playpen a piece of construction paper labeled with the following concepts: Infants, Toddlers, Preschoolers, Safety and Health, Babysitting, and Parenting.

Teaching Materials

Text
Chapters 10–15, pages 119–185

Student Activity Guide
Chapters 10–15

Teacher's Resource Guide/Binder
What Are Children Like? reproducible master
Growing Up! color transparency CT-10

Introductory Activities

1. *What Are Children Like?* reproducible master. Have students write down their impressions of what infants, toddlers, and preschoolers are like. Have students discuss these impressions as a class. You may wish to keep the students' worksheets and pass them back when you have finished studying the unit. Students could then discuss how their impressions of children may have changed.

2. Have students discuss any experiences they have had caring for children. Students should mention what they liked or disliked about these experiences.

3. *Growing Up!* color transparency CT-10. Have students identify characteristics of each stage of development. As students contribute their ideas, write the ideas on the transparency.

4. On an index card, have each student write down a question he or she has about how to care for children. Organize these questions to fit the order in which the answers would appear in the text chapters. Make a master list of the questions and distribute them to the class. Have students write down answers as they find them in the text. (If some questions are not covered in the text, list them on a separate page. You may have students do extra research for credit to find the answers.)

What Are Children Like?

Name _____ **Date** _____ **Period**_____

In the spaces below, write your impressions of what children are like. Discuss your responses with the class.

Infants

Physically, infants look like	Infants are able to	Infants like to play in these ways

Toddlers

Physically, toddlers look like	Toddlers are able to	Toddlers like to play in these ways

Preschoolers

Physically, preschoolers look like	Preschoolers are able to	Preschoolers like to play in these ways

How do you feel about caring for or being around children? _____

_____

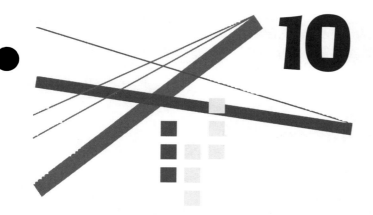

10 Taking Care of Infants

Objectives

After studying this chapter, students will be able to
■ list the four types of development and give examples as they apply to infants.
■ describe guidelines for caring for and playing with an infant.

Teaching Materials

Text, pages 120–131
Words to Know
Review It
Apply It
Think More About It
Student Activity Guide
A. *Infant Development*
B. *Caring for Infants*
C. *Choosing a Toy for an Infant*
Teacher's Resource Guide/Binder
Types of Development, reproducible master 10-1
Characteristics of a Newborn, transparency master 10-2
My Personal Journal, reproducible master 10-3
Chapter 10 Quiz

Introductory Activities

1. Have students bring in pictures of themselves as infants. Create a bulletin board with the photos. Use the pictures to discuss how infants are different from adults.
2. Have students think about two children they know who are the same age. Students should discuss how the two children are alike and how they are different.

Strategies to Reteach, Reinforce, Enrich, and Extend Text Concepts

■ **How Children Grow and Develop**

3. **RT** *Types of Development*, reproducible master 10-1. Have students determine whether given phrases describe physical, intellectual, social, or emotional development.
4. **ER** Invite a pediatrician to speak to your class about the way small children grow and develop. Have students prepare questions before the visit.
5. **RF** Collect some pictures of families including grandparents, parents, and children. Have students compare the features of family members and discuss traits that appear to have been inherited.

■ **Growth and Development of Infants**

6. **RT** *Characteristics of a Newborn,* transparency master 10-2. Use the transparency to discuss the physical characteristics of newborns.
7. **RF** Have a student stand a few inches behind a sheet of tough, clear plastic. Throw a large piece of wadded paper at the plastic while other students watch. Students should watch to see if the student behind the plastic blinks. Have students discuss how reflexes such as blinking protect people.
8. **ER** Arrange to have students view the nursery at a local hospital. Students should observe newborns' physical appearance as well as their reactions to their environment.
9. **RT** *Infant Development*, Activity A, SAG. Have students write examples of physical, intellectual,

social, and emotional growth in infants. Students should discuss their examples in class.

10. **EX**   Have students write a poem or short story about a baby. The poem or story should be written as if the baby is describing the people and events in his or her life.

■ Care Guidelines

11. **ER**   *My Personal Journal,* reproducible master 10-3. Have students write about interaction they might have had with an infant, how the infant made them feel, and how they feel this helped prepare them for parenting.

12. **RF**   *Caring for Infants,* Activity B, SAG. Have students describe how they would handle the given situations in caring for infants. Students should discuss their responses in class.

13. **RT**   Using a doll that is about the weight and size of a real baby, have students practice picking up and holding a baby.

14. **ER**   Invite the mother of an infant to demonstrate how to prepare formula, feed a baby, and burp a baby. Depending on the mother's wishes, you may want to allow one or two students to try feeding or burping.

15. **ER**   Have students make a poster describing the steps involved in changing a diaper.

16. **ER**   Using a doll that is about the weight and size of a real baby, have students practice giving a tub bath.

17. **ER**   Have several students ask parents of an older infant about the sleeping habits of their infant. Students should ask whether parents needed to adjust the infant's sleep schedule to get the infant to sleep through the night. Have the class discuss the students' findings.

■ Playing with Infants

18. **EX**   Have students try playing with an infant, not using any toys, for about five minutes. Students should try different facial expressions, sounds, or movements. Students should note how the infants respond to different actions and discuss their findings in class.

19. **ER**   *Choosing a Toy for an Infant,* Activity C, SAG. Have students select a toy they think is appropriate for an infant and evaluate it using the form provided.

20. **ER**   Have students interview a parent of an infant and ask how the parent selects toys for the infant. Students should also ask how the parent handles the problem of unsuitable gift toys. Have students report their findings to the class.

21. **EX**   Have students make a toy from inexpensive or free materials they think an infant would enjoy. (You may wish to supply materials or have students find their own.) Have each student explain to the class how they would use their toy with an infant.

Answer Key

■ Text

Review It, page 131

1. physical development—the growth or change in body size and ability; intellectual development—the development of the mind; social development—the development of communication skills and the ability to get along with others; emotional development—the development and expression of emotions
2. C
3. reflexes
4. Crying is a baby's first form of communication and is used to communicate discomfort, hunger, a need for changing, or a desire to have someone near. Cooing is a baby's second form of communication and is used to communicate pleasure or happiness. Babbling is a baby's third form of communication and is a first step toward speech.
5. false
6. to get rid of air in the baby's stomach that he or she swallowed during feeding
7. because their navels have not fully healed yet
8. to help the baby sleep through the night
9. false

■ Teacher's Resource Guide/Binder

Types of Development, reproducible master 10-1

1. B	4. A	7. C	10. A
2. A	5. C	8. D	11. B
3. D	6. B	9. A	12. D

Chapter 10 Quiz

1. T	9. F
2. F	10. T
3. F	11. emotional
4. F	12. physical
5. T	13. social
6. T	14. intellectual
7. F	15. newborn
8. T	16. reflexes

19. Parents may limit nap time so the infant will sleep through the night. Allowing the baby to sleep too long may cause the baby to wake up (and wake the parents up) in the middle of the night.
20. (Student response.)

Types of Development

Name _____ **Date** _____ **Period** _____

Children grow and develop in four main ways. These are listed below. Read each of the descriptions of growth and development that follow. Then place the letter of the type of development being described in the blank before it.

        A. physical
        B. intellectual
        C. social
        D. emotional

_____ 1. Eric can taste the difference between an orange and a peach.

_____ 2. Tanya can lift the stool that was too heavy for her a few months ago.

_____ 3. Juan cries when his mother leaves the house.

_____ 4. Jimmy's pants from last summer are too tight for him.

_____ 5. Kelly smiles and offers a cookie to a child she has just met.

_____ 6. When asked which is bigger, the cat or the kitten, Lamar points to the cat.

_____ 7. Although Alice wants to paint in her kindergarten class, she waits for her turn instead of rushing to an easel.

_____ 8. Keshia kisses her mother and says, "I love you."

_____ 9. Spicy foods no longer give Josh a stomachache.

_____ 10. Tamara can now hop on one foot without losing her balance.

_____ 11. Sam has figured out how to open doors by turning doorknobs.

_____ 12. Paul no longer has temper tantrums when he does not get his way.

Characteristics of a Newborn

- Large head compared to body

- Misshapen head

- Flattened nose

- Short neck

- Sloping shoulders

- Bulging abdomen

- Red, wrinkled skin

- Little hair

My Personal Journal

Think about any infants you have known or with whom you have had experience. How did the infant make you feel? How was the infant different from other children you have known? How might this experience help prepare you for parenting?

_____

_____

_____

_____

_____

_____

_____

_____

_____

_____

_____

_____

_____

_____

_____

_____

_____

_____

_____

_____

_____

_____

_____

_____

Taking Care of Infants

Name _____

Date _____ Period _____ Score _____

CHAPTER 10 QUIZ

☐ True/False: Circle *T* if the statement is true or *F* if the statement is false.

T F 1. Newborns may have colored marks on their skin.

T F 2. A newborn's heart rate is slower than an adult's.

T F 3. Most three-month-old babies can sit up without support.

T F 4. Infants who cannot say a few simple words by their tenth month are abnormal.

T F 5. Infants who throw objects over and over again are not trying to bother adults.

T F 6. Before infants can learn to care for others, they must understand they are separate people from their parents.

T F 7. Baby formula should be steaming hot when it is fed to an infant.

T F 8. Leaving wet diapers on a baby can cause a rash.

T F 9. Infants prefer playing with toys to playing with people.

T F 10. Toys with small parts attached with glue or thread are unsafe for infants.

☐ Fill in the Blank: Complete the statements below by filling in the blanks.

_____11. Learning how to express feelings is a part of _____ development.

_____12. _____ development involves changes in body size and ability.

_____13. _____ development includes learning to communicate and get along with others.

_____14. Improving the ability to think, reason, use language, and form ideas is _____ development.

_____15. A _____ is an infant who is less than one month old.

_____16. Reactions that happen automatically are called _____.

☐ Essay Questions: Provide the answers you feel best show your understanding of the subject matter.

17. Explain why it is important to follow parents' directions about nap time when caring for an infant.

18. Give two ways you could use a ball to play with an infant.

Reproducible Quiz

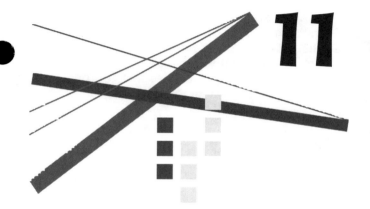

11 Taking Care of Toddlers

Objectives

After studying this chapter, students will be able to
- give examples of physical, intellectual, social, and emotional development in toddlers.
- discuss guidelines for caring for toddlers.
- describe the types of activities and toys to choose when playing with toddlers.

Teaching Materials

Text, pages 132–140
  Words to Know
  Review It
  Apply It
  Think More About It
Student Activity Guide
  A. *Toddler Development*
  B. *Caring for Toddlers*
  C. *Choosing a Toy for a Toddler*
Teacher's Resource Guide/Binder
  How Are Toddlers Different from Infants? transparency master 11-1
  Mealtime Tips, transparency master 11-2
  My Personal Journal, reproducible master 11-3
  Chapter 11 Quiz

Introductory Activities

1. Ask students to describe any toddlers they know. Ask them to explain how the toddlers are different from when they were infants.
2. Have students make a list of toys that interest toddlers. Have them think of reasons toddlers might enjoy these toys.

Strategies to Reteach, Reinforce, Enrich, and Extend Text Concepts

■ Growth and Development of Toddlers

3. **RT** *How Are Toddlers Different from Infants?* transparency master 11-1. Use this transparency to introduce a discussion on the development of toddlers.
4. **RF** Make or have some of your students make a videotape of toddlers walking. The toddlers should be filmed by age, starting with the youngest and ending with the oldest. Have the class view the tape and discuss how walking improves as toddlers grow.
5. **ER** Invite two to five parents of toddlers to discuss the speech patterns of toddlers with your class. Students should prepare questions in advance.
6. **ER** Have students interview the parents of a toddler about the toddler's social and emotional development. Students should write a short report based on their findings.
7. **ER** Invite a child psychologist to speak to your class about how to handle emotional problems of toddlers such as negative answers and temper tantrums. Students should write a short summary of the psychologist's presentation.
8. **RT** *Toddler Development*, Activity A, SAG. Have students give examples of physical, intellectual, social, and emotional growth in toddlers. Students should discuss their examples in class.

■ Care Guidelines

9. **RF** *Caring for Toddlers*, Activity B, SAG. Have students describe how they would handle each of the given situations in caring for toddlers. Students should discuss their responses in class.

10. **RT** *Mealtime Tips*, transparency master 11-2. Review the tips presented on the master with the class. Have students discuss why each tip is recommended. Also have students add tips they would recommend.

11. **EX** Have students role-play feeding toddlers. One student should be the toddler, with another student caring for the toddler. The caregiver should focus on making positive statements about food to get the toddler to eat, staying calm, and giving praise.

12. **ER** Have students interview parents of toddlers about the kinds of clothes their toddlers like and why. Students should also ask parents what kinds of clothes they prefer for their toddlers and why. Have students display pictures of the clothes with cards explaining why they are preferred by the toddler and/or parent.

13. **ER** Have students make a poster giving guidelines for bathing toddlers.

14. **RF** Have students discuss how their actions when babysitting could affect a parent's efforts with their child's toilet learning.

15. **RT** Have students make a list of ideas for quiet activities to use with a toddler before bedtime.

■ Toddlers and Play

16. **ER** Have students observe a group of toddlers playing. Students should make a list of typical characteristics they observed and compare their findings to the textbook description of toddlers at play.

17. **ER** *My Personal Journal*, reproducible master 11-3. Have students ask their parents about what toys or play activities the students enjoyed as toddlers. Ask them to relate this information to what they have learned about toddlers in this chapter.

18. **RF** Have students take a simple toy such as a ball or a block and list ways they could play with a toddler using the toy. Students should discuss their ideas in class.

19. **RF** Have students bring a book to class (from home or from the library) they think would be suitable for a toddler. Students should explain how and why they selected the book.

20. **ER** Have students make a poster related to toy safety for toddlers.

21. **RT** *Choosing a Toy for a Toddler*, Activity C, SAG. Have students select a toy they think is appropriate for a toddler and evaluate it using the form provided.

22. **RF** Have students make a chart listing household articles that would make good toys for toddlers and household articles that can be unsafe when used as toys for toddlers.

Answer Key

■ Text

Review It, page 140

1. (List four:) grow taller, gain weight, gain strength in bones and muscles, develop a more erect spine, lose baby fat, begin to walk, begin to climb, learn to run, gain more small and large motor coordination, begin to eat from a spoon and drink from a cup
2. true
3. false
4. Toddlers need clothing that allows them to move around comfortably. Clothes that are too tight make movement uncomfortable and can irritate the skin. Clothes that are too loose can cause toddlers to trip or get tangled in their clothes.
5. The water should be only a few inches deep and should be warm but not hot.
6. You should help toddlers clean up and change clothes without a fuss.
7. parallel
8. B
9. (List three:) coloring, drawing, reading, listening to soft music (Students may justify other responses.)
10. (List three:) should not have small parts that could break off easily, should be flame-resistant, should be free of sharp or rough edges (Students may justify other responses.)

Teacher's Resource Guide/Binder

Chapter 11 Quiz

1.	T	8.	F
2.	F	9.	T
3.	F	10.	C
4.	T	11.	B
5.	T	12.	A
6.	F	13.	C
7.	F		

14. (List two:) Choose clothes that are comfortable—not too tight or too loose. Allow the toddler to choose between a couple of outfits. Ask toddlers to help you as you dress them. Allow toddlers to do as much as they can on their own.
15. (Student response.)

How Are Toddlers Different from Infants?

- Toddlers are more independent

- Bones and muscles are much stronger

- Toddlers begin walking and climbing

- Listening and imitating lead to speaking

- Emotions are stronger

- Toddlers begin to enjoy playing with other children

Mealtime Tips

■ Avoid serving soups and foods with much sauce.

■ Cut fruits and vegetables into bite-size pieces.

■ Serve as many foods as possible that are easy to pick up with the fingers.

■ Put a bib on the toddler.

■ Put just a few spoonfuls of food on the toddler's plate at one time.

■ Pour only a small amount of liquid into the toddler's cup.

■ Make positive statements about the foods you serve a toddler.

■ Avoid asking the toddler whether he or she wants a food.

■ Be pleasant and understanding even if the toddler is messy.

■ Give some praise when toddlers do a good job with self-feeding.

■ Avoid playing games to get a toddler to finish eating.

My Personal Journal

Interview your parents about toys or play activities you enjoyed as a toddler. Are these toys and activities similar to those described in the chapter?

_____

_____

_____

_____

_____

_____

_____

_____

_____

_____

_____

_____

_____

_____

_____

_____

_____

_____

_____

_____

_____

_____

_____

Taking Care of Toddlers

Name _____

Date _____ **Period** _____ **Score** _____

CHAPTER 11 QUIZ

☐ True/False: Circle *T* if the statement is true or *F* if the statement is false.

T F 1. When toddlers walk, they may forget what they are doing and just fall over.

T F 2. Toddlers do better at eating foods with a spoon than eating foods with their fingers.

T F 3. Toddlers do not realize they can make things happen.

T F 4. Showing toddlers love is important even if toddlers throw temper tantrums.

T F 5. When you bathe a toddler, you should stay with the child the whole time he or she is in the tub.

T F 6. If a toddler who is in the process of toilet learning is wearing a diaper, you do not need to help him or her go to the bathroom.

T F 7. Playing tag is a good activity to use with toddlers just before bedtime.

T F 8. Repeating simple movements such as jumping up and down is boring for toddlers.

T F 9. Size is an important factor when choosing riding toys for toddlers.

☐ Multiple Choice: Choose the best answer and write the corresponding letter in the blank.

_____ 10. A likely first word for a toddler to learn would be _____.

A. run
B. kitty
C. daddy
D. ball

_____ 11. Which of the following is a good tip for feeding a toddler?

A. Serve soups for lunch.
B. Serve fresh fruits or vegetables that are cut into bite-size pieces.
C. Let toddlers decide whether or not they want a food.
D. If toddlers become tired of eating, use a game to get them to finish.

_____ 12. Playing next to but not with each other is called _____.

A. parallel play
B. cooperative play
C. non-interactive play
D. antisocial play

_____ 13. Which of the following is *not* a safety concern when choosing toys for toddlers?

A. Toys with small parts that could break off easily.
B. Toys with sharp edges.
C. Musical toys.
D. Flammable toys.

☐ Essay Questions: Provide the answers you feel best show your understanding of the subject matter.

14. Give two guidelines for helping a toddler dress.

15. Explain how you would handle a toddler who gets up in the middle of the night.

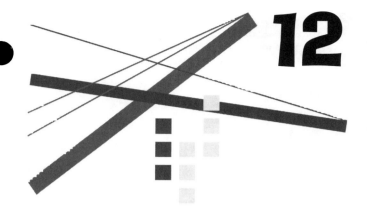

12 Taking Care of Preschoolers

Objectives

After studying this chapter, students will be able to
- give examples of physical, intellectual, social, and emotional development seen in preschoolers.
- discuss guidelines for caring for preschoolers.
- describe play activities and toys that are appropriate to use when playing with preschoolers.

Teaching Materials

Text, pages 141–149
  Words to Know
  Review It
  Apply It
  Think More About It
Student Activity Guide
  A. *Preschooler Development*
  B. *Caring for Preschoolers*
  C. *Choosing a Toy for a Preschooler*
Teacher's Resource Guide/Binder
  My Personal Journal, reproducible master 12-1
  A Story for a Preschooler, reproducible master 12-2
  Preschooler True and False, reproducible master 12-3
  Recipes for Fun and Snacks, color transparencies
CT-12A and CT-12B
  Chapter 12 Quiz

Introductory Activities

1. Have students bring in pictures of toddlers and preschoolers. (Students might even bring in pictures of themselves when they were toddlers and preschoolers.) Have students discuss how preschoolers differ from toddlers physically.
2. Have students describe what kind of games preschoolers enjoy playing. Have them explain why they think preschoolers enjoy these games.

Strategies to Reteach, Reinforce, Enrich, and Extend Text Concepts

■ Growth and Development of Preschoolers

3. **RF** Have students bring a sample of a preschooler's writing to class. Students should ask the preschooler to write his or her name. Students should also ask preschoolers to write anything else they want to. As a class, have students discuss the different writing samples and the abilities of the preschoolers.
4. **RF** Have students discuss what kinds of problems might be caused by preschoolers' inability to separate what is real and imagined. Students should also discuss how they might handle these problems.
5. **ER** Have students collect pictures of preschoolers who seem to be expressing emotions. Students should discuss the pictures and then make a bulletin board with captions for each picture.
6. **RT** *Preschooler Development,* Activity A, SAG. Have students give examples of physical, intellectual, social, and emotional growth in preschoolers. Students should discuss their examples in class.

■ Care Guidelines

7. **RF** *Caring for Preschoolers,* Activity B, SAG. Have students describe how they would handle each of the given situations in caring for preschoolers. Students should discuss their responses in class.
8. **ER** *My Personal Journal,* reproducible master 12-1. Have students write a letter to a caregiver they had

when they were preschoolers. Students should write about favorite and least-favorite activities.

9. **ER** Have students make a poster showing foods that can be substituted for others and still keep a meal balanced.

10. **RF** *Recipes for Fun and Snacks,* color transparencies CT-12A and CT-12B. Use these transparencies as an example of ways to introduce young children to food participation activities. Ask students to contribute additional ideas.

11. **ER** Have students prepare a display of clothing with self-dressing features. Students should label each self-dressing feature and explain how it helps make dressing easier.

12. **EX** Have students find and read an article or pamphlet on dealing with bedwetting. Students should write a short report based on what they have read.

13. **ER** Have students interview a parent about bad dreams their preschool-age child has had. Students should ask parents how they handled this problem. Students should discuss their findings with the class.

■ Preschoolers and Play

14. **RF** Have students discuss how cooperative play is important to a child's social development. What problems might result if a child has trouble with cooperative play?

15. **EX** Have students lead a small group of preschoolers in play. They should make arrangements to visit a preschool or child care center. Students should check their plans for play with you before the visit. Students should discuss their experiences with the class after the visit.

16. **ER** Have students bring in items they think would make good props for preschoolers to use when pretending. Donate the box to a local program for preschoolers and invite the program leader to report to the class on how the props were used.

17. **ER** *A Story for a Preschooler,* reproducible master 12-2. Have students use the form to write a story they think a preschooler would enjoy. Have the students write the story for a specific preschooler they know. Students should also write ideas for actions to go with the story. Have volunteers share their stories with the class.

18. **RF** *Choosing a Toy for a Preschooler,* Activity C, SAG. Have students select a toy they think is appropriate for a toddler and evaluate it using the form provided.

19. **ER** Invite a preschool teacher to share with the class examples of artwork done by preschoolers. Have the teacher discuss how preschoolers enjoy the different materials and feel about their finished products.

20. **RF** *Preschooler True and False,* reproducible master 12-3. Have students complete this activity as a review to the chapter.

Answer Key

■ Text

Review It, page 149

1. (List three:) hopping, skipping, riding swings, balancing on one foot, balancing while walking on a line, throwing, catching (Students may justify other responses.)

2. Preschoolers learn new words and begin to learn about grammar. They start to learn the rules for making words plural or singular and speaking in past or present tense.

3. because they can use language to express frustrations and wants and they can understand spoken reasons why they cannot do something

4. (List two:) avoid adding many seasonings to foods, serve stronger flavored vegetables raw or slightly cooked, offer different forms of foods children say they do not like for specific reasons, serve foods separately rather than in casseroles

5. A

6. true

7. try not to give preschoolers much to drink just before bedtime, remind them to go to the bathroom before going to bed, and leave a light on in the bathroom so they will be able to find their way in the night

8. Preschoolers' growing imaginations may cause them to confuse bad dreams with reality.

9. cooperative

10. (List four:) building blocks, simple construction sets, crayons, paste, blunt-end scissors, paper, finger paints, modeling clay, playdough (Students may justify other responses.)

■ Teacher's Resource Guide/Binder

Preschooler True and False, reproducible master 12-3

1. T	5. T	9. F	13. F
2. F	6. T	10. F	14. F
3. F	7. F	11. T	15. T
4. T	8. T	12. T	16. F

Chapter 12 Quiz

1. T	4. F	7. F	10. B
2. T	5. T	8. F	11. A
3. F	6. F	9. T	12. B

13. Preschoolers can express some of their frustrations through words rather than actions. Also, preschoolers can understand when explanations are given as to why they cannot do something.

14. (Student response.)

15. (Student response.)

My Personal Journal

Write a letter to a person who was your caregiver when you were a preschooler. Tell the caregiver how you feel about the care you received. What fun activities did you do? What was one of your favorite times? What was one of your least favorite times?

A Story for a Preschooler

Name _____ **Date** _____ **Period** _____

Preschoolers enjoy stories told by others, especially if the story is about them. Use the space below to develop a story a preschooler would like.

Preschooler's name: _____

Preschooler's interests: _____

_____

Theme of the story: _____

_____

Story: _____   Actions you would use with the story: _____

_____   _____

_____   _____

_____   _____

_____   _____

_____   _____

_____   _____

_____   _____

_____   _____

_____   _____

_____   _____

_____   _____

_____   _____

_____   _____

_____   _____

_____   _____

_____   _____

Preschooler True and False

Name _____ **Date** _____ **Period** _____

☐ Circle *T* if the statement is true or *F* if the statement is false.

T   F   1. Preschoolers are more confident than toddlers.

T   F   2. You can treat preschoolers the same way you would treat your peers.

T   F   3. Toddlers draw and color better than preschoolers.

T   F   4. Younger preschoolers can build towers from blocks, but the towers will most likely be crooked.

T   F   5. Preschoolers have longer attention spans than toddlers.

T   F   6. Preschoolers sometimes have trouble separating what is real and what is imagined.

T   F   7. Preschoolers are more likely to throw temper tantrums than toddlers.

T   F   8. By the time children reach the preschool years, they have some definite ideas about which foods they like and dislike.

T   F   9. You can avoid problems with food tastes by serving foods in casseroles.

T   F   10. You should never let preschoolers help prepare a meal.

T   F   11. Zippers with large pull tabs and elastic waistbands are examples of self-dressing features.

T   F   12. Preschoolers are able to bathe themselves, although they may need a little help.

T   F   13. Preschoolers need about six hours of sleep each night

T   F   14. If a preschooler has a bad dream, have the child describe the dream to you.

T   F   15. Preschoolers can imagine almost any situation.

T   F   16. Most preschoolers do not understand how to use props in play.

Taking Care of Preschoolers

Name _____

Date _____ **Period** _____ **Score** _____

CHAPTER 12 QUIZ

☐ True/False: Circle *T* if the statement is true or *F* if the statement is false.

T F 1. Preschoolers look thinner for their size than toddlers do.

T F 2. Preschoolers may believe what they dreamed has really happened.

T F 3. Preschoolers have a very good understanding of time.

T F 4. Preschoolers prefer foods with strong flavors.

T F 5. Bedwetting may be caused by fear of the dark.

T F 6. Cooperative play is playing next to but not with other children.

T F 7. Most preschoolers do not understand how to use props in play.

T F 8. Preschoolers do not remember stories they are told.

T F 9. Accidents may happen to preschoolers because they try activities they have seen older children doing.

☐ Multiple Choice: Choose the best answer and write the corresponding letter in the blank.

_____ 10. Which of the following is *not* a skill of most younger preschoolers?

    A. Cutting out shapes with scissors.
    B. Building a straight, high tower.
    C. Working a zipper.
    D. Balancing on one foot.

_____ 11. Which of the following is *not* a self-dressing feature?

    A. Shirt cuffs that button.
    B. A zipper with a large pull tab.
    C. A design on the front of a sweatshirt.
    D. An elastic waistband on pants.

_____ 12. About how many hours of sleep does a preschooler need each night?

    A. 8.
    B. 10.
    C. 12.
    D. 15.

☐ Essay Questions: Provide the answers you feel best show your understanding of the subject matter.

13. Explain why preschoolers can control their emotions better than toddlers.

14. How would you comfort a child who has had a bad dream?

15. Give two activities a preschooler would enjoy and explain why.

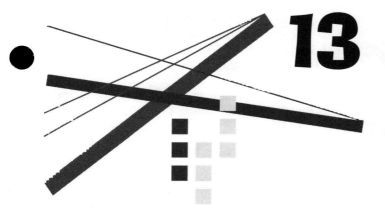

13 Safety and Health Concerns

Objectives

After studying this chapter, students will be able to
■ explain how to avoid situations that might threaten a child's safety.
■ discuss how to help children stay healthy and how to care for them when they are sick.
■ describe how to help meet the special needs of gifted children and children with disabilities.

Teaching Materials

Text, pages 150–160
  Words to Know
  Review It
  Apply It
  Think More About It
Student Activity Guide
  A. *Keeping Children Safe and Healthy*
  B. *Children with Special Needs*
Teacher's Resource Guide/Binder
  Emergency Phone Numbers, reproducible master 13-1
  My Personal Journal, reproducible master 13-2
  Dangerous and Poisonous Home Products Checklist, reproducible master 13-3
  Chapter 13 Quiz

Introductory Activities

1. *Keeping Children Safe and Healthy*, Activity A, SAG. Have students determine whether the statements listed describe safe or healthy practices. This activity can be used to stimulate interest in the chapter before students have studied the material.
2. Have students discuss accidents that occur in the home and ways they think these accidents could be prevented.

3. *Emergency Phone Numbers*, reproducible master 13-1. Have students fill in emergency phone numbers they should have easy access to in the home.

Strategies to Reteach, Reinforce, Enrich, and Extend Text Concepts

■ Safety

4. **ER** Have students visit a store specializing in items for children and find items related to childproofing a home. (Such items might include safety covers for electrical outlets or corner pads for furniture.) Have students report to the class on the types and prices of items available.
5. **ER** *My Personal Journal*, reproducible master 13-2. Have students write about an accident they have had or witnessed. Have them describe how they would prevent having that accident in the future.
6. **RT** *Dangerous and Poisonous Home Products Checklist*, reproducible master 13-3. Have students check a home using the checklist provided to see whether any unsafe products are left in locations that could be reached by children.
7. **ER** Have students collect empty cans, bottles, and packages that contained dangerous or poisonous products. Students should make an educational display using many of the items collected.
8. **EX** Divide the class into three groups. Each group should make a chart listing typical skills of children in one of the following age groups: infant, toddler, preschool. Across from each skill, group members should list possible safety hazards resulting from the skill. Have the class analyze and compare the finished lists.

9. **ER** Invite several parents to speak to the class about how they handle safety practices for their children. Parents of infants, toddlers, and preschoolers should be invited. Students should prepare questions related to safety concerns for each age group.

10. **ER** Have students make a poster outlining safety precautions for infants, toddlers, or preschoolers.

11. **ER** Invite a nurse to review with the class basic first aid for cuts, bruises, and burns. The nurse should also bring a good home first aid kit to show students.

12. **EX** Have students contact a doctor or pharmacist to find out how medicines can harm children if an overdose is taken. Students should also ask what to do in case of an overdose. Have students write a report based on their findings.

■ Health

13. **RF** Obtain four petri dishes with agar or another bacterial growth medium in them. (You may be able to borrow some from the science department.) Have two students cough on their hands and then place their fingers on the agar in separate dishes. Have the same students wash their hands thoroughly and place their fingers on the agar in the unused dishes. Label and cover the dishes. Keep the dishes on display for a week and have students check the growth of bacteria in the dishes. Discuss with students why washing hands is an important part of preventing illness.

14. **ER** Invite a pediatrician to discuss how treating a child's illness differs from treating the illness of a teen or an adult. The pediatrician should focus on how and why medications, amount of rest, and other factors involved in treatment differ.

15. **ER** Have students design a special treat they could share with a sick child. The treat might be a simple toy, game, story, or snack.

■ Children with Special Needs

16. **RF** *Children with Special Needs,* Activity B, SAG. Have students interview the parents of a child with special needs or the teacher of a child with special needs. Students should use the form provided to record information about the child's special needs.

17. **RF** All students have strengths and weaknesses. Have students think about weaknesses of theirs that might be considered "disabilities" of some sort. For instance, a student may not be able to draw well or run quickly. Have students discuss why it is unfair to assume that a person with disabilities cannot do much for himself or herself.

18. **ER** Have students research a national, state, or local organization that helps children with physical or mental disabilities. Students should report to the class on the goals and activities of the organization.

19. **RT** Have students discuss possible advantages and disadvantages of being a gifted child.

Answer Key

■ Text

Review It, page 160

1. putting unsafe items out of reach or behind locked doors; preventing falls, bumps, and cuts; checking toys and clothes to be sure they are safe
2. true
3. (Student response. Answers might include falling from a high place, choking on a small object, or drowning in a tub of water.)
4. keep poisonous substances out of toddlers' reach; label containers with "Mr. Yuk" stickers
5. (Student response.)
6. In a crash or sudden stop, the child could be thrown from your arms.
7. severe bleeding, head injuries, poisonings, sprains, and broken bones
8. (Student response. Answers might include meeting care needs properly, encouraging children to take care of their own health, and keeping your distance when you are sick.)
9. disability
10. D

■ Student Activity Guide

Keeping Children Safe and Healthy, Activity A
The following statements should have a + in the blanks:
1, 2, 5, 6, 7, 9, 11, 13, 15, 18, 19, 20
(Answers to questions are student response.)

■ Teacher's Resource Guide/Binder

Chapter 13 Quiz

1. T	6. T	11. F	16. A
2. F	7. T	12. T	17. D
3. F	8. T	13. F	18. C
4. T	9. F	14. B	
5. F	10. T	15. E	

19. As children grow and develop, their motor skills, thinking abilities, and interests change. These changes allow children to get into new situations that are potentially dangerous. Because toddlers can crawl and walk, they can reach objects that could not be reached by infants.
20. (Student response.)

Emergency Phone Numbers

Name _____ **Date** _____ **Period** _____

Parent's Work _____

Close Friend/Neighbor _____

Doctor _____

Ambulance _____

Hospital _____

Poison Control Center _____

Police Department _____

Fire Department _____

My Personal Journal

Write about a time when you had or witnessed an accident. What could have been done to prevent the accident? What would you do if you were in this situation in the future? What advice would you give to others in the same situation?

Dangerous and Poisonous Home Products Checklist

Name _____ Date _____ Period _____

Examine a home to see if the products listed below are kept in a place children could reach. Place a check mark by any items that children might be able to get into. At the bottom of the page, give suggestions for keeping the checked products away from children.

Kitchen

_____ drain cleaners
_____ furniture polish
_____ oven cleaner
_____ dishwasher detergent
_____ cleansing and scouring powders
_____ metal cleaners
_____ ammonia
_____ rust remover
_____ carpet and upholstery cleaners
_____ bleach

Bathroom

_____ all drugs, medications, and vitamins
_____ shampoo
_____ hair dyes and permanent solutions
_____ hair spray
_____ creams and lotions
_____ nail polish and remover
_____ suntan lotion
_____ deodorant
_____ shaving lotion
_____ toilet bowl cleaner
_____ hair remover
_____ bath oil
_____ rubbing alcohol
_____ room deodorizer

Storage Areas

_____ rat poison
_____ insecticides
_____ mothballs

Bedroom

_____ all drugs, medications, and vitamins
_____ jewelry cleaner
_____ cosmetics
_____ perfumes and colognes
_____ aftershave

Laundry

_____ bleaches
_____ soaps and detergents
_____ disinfectants
_____ bluing and dyes
_____ dry cleaning fluids

Garage/Basement

_____ lye
_____ kerosene
_____ gasoline
_____ lighter fluid
_____ turpentine
_____ paint remover and thinner
_____ antifreeze
_____ paint
_____ weed killer
_____ fertilizer
_____ plant spray

General

_____ flaking paint
_____ repainted toys
_____ broken plaster
_____ plants

Ways to keep unsafe products away from children:

_____

_____

_____

_____

Safety and Health Concerns

Name _____

Date _____ **Period** _____ **Score** _____

CHAPTER 13 QUIZ

☐ True/False: Circle *T* if the statement is true or *F* if the statement is false.

T   F   1. Shaving lotion can be a poisonous product.

T   F   2. A childproofed home is completely off limits to children.

T   F   3. To warn young children, "Mr. Yummy" symbols should be placed on containers of poisonous substances.

T   F   4. Children need to wear shoes when they play outside.

T   F   5. In a car, holding a child in your lap is as safe as putting a child in a car seat.

T   F   6. When a child gets a nosebleed, you should tilt the child's head forward.

T   F   7. If a child swallows a poisonous substance, you should have the container with you when you call the doctor.

T   F   8. You should not accept babysitting jobs when you are sick.

T   F   9. Playing tag is a good way to help cheer up a sick child.

T   F   10. Children with special needs should be treated just like other children in as many ways as possible.

T   F   11. A child with physical disabilities most likely has below normal intelligence.

T   F   12. Mental disabilities may affect social development.

T   F   13. Gifted children are just like adults in all areas of development.

☐ Matching: Match the following statements with the types of children they describe.

_____ 14. Children for whom an open stairway is a danger.

_____ 15. Children who may be more skilled or intelligent than most adults.

_____ 16. Children who cannot be left alone on beds or sofas.

_____ 17. Children who have one or more conditions that interfere with their abilities.

_____ 18. Children who are ready to learn to be more responsible for their own safety.

      A. infants
      B. toddlers
      C. preschoolers
      D. children with disabilities
      E. gifted children

☐ Essay Questions: Provide the answers you feel best show your understanding of the subject matter.

19. Explain why a home that has been childproofed for an infant may not be safe for a toddler.

20. Give two guidelines to remember when working with children with mental disabilities.

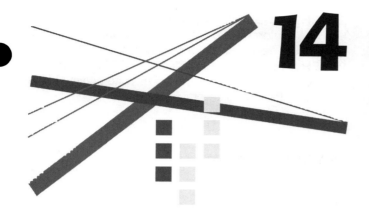

14 The Business of Babysitting

Objectives

After studying this chapter, students will be able to
- list ways of finding babysitting jobs.
- discuss the responsibilities babysitters have to the parents and children for whom they work.
- describe how to handle special child care concerns of babysitters.

Teaching Materials

Text, pages 161–172
   Words to Know
   Review It
   Apply It
   Think More About It
Student Activity Guide
   A. *Babysitting Experience*
   B. *Babysitting Do's and Don'ts*
   C. *Babysitting Responsibilities*
   D. *Babysitting Fun*
Teacher's Resource Guide/Binder
   Wanted: Qualified Babysitter, transparency master 14-1
   Information Babysitters Need from Parents, transparency master 14-2
   My Personal Journal, reproducible master 14-3
   The Reliable Babysitter, color transparency CT-14
   Chapter 14 Quiz

Introductory Activities

1. Have students discuss any experience they have working with children. Ask them if they enjoy working with children, and explain why or why not.
2. Have students complete the following sentence: "The most important responsibility of a babysitter is . . ."

Strategies to Reteach, Reinforce, Enrich, and Extend Text Concepts

■ Finding a Job

3. **RF** *Babysitting Experience,* Activity A, SAG. Have students answer the questions supplied based on their own experience or on an interview with another teen who babysits. Students should share their responses with the class.
4. **RT** *The Reliable Babysitter,* color transparency CT-14. Use this transparency as a basis for discussion. Discuss the points listed. Have students describe some of their own babysitting experiences.
5. **ER** Have students who are not babysitting or caring for siblings arrange to help as volunteers at a nursery service or to care for a child while a parent is home. Students should report on how the experience helped build their child care skills and on how they feel about caring for children after the experience.
6. **ER** Have students who are already babysitting or caring for siblings write a paper on some of their first experiences in caring for children.
7. **EX** Have students brainstorm a list of ways to find babysitting jobs.
8. **EX** Have students role-play meeting a new babysitting client for the first time. The role-play could be a phone conversation between babysitter and parent or a face-to-face meeting of babysitter, parent, and child.

■ Being a Responsible Sitter

9. **RF** *Wanted: Qualified Babysitter,* transparency master 14-1. Use this transparency to discuss qualities successful babysitters need to have.

10. **RT** *Babysitting Do's and Don'ts*, Activity B, SAG. Have students determine whether the given statements are items babysitters should do or should not do. Students should add five statements of their own and indicate whether each is a do or a don't. Have students discuss all the statements in class.

11. **ER** Invite a few parents to discuss with the class what they expect from babysitters. Without using names, parents may share some situations that happened with babysitters that they felt were handled well or could have been handled in a better way.

12. **ER** Have students prepare a questionnaire for parents in the community to find out what parents expect of sitters. Have the class work together to compile the results and write an article based on them. Place the article in a school paper or make copies for teachers to distribute in their classes.

13. **RF** *Information Babysitters Need from Parents*, transparency master 14-2. Have students discuss reasons each item is needed from parents before they leave the babysitter. Students should discuss other information they might want from parents.

14. **ER** Have students make a poster based on the theme "Babysitting Privileges Should Not Be Abused."

15. **RT** Have students practice taking telephone messages and preparing them for parents.

16. **RF** *Babysitting Responsibilities*, Activity C, SAG. Have students complete the given statements about being a responsible babysitter. Students should discuss their responses in class.

■ Caring for Children

17. **EX** Have students role-play meeting a child for the first time. Students should practice actions as well as words they would use.

18. **ER** Invite some experienced babysitters to discuss how they handle babysitting for more than one child. Students should prepare questions ahead of time.

19. **RF** Have students make a list of 20 statements beginning with "don't" that are often used in working with children. Students should reword the statements to use positive terms.

20. **ER** *My Personal Journal*, reproducible master 14-3. Have students write what they believe the most difficult part of babystting is, and how they could improve their skills.

21. **ER** Have students make items that could be included in a babysitter's bag of tricks. Make a display from all the students' items.

22. **RF** Have students plan two activities that require no equipment to entertain children. Students should demonstrate one activity to the class.

23. **ER** *Babysitting Fun*, Activity D, SAG. Have students use the form provided to write activity ideas for children of different ages.

Answer Key

■ Text

Review It, page 172
1. (List three:) spend time with younger relatives; read about child care, growth, and development; volunteer to help with nursery services provided at religious centers or community events; spend time with a neighbor's child
2. (Student response.)
3. C
4. Call the parent to see if he or she was expecting the repair person.
5. A babysitter cannot concentrate on watching children while he or she is on the phone. Also, parents or others may be trying to get through with important messages.
6. false
7. (Student response.)
8. Separate the children and ask what is wrong. Try to find a solution without favoring one child or the other.
9. role model
10. (Student response.)

■ Student Activity Guide

Babysitting Do's and Don'ts
Do's: 1, 5, 9, 11, 12, 13, 14, 15
Don'ts: 2, 3, 4, 6, 7, 8, 10
(Answers to questions 16-20 are student response.)

■ Teacher's Resource Guide/Binder

Chapter 14 Quiz

1. T	5. T	9. T	13. A
2. T	6. T	10. B	
3. F	7. F	11. C	
4. T	8. T	12. D	

14. Volunteer to help with nursery services provided at a religious center or community event; ask a neighbor if you can spend time with his or her children while the parent is home.
15. (Student response.)

Wanted: Qualified Babysitter

Babysitters should be

- dependable

- trustworthy

- responsible

- mature

- friendly

- punctual

- polite

Information Babysitters Need from Parents

■ Place and phone number where parents can be reached

■ Family doctor's name and phone number

■ Name and number of a close friend or neighbor

■ Number of police and fire department

■ Locations of

    Children's room or rooms

    Outside doors

    Light switches

    Phones

    Bathroom

    Kitchen

    First aid kit

    Flashlight

    Blankets

    Diapers and changes of clothes

■ Time of parents' return

■ Snack habits of children

■ House rules about play, television, etc.

■ Hygiene routines

■ Favorite songs or stories

■ Bedtime

■ Any family customs to be observed

■ Special habits or concerns of children (such as fear of dark)

My Personal Journal

If you babysit for children, what do you think is the most difficult part of babysitting? If you have never been a sitter, what do you think would be the most difficult part? Why? What could you do to improve your skills in this area?

The Business of Babysitting

Name _____

Date _____ **Period** _____ **Score** _____

CHAPTER 14 QUIZ

☐ True/False: Circle *T* if the statement is true or *F* if the statement is false.

T F 1. Spending time with children before babysitting helps build your confidence and skills.

T F 2. A person who babysits regularly for a toddler may not be prepared to babysit for an infant.

T F 3. Parents will not mind if you change their regular house rules on nights when you babysit.

T F 4. Canceling a babysitting appointment to attend a social activity can affect your ability to get future babysitting jobs.

T F 5. When babysitting, you should lock all outside doors as soon as parents leave.

T F 6. Babysitters have an obligation not to repeat any stories children tell them about private family matters.

T F 7. Once children are asleep, it is fine for you to take a nap while babysitting.

T F 8. When you babysit two children, you do not need to ignore the oldest child while you take care of the youngest.

T F 9. Admitting mistakes when you babysit for children is one way of being a good role model.

☐ Multiple Choice: Choose the best answer and write the corresponding letter in the blank.

_____ 10. After babysitting, if a parent has had too much alcohol or appears overtired, you should _____.
A. allow the parent to give you a ride home
B. call a family member for a ride home
C. let the parent know that you disapprove of his or her irresponsibility
D. yell at the parent

_____ 11. When parents return home after a babysitting job, you should _____.
A. tell them everything went fine
B. let them know verbally whether or not they had any phone calls
C. discuss any problems such as the child having a nightmare
D. complain to the parents if you did not enjoy babysitting for them

_____ 12. If a child seems scared or shy when meeting you for the first time, you should _____.
A. stand very close to the child, look down, and say hello
B. give the child a big hug
C. give up on ever getting the child to feel comfortable around you
D. try getting down on your knees and asking the child a question

_____ 13. Which of the following statements is least likely to harm a child's self-concept?
A. "Billy, try to hold the cup straight this time so the milk doesn't spill."
B. "That's a silly question, Jordan."
C. "Boy, Tina, are you clumsy!"
D. "Sally, you are so messy when you eat."

☐ Essay Questions: Provide the answers you feel best show your understanding of the subject matter.

14. Give two ways to get experience with children before babysitting.

15. List four items you should ask parents before they leave when you babysit.

15 Parenting

Objectives

After studying this chapter, students will be able to

- discuss the reasons to choose parenting and responsibilities of parenting.
- describe the impact having a child can have on a parent's time, energy, finances, and career.
- explain factors that affect the kind of relationship a parent has with a child.

Teaching Materials

Text, pages 173–185
  Words to Know
  Review It
  Apply It
  Think More About It
Student Activity Guide
  A. *The Impact of Parenting*
  B. *Reasons to Choose Parenting and Responsibilities of Parenting*
Teacher's Resource Guide/Binder
  My Personal Journal, reproducible master 15-1
  Parents Meet Children's Needs, transparency master 15-2
  The Cost of Parenting, transparency master 15-3
  Successful Parenting Requirements, color transparency CT-15
  Chapter 15 Quiz

Introductory Activities

1. Have students complete the following sentence: "I think the reason most people choose to become parents is . . ."
2. Have students make a list of their parents' responsibilities. Use this as the basis of a discussion about the responsibilities of parenting.

Strategies to Reteach, Reinforce, Enrich, and Extend Text Concepts

■ Reasons to Choose Parenting

3. **RF** Have students discuss the consequences of a person or couple having a child because they feel unloved and believe the child will make up for that feeling. (Parents may not be prepared for problems and negative feelings from children; parents may not be strong enough emotionally to give the child needed love and attention; the disappointment of not getting constant love from the child may even lead to neglect or abuse.)
4. **ER** Have students interview a parent about an experience that he or she saw differently because of his or her child. Students should write a short report based on the interview.
5. **RF** Have the class start a collection of quotes from children that are amusing or thought-provoking. These might be found in magazines or through interviews with parents. Have students discuss how these statements might be refreshing or rewarding to parents.
6. **ER** *My Personal Journal*, reproducible master 15-1. Have students write about reasons they might choose parenting, and how they think these opinions will change as they get older.

■ Responsibilities of Parenting

7. **RF** *Parents Meet Children's Needs,* transparency master 15-2. Use this transparency to discuss how parents meet the physical, intellectual, social, and emotional needs of their children.

8. **EX** Have students brainstorm specific responsibilities involved in meeting children's physical, intellectual, social, and emotional needs. Have one or two students compile a list of all the responsibilities named. Students should discuss the amount of time and effort that would be needed to fulfill all these responsibilities.

9. **EX** Have students work in small groups to plan skits that demonstrate effective ways for parents to be role models. Each group should present their skit and lead a class discussion on their skit afterwards.

10. **RF** *Reasons to Choose Parenting and Responsibilities of Parenting*, Activity B, SAG. Have students complete the given statements about the reasons to choose parenting and responsibilities of parenthood. Students should discuss their responses in class.

11. **RF** *Successful Parenting Requirements,* color transparency CT-15. Describe qualities that make successful parents. Discuss reasons teens are not yet ready to become parents.

■ Impact of Parenthood

12. **RF** *The Cost of Parenting*, transparency master 15-3. Assign different students to find out the cost of each item listed on the master. (For regular expenses, such as diapers, have students estimate a total expense for the baby's first year.) Use the master to record and total the various costs. Have students discuss other expenses parents might have as children grow.

13. **ER** Invite parents who have a young child to talk to the class about the impact of parenthood on them. Students should prepare questions in advance.

14. **ER** *The Impact of Parenting*, Activity A, SAG. Have students interview a parent about the impact of having a child. Students should use the form provided to record information. Students should compare their interview responses with those received by other members of the class.

■ The Parent-Child Relationship

15. **ER** Have students find and read an article that discusses some aspect of the mother's health and how it affects pregnancy and the child. Students should discuss their articles in class.

16. **RT** Have each student make a list of his or her ideas of maturity and responsibility in a parent. Students should compare their lists with those of other class members.

17. **RF** Have students discuss the importance of disciplining children. Students should discuss what they think a child who has no guidance from parents would be like.

18. **ER** Invite a family counselor or social worker to discuss the causes and effects of child abuse and neglect. The guest should also discuss sources of help for abused and neglected children.

19. **EX** Have students develop a list of resources for abused and neglected children. Students may use the information to produce a brochure to distribute to other students in the school.

Answer Key

■ Text

Review It, page 185

1. sharing love; having new experiences; seeing things from a child's perspective (Students may justify other responses.)
2. If parents do not decide how to share before they have children, they may be disappointed when they find they have to give up some of their time and other belongings. This could lead to resentment toward the child and other negative feelings. Such negative feelings can make a child feel insecure or unloved.
3. (Student response. List one for each need.)
4. Values are standards that guide actions, attitudes, and judgments. Children tend to accept the values that they see their parents living by.
5. (Student response.)
6. false
7. (Student response.)
8. (List three:) physical maturity; weight; eating habits; physical health; mental health
9. guidance
10. B

■ Teacher's Resource Guide/Binder

Chapter 15 Quiz

1.	F	10.	T
2.	T	11.	T
3.	T	12.	T
4.	F	13.	F
5.	T	14.	D
6.	F	15.	C
7.	T	16.	E
8.	F	17.	A
9.	T	18.	B
19.	(Student response.)		
20.	(Student response.)		

My Personal Journal

Think of some reasons you might want to choose parenting. Do you think they are good reasons? Do you think your opinions might change as you get older? How?

_____

_____

_____

_____

_____

_____

_____

_____

_____

_____

_____

_____

_____

_____

_____

_____

_____

_____

_____

_____

_____

_____

_____

_____

_____

_____

Parents Meet Children's Needs

Physical Needs

- provide food

- provide shelter

- provide clothing

- provide medical care

Intellectual Needs

- provide toys and other learning activities

- be active in schooling

- help children with studies

Social Needs

- trust other adults to care for children

- provide understanding and comfort

- help children learn from friendships

Emotional Needs

- show unconditional love

- show love openly

The Cost of Parenting

Having a Baby

Doctor's care for mother _____

Laboratory tests_____

Hospital/delivery fees _____

Feeding

Formula _____

Bottles _____

Cereal/solid food _____

Furnishings

Crib _____

Sheets/blankets _____

Car seat_____

Playpen _____

High chair _____

Health and Hygiene

Doctor's care for baby _____

Medicine _____

Vaccinations _____

Baby soap/powder/lotion _____

Clothing

Diapers _____

Cotton T-shirts _____

Play outfits_____

Footwear _____

Laundry supplies _____

Water/electricity for extra
    laundry_____

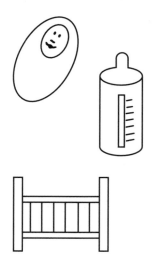

Cost for the First Year

Having a baby   _____

Feeding   _____

Furnishings   _____

Health and hygiene   _____

Clothing   _____

      Total   _____

Parenting

Name _____

Date _____ Period _____ Score _____

CHAPTER 15 QUIZ

☐ True/False: Circle *T* if the statement is true or *F* if the statement is false.

T F 1. Parents receive more love from children than they need to give to children.

T F 2. A couple needs to make many adjustments to their lifestyle to make room for a child.

T F 3. Parents must meet their children's physical needs by providing shelter, food, clothing, and medical care.

T F 4. As long as parents make sure their children get to school on time, they are meeting their children's intellectual needs.

T F 5. To meet children's social needs, parents may need to give up some time alone with their children.

T F 6. Children should not be shown love when they do not behave properly.

T F 7. If a parent tells lies in front of his or her child, the child may believe that there is nothing wrong with lying.

T F 8. Parents who put themselves down teach their children to feel good about themselves.

T F 9. Caring for a young child requires a great deal of physical energy.

T F 10. Family responsibilities may keep a parent from having the most successful career possible for him or her.

T F 11. Teen mothers are more likely to give birth to babies with low birthweights than mothers between 20 and 32 years of age.

T F 12. People who often change plans at the last minute without telling others should become more responsible before having children.

T F 13. Communication is a parenting skill that comes naturally to most parents.

☐ Matching: Match the following terms with their definitions.

_____ 14. Liking yourself and feeling that you are a good and worthwhile person.

_____ 15. All the words and actions parents use that affect their children's behavior.

_____ 16. The various methods parents use to teach children acceptable behavior.

_____ 17. Harm to a child that is done on purpose.

_____ 18. Failure to meet a child's needs.

A. child abuse
B. child neglect
C. guidance
D. self-esteem
E. discipline

☐ Essay Questions: Provide the answers you feel best show your understanding of the subject matter.

19. Explain two ways becoming a parent has an impact on a person's life.

20. Give three possible causes of child abuse or neglect.

Reproducible Quiz

Part Four

Your Health and Nutrition

Part goal: Students will learn ways to be as healthy, fit, well groomed, and well nourished as they can be.

Bulletin Board

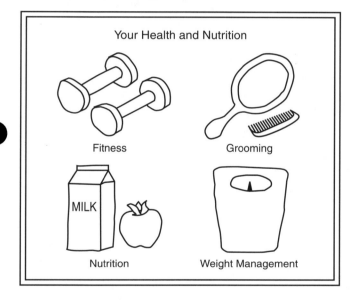

Your Health and Nutrition

Fitness   Grooming

MILK

Nutrition   Weight Management

Title: "Your Health and Nutrition"

Place symbols for fitness, grooming, nutrition, and weight management on the board as shown. Label each set of symbols.

Teaching Materials

Text
Chapters 16–20, pages 186–236

Student Activity Guide
Chapters, 16–20
Teacher's Resource Guide/Binder
How Do I Shape Up? reproducible master

Introductory Activities

1. *How Do I Shape Up?* reproducible master. Have students use the form to determine ways they care for their health and nutrition as well as ways they need improvement. As students work through the unit, have them fill in suggestions for improving their health and nutrition habits.
2. Have students write a short essay on what health and nutrition mean to them. Students should mention one person they know or know of who has good health and nutrition habits. Have students discuss their essays in class.
3. Invite a panel of speakers who portray aspects of wellness to speak to the class on their health habits. Speakers might include local high school or community college athletes, medical professionals, or health club personnel. Panelists should be prepared to discuss the importance of grooming, avoiding health risks, exercise, and healthy eating habits.

How Do I Shape Up?

Name _____ **Date** _____ **Period** _____

In the space below, write 10 habits you have that you think promote your own health and nutrition. Also write 10 areas of your health and nutrition habits that you think need improvement. As you study this unit, use this sheet to take notes on ways that you can improve your health and nutrition habits.

10 Good Health Habits	10 Health Habits To Improve	Suggestions From Text

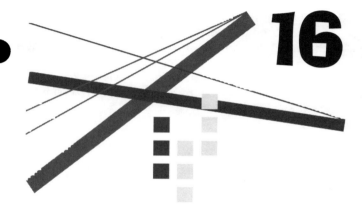

16 Promoting Good Health

Objectives

After studying this chapter, students will be able to
- describe personal health habits that promote wellness.
- identify health risks associated with the use of tobacco and alcohol and other drugs and list sources of help for dealing with these risks.
- discuss recommended treatments for minor injuries and common illnesses.

Teaching Materials

Text, pages 187–196
  Words to Know
  Review It
  Apply It
  Think More About It
Student Activity Guide
  A. *Promoting Wellness*
  B. *Saying No to Health Risks*
  C. *First Aid*
Teacher's Resource Guide/Binder
  Reasons to Avoid Alcohol, transparency master 16-1
  There's No Excuse, reproducible master 16-2
  My Personal Journal, reproducible master 16-3
  Promote Good Health, color transparency CT-16
  Chapter 16 Quiz

Introductory Activities

1. Have students define *wellness* in their own terms. Then have them look up the definition in the glossary and compare the two.
2. Create a list of health risks that have been discussed on the news lately. Discuss with students what type of health problem is associated with each risk.

Strategies to Reteach, Reinforce, Enrich, and Extend Text Concepts

■ The Wellness Revolution

3. **ER** Have students read a magazine or newspaper article on the current wellness trend and write a short report on its contents.
4. **RF** As a class, have students list factors in the environment that promote wellness and factors in the environment that can hamper wellness. Students should then discuss how they can control their exposure to different factors to achieve wellness.
5. **RF** *Promoting Wellness*, Activity A, SAG. Have students use the space provided to write an article describing personal health habits that promote wellness. Students should share and discuss their articles in class.

■ Health Risks

6. **RT** *Saying No to Health Risks*, Activity B, SAG. For each of the listed situations, have students write suggestions for how to say no to the health risks involved. Students should also list local sources of help in dealing with tobacco, alcohol, and drug abuse.
7. **ER** Invite one to three people who have quit smoking to talk to the class on why they started smoking, why they decided to quit, and what was involved in quitting.
8. **EX** Have students brainstorm a list of group activities that can be fun without drinking alcohol. Students should discuss why some people think they need alcohol at group activities to have fun. Have the students explain how each reason listed is really an excuse. Have them

summarize the legal implications of alcohol consumption by teens. They should also discuss what might happen if the only group activity is drinking.

9. **RF** *Reasons to Avoid Alcohol,* transparency master 16-1. Use this transparency to discuss reasons teens should avoid alcohol.

10. **ER** Have students research a program that helps alcohol or other drug abusers. Students should prepare and give an oral report.

11. **RF** *Promote Good Health,* color transparency CT-16. Use this transparency as a basis of discussion of healthy choices vs. unhealthy choices.

12. **RF** *There's No Excuse,* reproducible master 16-2. Have students write their responses to each of the excuses some teens give for using drugs. Students should discuss their responses in class.

13. **ER** Invite a law enforcement officer to speak to your class about the legal problems associated with drug abuse.

14. **ER** Have each student choose a health risk and create a poster that informs people about the potential dangers of that health risk.

■ When Treatment Is Needed

15. **ER** *First Aid,* Activity C, SAG. Invite an American Red Cross representative or a nurse to speak to the class about first aid. Students should use the forms provided to take notes on various first aid procedures.

16. **EX** Have students research and demonstrate a first aid technique to the class.

17. **ER** Have students make a bulletin board with pictures and drawings of poisonous plants and methods of treating symptoms from poisonous plants.

18. **ER** Have students interview doctors on how to treat a common illness and report their findings in class.

■ Terminal Illness

19. **ER** Invite a doctor who has had experience with cancer treatment to speak to the class. The doctor should discuss how treatment has advanced over the years, what types of treatment are currently being used, and what types of treatments are being studied for the future.

20. **RF** Have students read a magazine or newspaper article about AIDS and write a short report based on what they read.

21. **ER** *My Personal Journal,* reproducible master 16-3. Write a letter to someone 100 years in the future. Tell them about diseases that exist today and the ways we are trying to find cures for them. Predict advances that medicine will make in the future. Will diseases of today be cured? Will new ones exist?

Answer Key

■ Text

Review It, page 196
1. Wellness involves adopting good health habits that improve mental and social well-being as well as physical health.
2. (Student response. See pages 189–190 in the text.)
3. false
4. (List four:) mouth and throat tissues are harmed, stomach and heart are harmed, weight may be gained, nutrient deficiencies may occur, the liver may be harmed, babies of drinking mothers may suffer from birth defects
5. physically dependent
6. (List five:) clinics, state agencies, city and community agencies, churches, hospitals, school nurses, counselors, teachers, Alcoholics Anonymous, Al-Anon, Alateen (Students may justify other responses.)
7. The animal should be tested for rabies.
8. to avoid dehydration
9. A
10. early detection

■ Teacher's Resource Guide/Binder

Chapter 16 Quiz

1.	wellness	8.	cancer
2.	nicotine	9.	AIDS
3.	passive	10.	B
4.	depressant	11.	C
5.	alcoholism	12.	B
6.	abuse	13.	A
7.	psychologically		
14.	(Student response.)		
15.	(Student response.)		

Reasons to Avoid Alcohol

- Drinking alcohol is illegal for minors.

- Alcohol acts as a depressant—it slows down activity in the brain and spinal cord.

- Alcohol causes a lack of self-control and good judgment.

- Because alcohol stops people from responding quickly to pain or danger, use of alcohol increases the risks of being involved in accidents.

- Alcohol harms the tissues of the mouth and throat of heavy drinkers.

- Weight gain often occurs.

- Long-term use of alcohol harms the liver.

- Unborn babies can suffer from birth defects if their mothers drink while pregnant.

- People can become addicted to alcohol. This harms not only the person's health, but also their relationships with other people.

There's No Excuse

Name _____ **Date** _____ **Period** _____

Below are some excuses teens give for using drugs. In the space that follows, explain why you think each statement is no excuse for using drugs. Then write a suggestion for a more positive activity that would help meet the needs of teens using each excuse. Discuss your responses in class.

I want to be popular and accepted by friends.

_____

_____

My best friends use drugs, and they convinced me to start.

_____

_____

My parents or other family members use drugs.

_____

_____

I have the money to buy drugs, and they are easy to obtain.

_____

_____

Using drugs helps me escape from stress and other personal and family problems.

_____

_____

I like the thrill I get from taking drugs.

_____

_____

Using drugs gives me a good feeling and makes me happy.

_____

_____

Using drugs makes me feel better when I am bored or lonely.

_____

_____

Using drugs helps me overcome shyness and relax with people.

_____

_____

Drug use appears glamorous on TV and in movies, and using drugs makes me feel glamorous.

_____

_____

My Personal Journal

Write a letter to someone 100 years in the future. Tell them about diseases that exist today. Predict advances medicine will make in the future. Will diseases of today be cured? Will new ones exist?

_____

_____

_____

_____

_____

_____

_____

_____

_____

_____

_____

_____

_____

_____

_____

_____

_____

_____

_____

_____

_____

_____

_____

_____

Promoting Good Health

Name _____

Date _____ **Period** _____ **Score** _____

CHAPTER 16 QUIZ

☐ Fill in the Blank: Complete the statements below by filling in the blanks.

_____1. People whose lifestyles keep them in good physical, mental, and social health are in a state of _____.

_____2. When tobacco is used, a drug called _____ gives the body a lift.

_____3. The health of people who do not smoke can be harmed by _____ smoking.

_____4. Because alcohol is a _____, it slows down activity in the brain and spinal cord.

_____5. People who are unable to stop drinking alcohol have the disease called _____.

_____6. Using a drug for a purpose other than it is intended is called drug _____.

_____7. A person who craves a drug because it provides an escape from reality is _____ dependent on that drug.

_____8. When detected in its early stages, the uncontrolled growth of cells called _____ is often curable.

_____9. _____, a disease that affects the body's ability to resist infections, currently has no cure.

☐ Multiple Choice: Choose the best answer and write the corresponding letter in the blank.

_____ 10. Which of the following does *not* contain a drug?
A. Cigarettes.
B. Orange juice.
C. Coffee.
D. Nail polish remover.

_____ 11. Which of the following can be done without special training?
A. Giving cardiopulmonary resuscitation.
B. Treating a severe reaction to a poisonous plant.
C. Treating a scrape or cut.
D. Giving mouth-to-mouth resuscitation.

_____ 12. Which of the following should *not* be done when treating an insect bite?
A. Apply cold, wet compresses.
B. Leave the stinger in the skin.
C. Wash the area with soap and water.
D. Watch for an allergic reaction.

_____ 13. If a person is getting an electrical shock, you should *not* _____.
A. grab the person and pull him or her away from the source of the electric current
B. turn off the current by unplugging the appliance or turning off the circuit
C. use a wooden pole to pull the person away from the source of the electric current
D. call for medical help

☐ Essay Questions: Provide the answers you feel best show your understanding of the subject matter.

14. Choose a health risk and explain why it can be harmful to your health. Also explain why some people choose to take this health risk.

15. Choose a common illness and explain a recommended way of treating it.

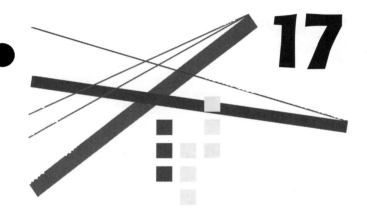

17 Looking Your Best

Objectives

After studying this chapter, students will be able to
- discuss basic health practices that contribute to good looks.
- explain how to clean and care for different parts of the body.

Teaching Materials

Text, pages 197–207
    Words to Know
    Review It
    Apply It
    Think More About It
Student Activity Guide
    A. *Grooming Products and Equipment*
    B. *Skin Care*
    C. *Grooming Skills*
Teacher's Resource Guide/Binder
    Warm Up to Exercise, reproducible master 17-1
    Do You Have Good Grooming Habits? transparency master 17-2
    My Personal Journal, reproducible master 17-3
    Chapter 17 Quiz

Introductory Activities

1. Have students discuss the types of exercises they do.
2. Have students discuss times they have not gotten enough sleep and how these times made them feel.

Strategies to Reteach, Reinforce, Enrich, and Extend Text Concepts

■ The Foundation of Good Looks

3. **ER** Have students find current articles from reliable sources about how certain nutrients affect the body. Students should discuss these articles in class.
4. **ER** Have students make a bulletin board that depicts different types of exercise. Benefits of exercise should be listed on the board.
5. **RF** Have students write down excuses people make for not exercising. As a class, have students come up with solutions to fit each excuse. (For example, the excuse may be that joining a health club is too expensive. Solutions would focus on exercise forms that are inexpensive, such as jogging or jumping rope.)
6. **RT** *Warm Up to Exercise*, reproducible master 17-1. Distribute the master and discuss with students how warming up should be a part of any exercise program. If possible, have the class try some of the exercises.
7. **ER** Have students try an exercise program for a month. Students should keep a record of what exercises they are doing and how often. Students should also record how they feel about the exercise. At the end of the month, have students write a short report on how they feel they benefited from

the exercise and whether or not they will continue the exercise program.

8. **EX** Have students keep records of their sleep habits for a week and analyze them in relationship to the text discussion of sleep.

9. **RT** Hold a class "slouch guard" contest. At the beginning of class, give each student an index card that has the word "posture" written on it. Throughout class, students should be allowed to indicate when they see a student slouching. The person who catches the sloucher should get the sloucher's index card. Slouchers who have more than one card must give up all their cards if they are caught. Award a prize to the person with the most cards at the end of the day.

■ Good Grooming Habits

10. **RF** *Do You Have Good Grooming Habits?* transparency master 17-2. Use this master to help students reflect on their personal grooming habits.

11. **RT** *Grooming Products and Equipment*, Activity A, SAG. Have students complete the given chart about grooming products and equipment they use or have used. Students should compare their charts with those of other students.

12. **RF** Have students collect newspaper and magazine advertisements for grooming aids. Students should compare the statements made about the products and discuss whether they think the statements are fact or just an effort to get people to buy the product.

13. **RF** Have students bring in different types of soaps and compare the ingredients. Students should discuss what affects they think the different ingredients have on the body.

14. **ER** *Skin Care*, Activity B, SAG. Invite a dermatologist to class or have students interview one about skin care. Students should write the answers to the listed questions.

15. **RF** Have students read a recent article about the sun's effects on the skin. Students should write a summary of the article.

16. **ER** Invite a dentist to speak to the class on proper dental care techniques.

17. **ER** Have students make a display of items used for manicures and pedicures and label each item according to how and why it is used.

18. **ER** Have students make a poster outlining the steps involved in hair care.

19. **RF** Have students collect and display pictures of different hairstyles for people in their age group. Have students discuss which hairstyles would work well for them and why.

20. **RT** *Grooming Skills*, Activity C, SAG. Have students set up a grooming schedule using the form provided.

21. **ER** *My Personal Journal,* reproducible master 17-3. Have students write letters to a model and ask for grooming advice.

Answer Key

■ Text

Review It, page 207

1. (List three:) strengthened muscles, strengthened heart and lungs, increased endurance, improved circulation and digestion, improved appearance, improved personality (Students can justify other answers.)
2. (Student response.)
3. A deodorant controls body odor but does not stop the flow of perspiration. An antiperspirant reduces the flow of perspiration in addition to controlling body odor.
4. oily, dry, normal, and combination
5. C
6. true
7. plaque
8. manicure
9. Suds left in the hair will dull the shine. Also, failure to rinse hair well could cause dandruff.
10. type of hair, face shape, and lifestyle

■ Teacher's Resource Guide/Binder

Chapter 17 Quiz

1.	F	10.	H
2.	T	11.	B
3.	F	12.	C
4.	T	13.	A
5.	T	14.	I
6.	F	15.	F
7.	T	16.	G
8.	T	17.	J
9.	D	18.	E

19. strengthens muscles and makes them more flexible, improving coordination; strengthens heart and lungs; improves endurance; improves blood circulation and digestion; improves appearance of skin; improves posture; makes it easier to relax and feel more comfortable
20. Brush hair to remove tangles and loosen dirt; clean scalp and hair as you shampoo; rinse thoroughly to remove all soap; follow with creme rinse if desired.

Warm Up to Exercise

Name _____ **Date** _____ **Period** _____

Warming up is an important part of any exercise program. Stretching and toning your muscles before you start vigorous exercise prevents stiffness, aches, and pains. Warm-up exercises can also help prevent injuries. The following exercises will help you warm up before you start exercising.

Stretcher Stand facing wall arms' length away. Lean forward and place palms of hands flat against wall, slightly below shoulder height. Keep back straight, heels firmly on floor, and slowly bend elbows until forehead touches wall. Tuck hips toward wall and hold position for 20 seconds. Repeat exercise with knees slightly flexed.

Reach and Bend Stand erect with feet shoulder-width apart and arms extended over head. Reach as high as possible while keeping heels on floor and hold for 10 counts. Flex knees slightly and bend slowly at waist, touching floor between feet with fingers. Hold for 10 counts. (If you can't touch the floor, try to touch the tops of your shoes.) Repeat entire sequence 2 to 5 times.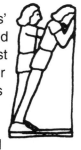

Knee Pull Lie flat on back with legs extended and arms at sides. Lock arms around legs just below knees and pull knees to chest, raising buttocks slightly off floor. Hold for 10 to 15 counts. (If you have knee problems, you may find it easier to lock arms behind knees.) Repeat exercise 3 to 5 times.

Situp Several versions of the situp are listed in reverse order of difficulty (easiest one listed first, most difficult one last). Start with the situp that you can do three times without undue strain. When you are able to do 10 repetitions of the exercise without great difficulty, move on to a more difficult version.

1. Lie flat on back with arms at sides, palms down, and knees slightly bent. Curl head forward until you can see past feet, hold for three counts, then lower to start position. *Repeat exercise 3 to 10 times.*

2. Lie flat on back with arms at sides, palms down, and knees slightly bent. Roll forward until upper body is at 45-degree angle to floor, then return to starting position. *Repeat exercise 3 to 10 times.*

3. Lie flat on back with arms at sides, palms down, and knees slightly bent. Roll forward to sitting position, then return to starting position. *Repeat exercise 3 to 10 times.*

4. Lie flat on back with arms crossed on chest and knees slightly bent. Roll forward to sitting position, then return to starting position. *Repeat exercise 3 to 10 times.*

5. Lie flat on back with hands laced in back of head and knees slightly bent. Roll forward to sitting position, then return to starting position. *Repeat exercise 3 to 15 times.*

Do You Have Good Grooming Habits?

Do You . . .

■ eat nutritious foods?

■ make time for exercise?

■ get enough sleep so you feel refreshed in the morning?

■ stand straight and tall?

■ bathe daily?

■ use deodorant or antiperspirant?

■ clean and care for skin, hands, and feet?

■ brush your teeth several times a day?

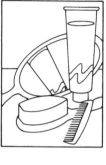

My Personal Journal

Write a letter to a famous model. What would you like to know about that person? What grooming questions would you ask? What advice could you give the model?

_____

_____

_____

_____

_____

_____

_____

_____

_____

_____

_____

_____

_____

_____

_____

_____

_____

_____

_____

_____

_____

_____

_____

_____

_____

Looking Your Best

Name _____

Date _____ **Period** _____ **Score** _____

CHAPTER 17 QUIZ

☐ True/False: Circle *T* if the statement is true or *F* if the statement is false.

T   F   1. A good guideline for eating nutritiously is to eat the same foods at each meal.

T   F   2. Exercising can make it easier for you to relax and feel comfortable.

T   F   3. Most young people need five to six hours of sleep each night.

T   F   4. Perspiration is odorless when it first appears on the body.

T   F   5. Shaving can be irritating to the skin.

T   F   6. People with oily skin often notice flakiness on their faces.

T   F   7. Ultraviolet rays from the sun can lead to dry, wrinkled skin and skin cancer.

T   F   8. A toothbrush with soft bristles is recommended for brushing your teeth.

☐ Matching: Match the following terms with their definitions.

_____ 9. Cleaning and caring for the body.

_____ 10. The way a person holds his or her body when walking, sitting, or standing.

_____ 11. A product that reduces the flow of perspiration and controls odor.

_____ 12. The appearance of the skin on a person's face.

_____ 13. A skin disorder that results in the appearance of blemishes on the face, neck, scalp, upper chest, or back.

_____ 14. A product for skin that filters out some of the sun's damaging rays.

_____ 15. A treatment for the care of feet.

_____ 16. An invisible film of bacteria that forms on teeth.

_____ 17. A hard, crusty substance that forms on teeth.

_____ 18. A treatment for the care of fingernails.

A. acne
B. antiperspirant
C. complexion
D. grooming
E. manicure
F. pedicure
G. plaque
H. posture
I. sunscreen
J. tartar

☐ Essay Questions: Provide the answers you feel best show your understanding of the subject matter.

19. How does exercise benefit your body?

20. What are the steps involved in washing your hair?

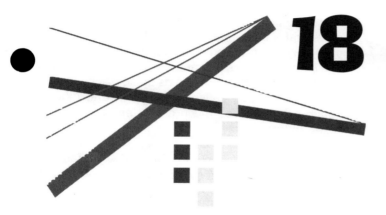

18 Nutrition and You

Objectives

After studying this chapter, students will be able to
- explain the importance of good nutrition.
- list the essential nutrients and describe their functions and sources.

Teaching Materials

Text, pages 208–216
 Words to Know
 Review It
 Apply It
 Think More About It
Student Activity Guide
 A. *Nutrition Puzzle*
 B. *Nutrients*
Teacher's Resource Guide/Binder
 What Does the Body Need? transparency master 18-1
 Nutrient Sources, transparency master 18-2
 My Personal Journal, reproducible master 18-3
 Water, color transparencies CT-18A and CT-18B
 Chapter 18 Quiz

Introductory Activities

1. As a class, have students develop a list of characteristics associated with good nutrition and a list of characteristics associated with poor nutrition.
2. Have students write a short story based on the theme "You Are What You Eat."

Strategies to Reteach, Reinforce, Enrich, and Extend Text Concepts

■ Foods for Good Health

3. **ER** Have students survey teens and adults to find out what the word *nutrition* means to each of them. Then have a group of students use the survey results to develop a newscast style skit reporting the findings.
4. **ER** Have students make posters based on the theme "Good Nutrition is for Now and for the Future."

■ Understanding Nutrients

5. **RF** *What Does the Body Need?* transparency master 18-1. Use this transparency to introduce the different nutrients included in the chapter. Ask students to give examples of possible sources for each nutrient.
6. **RF** *Nutrient Sources,* transparency master 18-2. Have students use the appendix to find foods high in the nutrients given on the master. List or have a student list these foods on the transparency as students name them.
7. **ER** Have students read articles on vegetarianism and discuss these articles in class. Have students discuss how vegetarians get enough protein even without eating meat.
8. **ER** Invite a dietitian to speak to the class on carbohydrates in the diet. The speaker should focus on how different forms of carbohydrates affect the

body. The speaker should also talk about any current findings on the functions of fiber in the body.

9. **RF** Have students list foods they eat frequently and find out how much fat is in each of them. Students should then compare their lists and develop a list of the ten foods that are highest in fat. Students should discuss ways of cutting down on the amounts of these foods they eat.

10. **ER** Have students design a bulletin board depicting how specific vitamins and minerals work in the body.

11. **RF** *Nutrition Puzzle*, Activity A, SAG. Have students fill in the puzzle by finding the terms described in the given statements.

12. **RT** *Nutrients*, Activity B, SAG. Have students complete the chart with various nutrients listed. For each nutrient, students should give the reason the nutrient is needed and food sources of the nutrient.

13. **RF** *Water,* color transparencies CT-18A and CT-18B. Review the necessity of water for life. Then, through class discussion or buzz groups, have students use their creativity and problem-solving skills to answer the questions concerning water problems.

■ Nutritional Needs

14. **ER** *My Personal Journal*, reproducible master 18-3. Have students write about the nutrients in their favorite food. Have them refer to the appendix for additional information.

15. **EX** Have students discuss how much they have grown in the last few years. Students should include changes in size and weight, but also changes in abilities, coordination, voice, body proportions, etc. Have students discuss which nutrients were especially important in helping their bodies grow in these ways.

16. **ER** Have students find a copy of RDA charts and report on the nutrient needs for their age group.

Answer Key

■ Text

Review It, page 216
1. B
2. false
3. nutrients
4. proteins, carbohydrates, fats, vitamins, minerals, water

5. Complete protein supplies all the essential amino acids that a body needs. Incomplete protein supplies only some essential amino acids.
6. The carbohydrates sugar and starch provide energy for physical activities. Fiber aids in digestion.
7. Too much fat can cause weight gain and other health problems. Too much cholesterol has been linked to heart disease.
8. true
9. vitamin A—C; vitamin C—F; vitamin D—A; vitamin K—B; calcium and phosphorous—E; iron—D

■ Student Activity Guide

Nutrition Puzzle, Activity A

1	A	L	L	O	W	A	N	C	E	S					
2						N	U	T	R	I	E	N	T	S	
3				F	A	T	S								
4		M	I	N	E	R	A	L	S						
5					D	I	E	T							
6	M	A	L	N	U	T	R	I	T	I	O	N			
7				V	I	T	A	M	I	N	S				
8		C	A	R	B	O	H	Y	D	R	A	T	E	S	
9	P	R	O	T	E	I	N	S							

■ Teacher's Resource Guide/Binder

Chapter 18 Quiz

1. T
2. F
3. T
4. T
5. F
6. F
7. T
8. T
9. F
10. diet
11. nutrition
12. Malnutrition
13. protein
14. fiber
15. fortified
16. deficiencies
17. water
18. RDA (Recommended Dietary Allowances)
19. (Student response.)
20. Fat-soluble vitamins can be stored by the body. Therefore, food sources do not need to be eaten every day. Also, getting too much of these vitamins can lead to illness. Water-soluble vitamins cannot be stored in the body. Therefore, food sources should be eaten every day.

What Does the Body Need?

■ Proteins

■ Carbohydrates

■ Fats

■ Vitamins

■ Minerals

■ Water

Nutrient Sources

Vitamin A	B Vitamins

Vitamin C	Vitamin D

Calcium	Iron

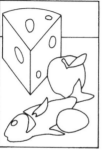

My Personal Journal

Write about your favorite food. How nutritious is this food? (Refer to the appendix for more specific nutrient information.) Based on you findings, should you eat this food often? Why or why not?

_____

_____

_____

_____

_____

_____

_____

_____

_____

_____

_____

_____

_____

_____

_____

_____

_____

_____

_____

_____

_____

_____

_____

_____

_____

_____

Nutrition and You

Name _____

Date _____ **Period** _____ **Score** _____

CHAPTER 18 QUIZ

☐ True/False: Circle *T* if the answer is true or *F* if the answer is false.

T F 1. People who do not eat enough protein recover from illnesses at a slower rate than people who do eat enough protein.

T F 2. If you eat more carbohydrates than you need, you may feel tired due to lack of energy.

T F 3. Many baked goods contain a lot of fats.

T F 4. People should try to get their vitamins from foods rather than from pills.

T F 5. Vitamin A cannot be stored by the body.

T F 6. Fruits and vegetables are good sources of vitamin D.

T F 7. Calcium and phosphorus are important for normal heart and muscle formation.

T F 8. Anemia may be caused by a lack of iron in the diet.

T F 9. The nutritional needs of the body are very low during the teen years.

☐ Fill in the Blanks: Complete the statements below by filling in the blanks.

_____10. All the foods you regularly eat make up your _____.

_____11. Practicing good _____ involves eating the right foods to keep your body operating properly.

_____12. _____ can be caused by not eating the right amount or the right selection of foods over time.

_____13. Amino acids are the building blocks for _____.

_____14. The type of carbohydrate that does not supply the body with energy but aids in digestion is called _____.

_____15. When nutrients are added to a food product, the product has been _____.

_____16. People who have shortages of certain vitamins suffer from _____.

_____17. The single most important substance you take into your body is _____.

_____18. Standards set up by the United States government to let you know your daily nutrient needs are known as the _____.

☐ Essay Questions: Provide the answers you feel best show your understanding of the subject matter.

19. Choose a nutrient and explain why it is needed by the body. Also list sources of that nutrient.

20. Explain the difference between fat-soluble and water-soluble vitamins.

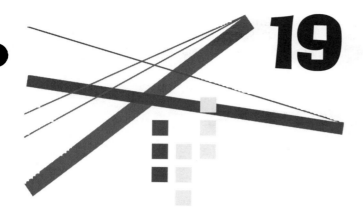

19 Eating Nutritiously

Objectives

After studying this chapter, students will be able to
- explain factors that affect food choices.
- identify the groups in the Food Guide Pyramid and give the recommended number of daily servings for each group.
- describe the main points to consider when planning nutritious, appealing meals.

Teaching Materials

Text, pages 217–226
Words to Know
Review It
Apply It
Think More About It
Student Activity Guide
A. *Dietary Guidelines for Americans*
B. *Using the Food Guide Pyramid*
C. *Planning Appealing Meals and Snacks*
Teacher's Resource Guide/Binder
How Does Food Meet Needs? transparency master 19-1
My Personal Journal, reproducible master 19-2
Dietary Guidelines for Americans, transparency master 19-3
Food Guide Pyramid, color transparency CT-19
Chapter 19 Quiz

Introductory Activities

1. Have students explain how their culture influences their food choices.
2. Ask students to describe their favorite meals. Use this as the basis for a discussion on texture, flavor, shape, and color.

Strategies to Reteach, Reinforce, Enrich, and Extend Text Concepts

■ Why You Eat What You Eat

3. **RF** *How Does Food Meet Needs?* transparency master 19-1. Use this transparency to discuss how food meets physical, social, and emotional needs. Have students suggest examples for each.
4. **RT** Have students write down some of the common meals that they have at home. Students should discuss some of the factors that have made these meals so common for them.
5. **RF** Have students collect magazine ads for different food items. Students should discuss how these ads might persuade people to eat the foods advertised.
6. **ER** *My Personal Journal*, reproducible master 19-2. Have students describe one food they believe describes their personality and explain why.

■ Making Wise Food Choices

7. **RT** *Dietary Guidelines for Americans*, transparency master 19-3. Use this transparency to introduce students to the Dietary Guidelines for Americans. Discuss ways these guidelines can be followed.
8. **RT** *Dietary Guidelines for Americans*, Activity A, SAG. Have students write examples of ways to follow each Dietary Guideline.
9. **RF** *Food Guide Pyramid*, color transparency CT-19. Have students discuss whether or not they get the recommended number of daily servings from each group in the Food Guide Pyramid. Have them discuss ways they might include any servings they are missing.

10. **RT** *Using the Food Guide Pyramid,* Activity B, SAG. Have students define *Food Guide Pyramid.* Then have students complete the given chart by filling in the food group, number of daily servings recommended, and major nutrients supplied for each list of food examples given.

11. **RF** As a class, have students list popular foods that are in the fats, oils, and sweets segment of the Food Guide Pyramid. Then have them list possible substitute snack foods from the five food groups.

12. **EX** Have students keep a food diary for a week, writing down the types and amounts of foods eaten each day. Students should then evaluate the diary by checking to see whether or not they ate the recommended number of servings from each food group each day.

13. **ER** Have students conduct a survey throughout the school to find out what are students' favorite snack foods. Students should then determine the food group of the Food Guide Pyramid in which each snack belongs. Students may write a brochure with the results of the survey to distribute throughout the school.

■ Planning Meals

14. **EX** Have students brainstorm ideas for quick, nutritious breakfast meals. Students should choose some of the best ideas and develop a bulletin board called "Breakfast on the Run."

15. **ER** Have students interview other students in the school cafeteria who bring their lunches from home. Students should ask "brown baggers" what they typically bring and how they feel about their lunches. As a class, discuss the different lunches and have students suggest ways of improving the lunches.

16. **ER** Have students demonstrate making a simple, nutritious snack. Students should distribute copies of the recipe to the class.

17. **EX** Have students find a magazine picture of a meal that they think is appealing. Students should evaluate the meal in terms of color, flavor, texture, shape, size, and temperature.

18. **RT** *Planning Appealing Meals and Snacks,* Activity C, SAG. Have students use the forms provided to plan and evaluate a breakfast, lunch, dinner, and snack.

Answer Key

■ Text

Review It, page 226

1. true
2. (List three:) family members, friends, culture, advertising (Students may justify other responses.)
3. Such a diet may reduce your risk of heart disease, stroke, and certain cancers.
4. (See Chart 19-5. Response should be appropriate for gender.)
5. Fats, oils, and sweets contribute little more than calories to the diet.
6. The longest time between meals is from dinner one night to breakfast the next morning.
7. false
8. color, flavor, texture, shape, size, temperature
9. garnish

■ Student Activity Guide

Using the Food Guide Pyramid, Activity B
Food Guide Pyramid: A plan to help people choose foods that will provide them with the nutrients they need. (See chart on page 153.)

■ Teacher's Resource Guide/Binder

Chapter 19 Quiz

1. F	8. T
2. T	9. F
3. F	10. D
4. T	11. C
5. F	12. A
6. T	13. B
7. F	

14. (Student response.)
15. (Student response.)

Food Guide Pyramid for You						
Groups:	**Bread**	**Vegetable**	**Fruit**	**Milk**	**Meat**	**Fats & Sweets**

Examples of foods in this group:	Wheat bread
	Oatmeal
	Rice
	Tortilla
	Cracker
	Pasta
	Muffin
	Pancake
		Potato
		Broccoli
		Spinach
		Carrot
		Cucumber
		Pepper
		Green beans
		Onion
			Apple
			Grapes
			Banana
			Orange
			Cherries
			Kiwifruit
			Peach
			Apricot
				Milk
				Cheddar
				  cheese
				Cottage cheese
				Ice cream
				Yogurt
				Pudding
				Cream soups
				Custard
					Lean, cooked
					  meat
					Poultry
					Fish
					Eggs
					Dried legumes
					  or peas
					Peanut butter
						Candy bar
						Butter
						Soft drink
						Salad dressing
						Cookies
						Potato chips

Number of daily servings recommended for you:	See chart 19-5 in text.	See chart 19-5 in text.	See chart 19-5 in text.	See chart 19-5 in text.	See chart 19-5 in text.	See chart 19-5 in text.

Major contribution of nutrients supplied in diet:	B vitamins
	Iron
	Carbohydrates
	Fiber
		Vitamins
		(especially
		  A and C)
		Minerals
		Carbohydrates
			Vitamins
			(especially
			  A and C)
			Minerals
			Carbohydrates
				Calcium
				Phosphorus
				Protein
				Vitamins
					Protein
					Iron
					B vitamins
						Calories

How Does Food Meet Needs?

● Physical:

Social:

●

Emotional:

●

My Personal Journal

What one food do you feel describes your personality? In what way does it relate to your personality? How does this reflect on the importance of nutrition in your lifestyle?

_____

_____

_____

_____

_____

_____

_____

_____

_____

_____

_____

_____

_____

_____

_____

_____

_____

_____

_____

_____

_____

_____

_____

Dietary Guidelines for Americans

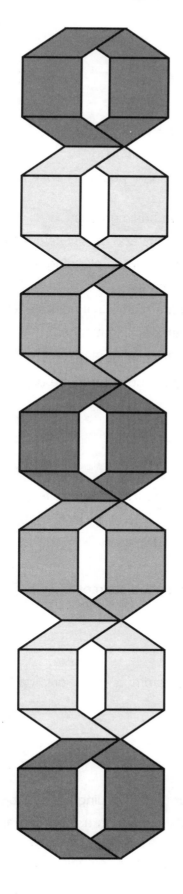

Eat a variety of foods.

Balance the food you eat with physical activity—maintain or improve your weight.

Choose a diet with plenty of grain products, vegetables, and fruits.

Choose a diet low in fat, saturated fat, and cholesterol.

Choose a diet moderate in sugars.

Choose a diet moderate in salt and sodium.

If you drink alcoholic beverages, do so in moderation.

Eating Nutritiously

Name_____

Date _____ Period _____ Score _____

CHAPTER 19 QUIZ

☐ True/False: Circle *T* if the statement is true or *F* if the statement is false.

T F 1. Friends do not affect people's food choices.

T F 2. The Dietary Guidelines for Americans recommend that people choose a diet low in fat, saturated fat, and cholesterol.

T F 3. The Food Guide Pyramid divides foods into seven basic groups.

T F 4. Foods that are considered to be fats, oils, and sweets add mostly calories to the diet.

T F 5. Nutrition is the only factor that should be considered when planning meals.

T F 6. Changes in your schedule can affect your eating pattern.

T F 7. Breakfast should give your body at least half of the nutrients it needs each day.

T F 8. Protecting foods from spoilage is a concern when packing lunches.

T F 9. Meals are more pleasing if all the foods served are similar in color.

☐ Multiple Choice: Choose the best answer and write the corresponding letter in the blank.

_____ 10. The serving size for rice or pasta is _____.
   A. 1 ounce cooked
   B. 1 cup cooked
   C. ½ cup uncooked
   D. ½ cup cooked

_____ 11. The number of recommended daily servings from the fruit group for teens is _____.
   A. three for both girls and guys
   B. four for girls, three for guys
   C. three for girls, four for guys
   D. four for girls, five for guys

_____ 12. Foods in the milk and milk products group are not good sources of _____.
   A. fiber
   B. calcium
   C. vitamins
   D. protein

_____ 13. Foods in the meat, poultry, fish, dry beans, eggs, and nuts group provide high levels of _____.
   A. vitamin A
   B. B vitamins
   C. vitamin C
   D. vitamin D

☐ Essay Questions: Provide the answers you feel best show your understanding of the subject matter.

14. Select one of the Dietary Guidelines for Americans. Explain why it is a guideline and how the guideline can be met.

15. Write a dinner menu and explain how it meets the six guidelines for planning appealing meals.

Reproducible Quiz

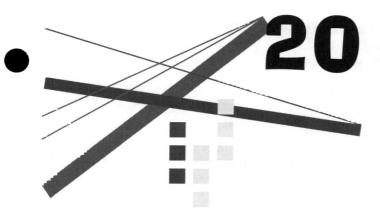

20 Managing Your Weight

Objectives

After studying this chapter, students will be able to
■ determine what weight is healthy for them.
■ list guidelines for sensible dieting.
■ discuss dieting dangers.

Teaching Materials

Text, pages 227–236
  Words to Know
  Review It
  Apply It
  Think More About It
Student Activity Guide
  A. *Dieting Do's and Don'ts*
  B. *Ask a Diet Expert*
Teacher's Resource Guide/Binder
  Causes of Being Overweight or Underweight, transparency master 20-1
  Calorie Burning, reproducible master 20-2
  My Personal Journal, reproducible master 20-3
  Energy Balance, color transparency CT-20
  Chapter 20 Quiz

Introductory Activities

1. Ask students to explain how they think behavior affects weight management.
2. Have students find an article in a medical journal or consumer magazine about various dieting aids. Use the articles to begin a discussion on healthy dieting.

Strategies to Reteach, Reinforce, Enrich, and Extend Text Concepts

■ You and Your Weight

3. **EX** Have students develop and present a skit that encourages students to be satisfied with their body structures. The skit should emphasize that some things about a person's body can't be changed even by losing weight. Therefore, people should strive to be the proper weight for their body structure and play up their good features without worrying about the features they can't change.
4. **RF** *Energy Balance,* color transparency CT-20. Use this transparency to illustrate the concept of energy balance.
5. **ER** Invite a physical education teacher to speak to the class about basic exercises for keeping the body toned. The teacher may also talk about developing total fitness programs.
6. **ER** Have students develop an exercise program for themselves and try following the program for a month. At the end of the month, students should write a report on any changes that resulted from the exercise program.

■ Teenage Dieting

7. **RT** *Causes of Being Overweight or Underweight,* transparency master 20-1. Use the transparency to have students discuss each of the causes of being overweight, giving suggestions for overcoming each of the causes.

8. **RF** *Calorie Burning*, reproducible master 20-2. Have students use the form to keep track of how many calories they burn for five days.

9. **RT** Have students choose a favorite food that is high in calories and list activities they could do to burn off the number of calories in the food. Students should list types of activities with the length of time they would need to be done.

10. **RF** Have students discuss habits they have. Students should analyze how hard it is to break habits. Then have students discuss why behavior modification needs to be part of any weight loss program for it to be successful in the long run.

11. **ER** Have students interview someone who has been successful at losing weight. Students should report to the class any helpful dieting tips given by the person interviewed.

12. **RF** *Dieting Do's and Don'ts*, Activity A, SAG. Have students evaluate whether the listed statements are "Dieting Do's" or "Dieting Don'ts." Then have students choose the statement they think is most important to dieting and explain why.

13. **ER** Have students prepare their own personal calorie counting booklet. Students should list foods they eat often plus foods they need to include in their daily diet. Students can use the text appendix and other resources to find the calorie count for each food.

14. **ER** Have students write a one-day menu for a person trying to lose weight (1200 to 1500 calories), maintain weight (2500 calories), or gain weight (3500 calories). Students should use the Food Guide Pyramid to plan meals. Have students list the amount and calorie content of each menu item and give the total calories for the meal.

15. **ER** *My Personal Journal*, reproducible master 20-3. Have students evaluate their own weight using Chart 20-2 and answer questions about personal weight management. (These evaluations should not be shared with the rest of the class.)

■ Dieting Dangers

16. **EX** Have students discuss different fad diets with which they are familiar. For each diet, have students analyze whether or not the diet is nutritionally sound and whether it teaches behavior modification.

17. **ER** Invite a counselor who works with anorexics and bulimics to speak on the causes and effects of these problems. The speaker should also recommend ways of detecting these problems and finding help for people with these problems.

18. **ER** *Ask a Diet Expert*, Activity B, SAG. Have students interview a dietitian and write the answers to the questions provided. Students should also write questions of their own and record the answers.

Answer Key

■ Text

Review It, page 236

1. physical body structure, daily eating habits, level of physical activity
2. energy balance
3. (Describe two:) Weight charts can be used to compare your weight with the weights of other people your age. The pinch test can be used to measure the amount of fat stored under the skin. The mirror test can help you determine whether or not you look overweight or underweight.
4. one hour, three times a week
5. B
6. (List four:) poor eating habits, inactivity, social pressures, personal problems, lack of knowledge, heredity
7. false
8. (List three:) eat nutritious, high-calorie foods; eat a good breakfast; avoid filling up on sweets and snacks near mealtime; increase the size of portions at meals (Students may justify other responses.)
9. Many fad diets lack variety. People become bored with the diet and resume their old eating habits.
10. Anorexia nervosa causes people to starve themselves. Bulimia causes an uncontrollable urge to eat large amounts of food, then eliminate the food by forced vomiting or use of laxatives.

■ Student Activity Guide

Dieting Do's and Don'ts, Activity A
Do's: 1, 2, 6, 7, 9, 13, 14, 16, 18, 20
Don'ts: 3, 4, 5, 8, 10, 11, 12, 15, 17, 19

■ Teacher's Resource Guide/Binder

Chapter 20 Quiz

1.	F	10.	D
2.	T	11.	E
3.	T	12.	I
4.	T	13.	H
5.	F	14.	B
6.	F	15.	F
7.	T	16.	G
8.	T	17.	A
9.	T	18.	C

19. eating in front of the TV, having snacks between meals that are high in calories and low in nutrients, eating when not hungry (Students may justify other responses.)
20. (Student response.)

Causes of Being Overweight or Underweight

Physical reasons:

- ■ poor eating habits

- ■ large or small amounts of physical activity

- ■ heredity

Social reasons:

- ■ eating in restaurants

- ■ eating with friends

- ■ media (advertisements, magazines, etc.)

Emotional reasons:

- ■ personal crises

- ■ depression

- ■ stress

Calorie Burning

Name _____ **Date** _____ **Period** _____

Many of your daily activities burn calories. Use the form below to record the number of calories you burn for five days. Then analyze your activity level by answering the questions that follow.

Activity	Calories Burned Per Hour	Day 1 Hours Spent	Day 1 Total Calories	Day 2 Hours Spent	Day 2 Total Calories	Day 3 Hours Spent	Day 3 Total Calories	Day 4 Hours Spent	Day 4 Total Calories	Day 5 Hours Spent	Day 5 Total Calories
Badminton— singles	233–310										
Baking— using mixer	75–100										
Bicycling— 10 mph	278–370										
Dancing	165–225										
Eating	60–80										
Jogging— 5.5 mph	439–585										
Resting	49–65										
Jumping rope	341–455										
Shopping	113–150										
Sitting	60–80										
Standing still	68–90										
Swimming— 30 yards per minute	281–375										
Talking on telephone	60–80										
Watching TV	53–70										
Walking— 3.5 mph	210–280										
Writing	60–80										
Other:											
			Total		Total		Total		Total		Total

Do you think your activity level is high enough? If so, why?

_____

_____

If not, list some specific ways that you could increase your activity level. _____

_____

_____

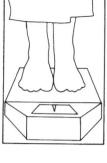

My Personal Journal

Using Chart 20-2 in the text, evaluate your present weight. Is your weight appropriate for your body structure? If not, what steps can you take to gain or lose weight? If your weight is appropriate for your body structure, what steps can you take in the future to maintain your weight?

_____

_____

_____

_____

_____

_____

_____

_____

_____

_____

_____

_____

_____

_____

_____

_____

_____

_____

_____

_____

_____

_____

_____

_____

Managing Your Weight

Name _____

Date _____ Period _____ Score _____

CHAPTER 20 QUIZ

☐ True/False: Circle *T* if the statement is true or *F* if the statement is false.

T   F   1. Exercise and weight loss will change your basic body structure.

T   F   2. Calorie needs are determined by a person's age, rate of growth, body size, and level of physical activity.

T   F   3. Standard weight charts should only be used as guidelines in determining healthy weight.

T   F   4. In a healthy exercise program, you should not exercise until you feel pain in your muscles and joints.

T   F   5. Dieting only involves eating fewer calories than usual.

T   F   6. Exercise causes a person to eat more and gain weight.

T   F   7. A safe weight loss goal is to lose one pound per week.

T   F   8. The problem of being underweight is just as important as the problem of being overweight.

T   F   9. Many diet pills have serious side effects.

☐ Matching: Match the following terms with their definitions.

_____ 10. Units of energy or body fuel provided by carbohydrates, fats, and proteins in foods.

_____ 11. Taking in and burning an equal number of calories.

_____ 12. A method of measuring the amount of fat stored under the skin.

_____ 13. Being 20 percent or more above normal weight.

_____ 14. Getting rid of problem eating habits and learning new eating habits that are kept for life.

_____ 15. Popular, often unsafe, diet plans that promise quick weight loss.

_____ 16. Going without food for a certain amount of time.

_____ 17. An eating disorder that causes people to starve themselves.

_____ 18. An eating disorder in which people are obsessed with being thin but cannot control the urge to eat large quantities of food.

A. anorexia nervosa
B. behavior modification
C. bulimia
D. calories
E. energy balance
F. fad diets
G. fasting
H. obese
I. pinch test

☐ Essay Questions: Provide the answers you feel best show your understanding of the subject matter.

19. List three poor eating habits that teens commonly have.

20. Give four guidelines for sensible dieting.

Part Five

Working in the Kitchen

Part goal: Students will learn safe and appropriate ways to plan, shop for, prepare, serve, and enjoy meals.

Bulletin Board

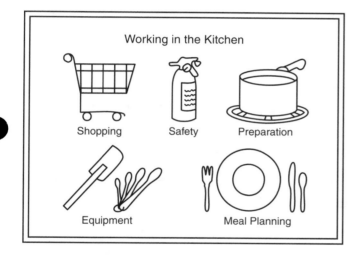

Working in the Kitchen

Shopping   Safety   Preparation

Equipment   Meal Planning

Title: "Working in the Kitchen"

Draw symbols for shopping, safety, preparation, equipment, and meal planning on the bulletin board. Place the appropriate label under each symbol.

Teaching Materials

Text
Chapters 21–32, pages 237–349

Student Activity Guide
Chapters 21–32

Teacher's Resource Guide/Binder
Kitchen Skills Survey, reproducible master

Introductory Activities

1. *Kitchen Skills Survey*, reproducible master. Have students answer the questions about their experience and knowledge in working with foods. Students should also list areas of foods about which they would like to learn more. Use the answers on the survey to gear teaching of this unit to the students' skill levels and interests.
2. Have students write a short essay describing their favorite meal. Students should explain why they enjoyed the meal so much. Have students discuss their essays and try to determine what skills went into planning and serving the meals.
3. Invite a culinary arts professional or student to demonstrate some food preparation techniques to the class. Sources may include local restaurants or community colleges. If you are unable to arrange for a speaker, show a videotape on culinary skills.

Kitchen Skills Survey

Name _____ **Date** _____ **Period** _____

Answer the following questions about your experience with food preparation. Then list some skills about which you would like to learn more.

Do you help with grocery shopping in your family? _____

How would you go about finding the best foods for the best prices at a grocery store? _____

_____

_____

_____

List five actions you should take to keep the kitchen safe and sanitary. _____

_____

_____

_____

_____

What kitchen appliances do you know how to use? _____

_____

Describe a cooking experience you have had. Explain whether or not you enjoyed it and why. _____

_____

_____

_____

What types of foods have you prepared? (If you prepared a food with help, note that next to the food listed.)

_____

_____

_____

What cuisines from other countries have you tried? _____

_____

_____

List five actions that you know are good table manners. _____

_____

_____

_____

I want to learn more about the following foods skills (related to meal planning; food selection, storage, and preparation; foods of different cultures; eating meals at home or at restaurants): _____

_____

_____

_____

_____

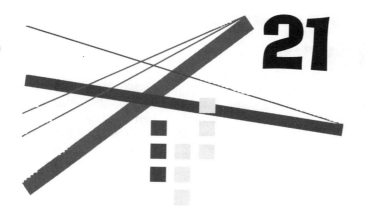

21 Getting Your Money's Worth

Objectives

After studying this chapter, students will be able to
■ describe guidelines for making grocery shopping decisions.
■ list factors to consider when comparing prices of products.
■ explain how consumers can use label information when making grocery purchases.

Teaching Materials

Text, pages 238–247
Words to Know
Review It
Apply It
Think More About It
Student Activity Guide
A. *Comparing Food Stores*
B. *Getting the Best Buy*
C. *Reading Labels*
D. *The Grocery Cart*
Teacher's Resource Guide/Binder
Avoiding Impulse Buying, reproducible master 21-1
Factors Affecting the Cost of Food, transparency master 21-2
My Personal Journal, reproducible master 21-3
Food Label Analysis, color transparency CT-21A
Nutrition Label Information, color transparency CT-21B
Chapter 21 Quiz

Introductory Activities

1. Survey the class to find out how many students are responsible for at least part of the grocery shopping in their families.
2. Ask students what they think makes someone a wise grocery shopper.

Strategies to Reteach, Reinforce, Enrich, and Extend Text Concepts

■ Grocery Shopping Guidelines

3. **RF**   Have students gather recipes needed to plan menus for three days. Then have them make up a shopping list of all the items they would need to buy to prepare those menus. Ask them to organize their lists, grouping together items that would be found in the same department of the store.
4. **RT**   Have students look through grocery store sales fliers to see if any of the items on the shopping lists they made in Learning Experience 3 are on sale. Discuss with students how taking advantage of store sales can help them stretch their family food budgets.
5. **RF**   *Comparing Food Stores*, Activity A, SAG. Have students prepare a grocery list that might be used when doing the family food shopping. Then have students visit two types of food stores to complete the chart and answer questions comparing the two stores.
6. **RF**   *Avoiding Impulse Buying*, reproducible master 21-1. Have students read the case studies of teens who made unplanned purchases when shopping for food. Then have them answer the questions that follow.

■ Comparing Prices

7. **RT**   *Factors Affecting the Cost of Food*, transparency master 21-2. Use the transparency to illustrate factors that affect food costs. Ask students to cite specific examples of each factor.

8. **RT** *Getting the Best Buy*, Activity B, SAG. Have students use unit pricing to compare different brands, sizes, and forms of the products specified.
9. **RF** Display pairs of the same food items that differ in terms of packaging, size, brand, or form. Have students guess which item in each pair has the higher unit cost and give a reason for their choice.

■ Reading Labels

10. **RT** *Food Label Analysis,* color transparency CT-21A. Use the transparency to discuss with students how the various types of information on food product labels can be used. Then ask students specific questions about the label, such as the following: What is the serving size? How many servings are in this container? How many grams of fat are in one serving of this product? How much sodium is in one serving of this product?
11. **RT** *Nutrition Label Information,* color transparency CT-21B. Use this transparency to identify the features on nutrition labels.
12. **RF** *Reading Labels,* Activity C, SAG. Have each student mount a nutritional label on his or her activity sheet and use it to answer the questions.
13. **ER** Have each student find the name of an additive on a food product ingredient list. Then have students use library resources to learn the functions of their additives and report their findings to class.

■ Buying and Storing Food

14. **RF** Design a grocery store scavenger hunt. Divide the class into teams of three and give each team a list of items they must find in a grocery store. Items might include an example of a technique used to encourage impulse buying, a food product for which the unit cost differs by more than $.50 between sizes, a food product that provides more than 25 percent of the U.S. RDA for protein, a package with a freshness date for the following year, etc.
15. **ER** *My Personal Journal,* reproducible master 21-3. Students are to list smart shopping techniques they use to help them get the most for their money. Then they are to describe how they could be more careful consumers and explain why it would be worthwhile to improve their shopping skills.
16. **RF** *The Grocery Cart*, Activity D, SAG. Have students complete the statements about shopping for food. They are then asked to list food buying tips.

Answer Key

■ Text

Review It, page 247
1. (List two:) helps you avoid forgetting needed grocery items, saves you time in the store trying to decide what to buy, saves money by helping you avoid buying items that are not on your list, saves energy from running back and forth in the store looking for items
2. B
3. impulse buying
4. Consumers can use unit pricing to compare the cost per unit of measure or weight of different brands, sizes, and forms of products.
5. the ingredient present in the largest amount by weight
6. serving size, servings per container, dietary components, percent Daily Values
7. (List three:) to maintain or improve nutritional value, to maintain freshness, to make foods more appealing and attractive, to help in processing or preparation
8. (List two:) shoppers get a detailed grocery tape so they can keep track of their purchases, checkout is faster, there are fewer checkout errors, reduced inventory costs save shoppers money
9. true
10. Food rotation is putting the foods you have bought most recently on the back part of the shelf so you use older foods first.

■ Student Activity Guide

The Grocery Cart, Activity D

1. list	8. impulse	15. universal
2. coupons	9. national	16. open
3. supermarkets	10. store	17. freshness
4. warehouse	11. generic	18. pack
5. convenience	12. unit	19. pull
6. specialty	13. labels	20. expiration
7. roadside	14. additive	

(Tips are student response.)

■ Teacher's Resource Guide/Binder

Chapter 21 Quiz

1. T	5. T	9. F	13. C
2. T	6. F	10. T	
3. F	7. F	11. B	
4. F	8. T	12. C	

14. (List three:) displays, specialty departments, free samples, demonstrations
15. National brand products tend to cost more because they include advertising costs that are passed along to consumers.

Avoiding Impulse Buying

Name _____ **Date** _____ **Period** _____

Read each of the following cases of teens who made unplanned purchases when shopping for food. Then answer the questions that follow.

1. Janet stopped at the supermarket on her way home from school. It had been hours since lunch. She had intended to pick up pork chops and potatoes for dinner. However, Janet also ended up buying a box of cookies, which she started eating on her way home.

   What could Janet do to avoid making this type of impulse buy in the future? _____

   _____

   _____

2. Ethan's mother sent him to the grocery store to buy some chicken breasts for dinner. She was surprised when he came home with a box of Kramer's Frozen Fish Pops instead. Ethan explained that a woman at the store was demonstrating how easy the fish pops were to prepare. However, Ethan's enthusiasm for his purchase diminished when his mother reminded him that nobody in their family liked fish.

   What could Ethan do to avoid making this type of impulse buy in the future? _____

   _____

   _____

3. Zachary went to the supermarket to buy some eggs, milk, and cereal. Besides those items, Zachary brought home a tray of fresh breakfast rolls. His father asked why Zachary had made this unplanned purchase. Zachary said he hadn't been able to resist the delicious smell from the in-store bakery.

   What could Zachary do to avoid making this type of impulse buy in the future? _____

   _____

   _____

4. Lupe came home from the store with the cheese her sister asked her to buy. She also had a box of snack crackers. Her sister asked Lupe why she had bought the crackers when they already had crackers at home. Lupe said there was a display of crackers next to the cheese, and she thought they would taste good together.

   What could Lupe do to avoid making this type of impulse buy in the future? _____

   _____

   _____

5. Candice's brother helped her unpack the groceries she brought home from the store. When he pulled three magazines and a candy bar out of the bag, he said, "I know *these* weren't on your shopping list. Mom's going to be mad when she finds out you spent our food money on this stuff."

   What could Candice do to avoid making this type of impulse buy in the future? _____

   _____

   _____

Factors Affecting the Cost of Food

degree of preparation

availability

freshness

packaging

My Personal Journal

Think about your behavior when you shop for food. What smart shopping techniques do you use to help you get the most for your money? In what ways could you be a more careful consumer? Why would it be worthwhile for you to improve your shopping skills?

_____

_____

_____

_____

_____

_____

_____

_____

_____

_____

_____

_____

_____

_____

_____

_____

_____

_____

_____

_____

_____

_____

_____

Getting Your Money's Worth

Name _____

Date _____ Period _____ Score _____

CHAPTER 21 QUIZ

☐ True/False: Circle *T* if the statement is true or *F* if the statement is false.

T　F　1. Having a shopping list can help you save time and money at the grocery store.

T　F　2. Not all foods listed in newspaper ads and store sales fliers are on sale.

T　F　3. Fruits and vegetables tend to cost more at farmers' markets because they are fresher and higher in quality.

T　F　4. Items that are individually wrapped or packaged in serving-size portions tend to be better buys than items sold in larger quantities.

T　F　5. Serving sizes listed on nutrition labels for similar food products are the same.

T　F　6. A product labeled "fat free" contains 3 grams or less fat per serving.

T　F　7. Additives are harmful, unnecessary ingredients that are added to foods.

T　F　8. Checkout with the universal product code system is faster and there are fewer errors.

T　F　9. A good way to save money at the grocery store is to buy reduced-price, dented canned goods.

T　F　10. Recently purchased food should be stored on the back part of the shelf.

☐ Multiple Choice: Choose the best answer and write the corresponding letter in the blank.

_____ 11. What is the unit price of a box of six ice cream bars that sells for $2.49?

A. $.34 per bar.
B. $.42 per bar.
C. $.49 per bar.
D. $.72 per bar.

_____ 12. Which of the following is not required on a food product label?

A. The name and form of the food.
B. The weight of the contents.
C. Directions for preparing the product.
D. The name and address of the manufacturer, packer, or distributor.

_____ 13. The last day a product should be sold is identified by the _____.

A. freshness date
B. pack date
C. pull date
D. expiration date

☐ Essay Questions: Provide the answers you feel best show your understanding of the subject matter.

14. List three techniques stores use to encourage impulse buying.

15. Why are national brand products likely to cost more than house brand or generic products?

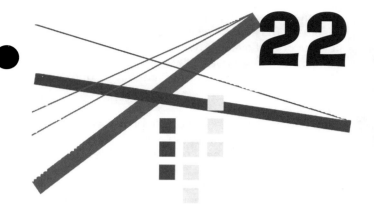

22 Kitchen Safety and Sanitation

Objectives

After studying this chapter, students will be able to
- list safety practices to follow to help prevent accidents in the kitchen.
- describe procedures to follow in the event of kitchen accidents.
- explain proper food handling techniques to prevent contamination.

Teaching Materials

Text, pages 248–255
  Words to Know
  Review It
  Apply It
  Think More About It
Student Activity Guide
  A. *How Many Hazards Can You Spot?*
  B. *Preventing Kitchen Accidents*
  C. *Handling Food Safely*
Teacher's Resource Guide/Binder
  Causes of Kitchen Injuries, transparency master 22-1
  Pack It Safely, transparency master 22-2
  My Personal Journal, reproducible master 22-3
  Chapter 22 Quiz

Introductory Activities

1. Ask students to explain what they think is meant by the phrase "Safety is no accident."
2. *Causes of Kitchen Injuries*, transparency master 22-1. Use the transparency master to introduce students to the five major causes of injuries in the kitchen. Ask students to identify hazards that could cause each of these types of injuries. List their responses on the master.

Strategies to Reteach, Reinforce, Enrich, and Extend Text Concepts

■ Preventing Kitchen Accidents

3. **RT** *Preventing Kitchen Accidents*, Activity B, SAG. Have students read the situations on the worksheet and suggest ways accidents can be prevented.
4. **ER** Have students make posters about preventing accidents in the kitchen.
5. **ER** Have students write a skit or puppet show to teach young children about kitchen safety. Make arrangements for students to give their presentation to a preschool or kindergarten class.
6. **ER** Invite a paramedic to demonstrate basic first aid procedures for your students. Ask the speaker to discuss how to treat shock, burns, broken bones, cuts, and poisonings.
7. **RF** Have students make a checklist of potential hazards in the kitchen. Have them use the checklist to evaluate the safety of their foods labs and their kitchens at home.
8. **RF** Have students examine nonfood items stored in their kitchens at home to determine whether any of these products might be poisonous.
9. **ER** Invite someone from the fire department to speak to your class about kitchen fire safety. Ask the speaker to demonstrate how to operate a fire extinguisher.
10. **ER** Invite a speaker from the American Red Cross to teach your students how to perform the abdominal thrust (Heimlich Maneuver).

■ Preparing Safe Food

11. **ER** Divide the class into groups. Ask each group to use library resources to research a different type of food-borne illness. Ask them to find out

about causes, symptoms, and prevention and report their findings in class.

12. **EX** Obtain petri dishes filled with agar from the science department. Have students press unwashed fingers, hair samples, and swabs moistened with saliva on the agar. Label the dishes and cover them for one week to allow bacterial cultures to grow. Have students examine the cultures. Use their observations as the basis for a discussion on why they should wash hands, tie back hair, and avoid licking utensils when cooking.

13. **ER** Invite someone from the health department to speak to your class about what he or she looks for when inspecting commercial food kitchens.

14. **RT** *How Many Hazards Can You Spot?* Activity A, SAG. Have students list all the safety and sanitation hazards they can identify in the illustration on the worksheet. Then discuss with students how these hazards could be eliminated.

15. **RT** *Handling Food Safely*, Activity C, SAG. Have students list safety guidelines to follow when buying, preparing, serving, and storing foods.

16. **RT** *Pack It Safely*, transparency master 22-2. Use the transparency to review guidelines students should follow when packing food to be eaten away from home.

17. **ER** *My Personal Journal*, reproducible master 22-3. Students are to describe a time when they or someone they know got sick from eating something. Then they are to explain how they could improve sanitation and food handling practices.

Answer Key

■ Text

Review It, page 255
1. hazard
2. electrical shocks, burns, falls, cuts, and poisonings
3. Pouring water on a grease fire can cause the fire to spread.
4. Do not run. Instead, drop to the floor and roll over to smother the flames.
5. The victim cannot speak or breathe, the victim's face will turn blue, the victim will collapse.
6. true
7. Wash hands with soap and warm water.
8. no more than two hours
9. protein foods, such as meat, poultry, fish, and eggs
10. (Student response.)

■ Student Activity Guide

How Many Hazards Can You Spot? Activity A
The hazards included in the illustration are: (In any order.)
    Frayed electric cord on ceiling light.

Hammer extending from wall shelf.
    Electric cords from small appliances extending under water faucet and over burners on the range.
    Aerosol container near lighted range burner.
    Roach powder stored near cooking equipment and food.
    Water on floor.
    Mop handle extending across floor.
    Open box of matches on table.
    Open box of matches near flammable cleaning products.
    Cleaning supplies near food on table.
    Food that requires refrigeration unwrapped and left at room temperature.
    Cleaver on table, extending over edge.
    Newspaper on floor.
    Pull toy on floor.
    Wagon under ladder.
    Ladder not fully open, unsteady position.
    One leg of ladder on newspaper.

Preventing Kitchen Accidents, Activity B
1. She should unplug the toaster before trying to dislodge the food. This can prevent an electrical shock.
2. The pan handle should be turned toward the center of the range. This is done to prevent burns.
3. She should wipe up the spill immediately. This is done to prevent falls.
4. He should carefully place the can lid in the bottom of the empty can before throwing them in the trash. This will help prevent cuts.
5. He should store them away from food storage areas. This will help to prevent poisonings.
6. He should be sure his hands are dry before plugging in the radio. This will help prevent an electrical shock.
7. He should lift the lid away from himself. This will help prevent burns.
8. He should use a sturdy step stool. This will help prevent falls.
9. She should sweep the broken glass onto a piece of paper or cardboard to throw away. Then she should use a damp paper towel to wipe up tiny slivers. This will help prevent cuts.
10. She should keep food out of range when spraying. When finished spraying, she should wipe food preparation areas thoroughly. This will help prevent poisonings.

Handling Food Safely, Activity C
(See chart 22-5 in the text.)

■ Teacher's Resource Guide/Binder

Chapter 22 Quiz
1. T		3. T	
2. T		4. T	

5. F
6. F
7. F
8. T
9. F
10. F
11. B
12. D
13. C
14. (Student response. See chart 22-1.)

15. (List two:) Use a thermos; pack something cold in the lunch bag, such as a well-chilled drink or a refreezable gel pack; make sandwiches ahead of time and freeze them. (Students may justify other responses.)

Causes of Kitchen Injuries

 Electrical Shocks

 Burns and Fires

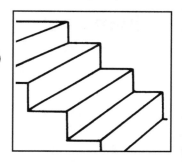 Falls

 Cuts

 Poisonings

Pack It Safely

■ Use a thermos to keep foods at safe temperatures.

■ Freeze sandwiches to keep them cool.

■ Pack a chilled drink or refreezable gel pack to keep food cool.

My Personal Journal

Think about a time when you or someone you know got sick from eating something. What caused the illness? How was the illness treated? What could you do to your kitchen work area to prevent food-borne illnesses in the future? How could you improve your personal cleanliness when working with food? How could you handle food more carefully to prevent food-borne illnesses?

_____

_____

_____

_____

_____

_____

_____

_____

_____

_____

_____

_____

_____

_____

_____

_____

_____

_____

_____

_____

_____

_____

_____

_____

_____

_____

Kitchen Safety and Sanitation

Name_____

Date _____ Period _____ Score _____

CHAPTER 22 QUIZ

☐ True/False: Circle *T* if the statement is true or *F* if the statement is false.

T F 1. Many kitchen accidents can be avoided.

T F 2. An ABC class-rated fire extinguisher can be used to take care of all types of fires.

T F 3. When getting away from a fire, you should drop to the floor to avoid breathing in smoke.

T F 4. Choking victims can perform the abdominal thrust (Heimlich Maneuver) on themselves.

T F 5. Food most often becomes contaminated during processing.

T F 6. Symptoms of food-borne illnesses often include a rash and blurred vision.

T F 7. Starchy foods, such as breads and cereals, are most likely to become contaminated.

T F 8. Hands should be washed with soap and warm water before handling any food and again after handling uncooked protein foods.

T F 9. When shopping, put refrigerated and frozen foods in your cart first.

T F 10. If stored properly, most foods can be stored indefinitely.

☐ Multiple Choice: Choose the best answer and write the corresponding letter in the blank.

_____ 11. Which of the following should *not* be used to put out a grease fire?

    A. Fire extinguisher.
    B. Water.
    C. The lid of a pan.
    D. Baking soda.

_____ 12. Which of the following is an indication that a person is choking?

    A. He or she cannot speak or breathe.
    B. His or her face turns blue.
    C. He or she collapses.
    D. All of the above are indications of choking.

_____ 13. At what temperatures do bacteria multiply rapidly?

    A. Between 20 and 40°F.
    B. Between 40 and 120°F.
    C. Between 40 and 140°F.
    D. Between 140 and 160°F.

☐ Essay Questions: Provide the answers you feel best show your understanding of the subject matter.

14. List five safety guidelines that can help prevent the most common types of kitchen accidents.

15. Give two suggestions for packing food safely when heating or cooling facilities are not available.

           Reproducible Quiz

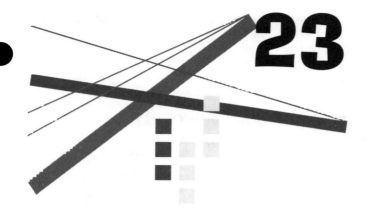

23 Kitchen Utensils and Appliances

Objectives

After studying this chapter, students will be able to
■ identify basic kitchen utensils and pieces of cookware and bakeware and explain their uses.
■ describe the purposes of common kitchen appliances.

Teaching Materials

Text, pages 256–263
Words to Know
Review It
Apply It
Think More About It
Student Activity Guide
A. *Kitchen Utensils*
B. *Using Appliances*
C. *Cook's Tools*
Teacher's Resource Guide/Binder
The Right Tool for the Task, transparency master 23-1
Which Tool Would You Use? reproducible master 23-2
My Personal Journal, reproducible master 23-3
Chapter 23 Quiz

Introductory Activities

1. Ask students to define *utensil* and *appliance*. Note how closely their definitions match the definitions used in the text.
2. *The Right Tool for the Task*, transparency master 23-1. Ask students to name the different utensils and appliances they think belong in each of the groups on the transparency master. List their responses in the appropriate spaces. (After studying this chapter, you may want to use this master again to help students evaluate their learning.)

Strategies to Reteach, Reinforce, Enrich, and Extend Text Concepts

■ Kitchen Utensils

3. **RT** Have students practice using measuring tools by measuring a variety of ingredients.
4. **RT** Prepare a salad or vegetable tray for students to demonstrate the use of various cutting tools.
5. **ER** Have students prepare a simple recipe that will require them to use a variety of kitchen utensils. After the lab, ask students to evaluate the usefulness of the utensils they used.
6. **ER** Have students go to the kitchen equipment and appliance section of a local department store. Ask each student to find a utensil with which he or she is not familiar. Then have students give brief oral reports about what their chosen utensils do, how much they cost, and what features they have.
7. **ER** *Which Tool Would You Use?* reproducible master 23-2. Have students identify which kitchen utensil they would choose to do listed tasks.

■ Cookware and Bakeware

8. **EX** Have students visit the cookware and bakeware section of a department store. Ask them to note the different materials used to make the different types of items. Ask them to also note the features described on the packaging of these items. Have them report their findings in class and draw conclusions about why certain materials are most often used for certain types of items.
9. **RT** *Kitchen Utensils*, Activity A, SAG. Have students identify the kitchen utensils shown on the worksheet and describe their uses.

10. **RF** Make a bingo-type game to help students learn the names and functions of kitchen utensils and cookware and bakeware pieces. Write the names of the utensils in the squares on the bingo cards. (Be sure to arrange the names in different order on different cards.) Play the game by holding up a utensil or reading a function. Have students cover the appropriate squares on their cards if they can identify the utensils. The winner is the first student to cover five squares in a row.

■ Small Appliances

11. **RF** Obtain use and care booklets for portable appliances from dealers or manufacturers. Have students look through them to see the kinds of information they provide.
12. **RF** *Using Appliances,* Activity B, SAG. Have students mount a picture of a small appliance on the worksheet. Have them complete the exercise by describing the features, uses, safety considerations, and other information about the appliance.
13. **ER** *My Personal Journal,* reproducible master 23-3. Students are to describe how a portable kitchen appliance makes it easier to prepare foods. They are also to explain why it is important for them to know how to use and care for the appliance properly.

■ Large Appliances

14. **ER** Have each student select a major kitchen appliance. Then have students visit an appliance store to learn about the styles, features, and sizes that are available for their chosen appliances. Discuss their findings in class.
15. **RF** *Cook's Tools,* Activity C, SAG. Have students find a recipe and list all the kitchen utensils and appliances they would need to prepare it.

Answer Key

■ Text

Review It, page 263
1. (Student response. Answers might include flour, sugar, brown sugar, and cocoa.)
2. C
3. rubber scraper
4. A wide spatula is used to flip foods like hamburgers, pancakes, and eggs while cooking. A narrow spatula is used to level dry ingredients in dry measuring cups and measuring spoons.
5. false
6. Food is placed in a small pan that fits inside a larger pan filled with water. The food is cooked by the heat of steam from the water in the larger pan.

7. (List three:) square pan, round pan, tube pan, jelly roll pan, muffin pan
8. true
9. portable
10. true

■ Student Activity Guide

Kitchen Utensils, Activity A

1.	tongs	21.	grater
2.	round pan	22.	measuring spoons
3.	double boiler	23.	rotary beater
4.	rubber scraper	24.	slotted spoon
5.	thermometer	25.	timer
6.	kitchen fork	26.	paring knife
7.	rolling pin	27.	can opener
8.	covered cake server	28.	muffin pan
9.	cooling racks	29.	large spoon
10.	pie pan	30.	tube pan
11.	strainer	31.	pizza pan
12.	bottle opener	32.	cutting board
13.	ladle	33.	wide spatula(turner)
14.	dry measuring cups	34.	cookie sheet
15.	narrow spatula	35.	mixing bowls
16.	serrated knife	36.	kitchen shears
17.	peeler	37.	liquid measuring cups
18.	skillet	38.	chef's knife
19.	jelly roll pan	39.	saucepan
20.	square pan	40.	colander

■ Teacher's Resource Guide/Binder

Which Tool Would You Use? reproducible master 23-2

1.	narrow spatula	11.	rolling pin
2.	chef's knife	12.	liquid measuring cup
3.	peeler	13.	ladle
4.	grater	14.	cutting board
5.	measuring spoon	15.	kitchen fork
6.	rubber scraper	16.	thermometer
7.	wide spatula/turner	17.	timer
8.	kitchen shears	18.	dry measuring cup
9.	tongs	19.	rotary beater
10.	colander	20.	can opener

Chapter 23 Quiz

1.	F	7.	C	13.	B
2.	T	8.	H	14.	A
3.	T	9.	D	15.	I
4.	F	10.	G	16.	E
5.	T	11.	F		
6.	T	12.	J		

17. Cookware refers to pots and pans used on top of the range. Bakeware refers to items that are used in an oven. (Examples are student response.)
18. This helps people learn how to use and care for appliances properly. This will help avoid accidents and safety problems and keep appliances working longer and better.

The Right Tool for the Task

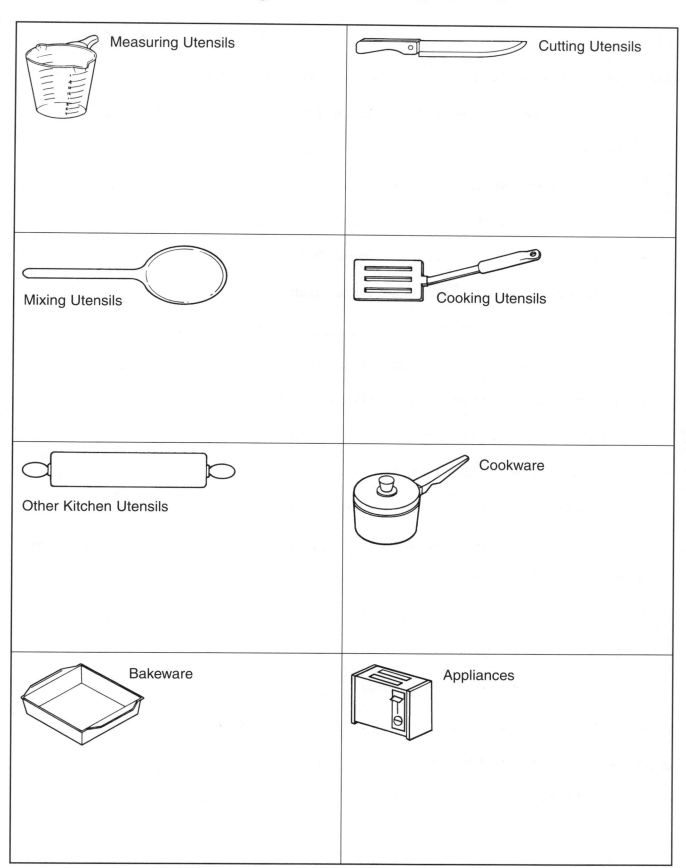

Measuring Utensils

Cutting Utensils

Mixing Utensils

Cooking Utensils

Other Kitchen Utensils

Cookware

Bakeware

Appliances

Which Tool Would You Use?

Name _____**Date** _____**Period** _____

Identify which kitchen utensil you would choose to do each of the following tasks.

1. You want to level powdered sugar you have measured in a dry measuring cup. _____

2. You want to chop celery to add to a casserole. _____

3. You want to peel carrots for a vegetable tray. _____

4. You want to shred cabbage to make coleslaw. _____

5. You want to measure a teaspoon of cinnamon to add to a coffee cake. _____

6. You want to fold whipped cream into chocolate pudding. _____

7. You want to flip hamburgers on the grill. _____

8. You want to cut dried apricots to add to a trail mix. _____

9. You want to lift ears of corn out of a pot of boiling water. _____

10. You want to drain spaghetti after it has finished cooking. _____

11. You want to flatten dough to make sugar cookies. _____

12. You want to measure fi cup of milk to add to pancake batter. _____

13. You want to serve vegetable soup into bowls. _____

14. You want to protect the countertop when slicing tomatoes. _____

15. You want to hold a roast while you slice it. _____

16. You want to cook a candy syrup to 290°F. _____

17. You want to bake a cake for 35 minutes. _____

18. You want to measure 2 cups of flour to add to a recipe for banana bread. _____

19. You want to beat eggs to make an omelet. _____

20. You want to open a can of peaches. _____

My Personal Journal

Think of a portable appliance in your kitchen. How does this appliance make it easier to prepare foods? What foods do you prepare with this appliance? How would you prepare these foods if you didn't have this appliance? Why is it important for you to know how to use and care for this appliance properly?

_____

_____

_____

_____

_____

_____

_____

_____

_____

_____

_____

_____

_____

_____

_____

_____

_____

_____

_____

_____

_____

_____

_____

_____

_____

Kitchen Utensils and Appliances

Name _____

Date _____ Period _____ Score _____

CHAPTER 23 QUIZ

☐ True/False: Circle *T* if the statement is true or *F* if the statement is false.

T   F   1. Skillets are used for cooking delicate foods.

T   F   2. A cooling rack allows baked goods to cool faster and more evenly.

T   F   3. Cookware used on top of the range is often made of copper, aluminum, and stainless steel.

T   F   4. Most small appliances perform only one task.

T   F   5. Standard mixers are larger and heavier than hand mixers.

T   F   6. Ranges, refrigerators, and dishwashers are major appliances.

☐ Matching: Match the following kitchen utensils with their functions.

_____ 7. Used to level dry ingredients in dry measuring utensils.

_____ 8. Used to slice bread and tender vegetables.

_____ 9. Used to thinly peel vegetables and fruits, such as carrots and apples.

_____ 10. Used to clean the sides of mixing bowls.

_____ 11. Used to beat, blend, and whip foods.

_____ 12. Used to turn foods while broiling or frying.

_____ 13. Used to serve punches, soups, and stews.

_____ 14. Used for rinsing fruits and vegetables.

_____ 15. Used to separate solids from liquids.

_____ 16. Used to flatten dough into a thin, even layer.

A. colander
B. ladle
C. narrow spatula
D. peeler
E. rolling pin
F. rotary beater
G. rubber scraper
H. serrated knife
I. strainer
J. tongs

☐ Essay Questions: Provide the answers you feel best show your understanding of the subject matter.

17. Explain the difference between cookware and bakeware and give two examples of each.

18. Why is it important to read the instruction booklets that come with appliances?

24 Convenience in the Kitchen

Objectives

After studying this chapter, students will be able to
■ discuss suggestions for organizing space, equipment, and tasks in the kitchen.
■ explain how appliances, such as microwave and convection ovens, can save time and energy in the kitchen.
■ compare the cost of convenience food products with the amount of food preparation time they save.

Teaching Materials

Text, pages 264–270
   Words to Know
   Review It
   Apply It
   Think More About It
Student Activity Guide
   A. *Task Planning*
   B. *Convenience Foods*
Teacher's Resource Guide/Binder
   Kitchen Work Triangle, transparency master 24-1
   My Personal Journal, reproducible master 24-2
   Consider Convenience, reproducible master 24-3
   Microwave Oven, color transparency CT-24
   Chapter 24 Quiz

Introductory Activities

1. Have students brainstorm a list of all the different types of activities that take place in the kitchen. Write their responses on the chalkboard. Ask them what types of problems might arise when a kitchen is used for a variety of functions.
2. Ask students to define the term *organization*. Ask them how they think being organized would help them work in the kitchen.

Strategies to Reteach, Reinforce, Enrich, and Extend Text Concepts

■ Getting Organized

3. **RT** *Kitchen Work Triangle*, transparency master 24-1. Use the master to illustrate for students the triangular path that is formed between the three major work centers in the kitchen.
4. **EX** Have students inventory the kitchens in their homes to find out what types of items are stored in each of the three basic work areas. Ask them to write a one-page report evaluating the organization of their kitchens and giving suggestions for increased efficiency.
5. **ER** Ask students to visit the housewares section of a department store. Have them make a list of all the different types of special racks and storage units designed for use in the kitchen. Have students report their findings in class. Discuss how useful some of these items would be for organizing space in the kitchen.
6. **EX** Ask students to use their imaginations to design racks or storage units that could be made from common, inexpensive materials to organize equipment and supplies in the kitchen.
7. **RF** *Task Planning*, Activity A, SAG. Have each student plan a meal that can be prepared and served in 45 minutes. Ask students to write menus and time schedules for preparing their meals.

■ Time-Saving Appliances

8. **RF** Have students design and conduct experiments to evaluate the time savings of using certain portable appliances. For instance, students might

time how long it takes to beat an egg white to the stiff peak stage using a whisk, a rotary beater, and an electric mixer.

9. **RT** *Microwave Oven,* color transparency CT-24. Use this transparency to introduce microwave cookery to the class. Explain how microwaves are generated by the magnetron tube and are spread throughout the oven interior by a stirrer fan, reflecting off the walls and floor of the oven so they can hit food at all angles. Also explain that as microwaves penetrate food, molecules in the food vibrate and generate heat through friction.

10. **RT** Prepare a simple recipe to demonstrate for students how to use a microwave oven. During the demonstration, emphasize not only the ease and convenience, but also cooking techniques and special considerations, of microwave cooking.

11. **RF** Obtain a class set of use and care booklets for your classroom microwave(s) from the manufacturer(s). After students have read through the booklets, ask them to individually demonstrate how to set the cooking time and power level on your classroom model(s).

12. **ER** Have students visit an appliance store or read consumer magazines to learn about the features, cost, and safety of various models of microwave and convection ovens. Then have each student write an advertisement for one particular model that emphasizes the consumer information he or she has gathered.

13. **ER** *My Personal Journal,* reproducible master 24-2. Students are to describe their microwave cooking experience and explain how learning more about microwave cooking could help them save time and effort in the kitchen.

■ Convenience Food Products

14. **RF** Have students keep a record of all the foods they eat for one day. Ask them to identify which foods were made from convenience products.

15. **ER** *Consider Convenience,* reproducible master 24-3. Have students use the master to interview an adult who is responsible for meal preparation about use of convenience food products. Then have students compile their findings and write a summary article for the school newspaper.

16. **ER** Have students make a bulletin board or showcase display about popular convenience food products.

17. **ER** *Convenience Foods,* Activity B, SAG. Have students compare the cost, preparation

time, appearance, and flavor of the finished, semi-prepared, and homemade forms of a food.

Answer Key

■ Text

Review It, page 270
1. food storage area—refrigerator, cleanup area—sink, cooking and serving area—range
2. A well-planned kitchen allows for easy movement from one work area to another. It has a small work triangle to save steps while you are working.
3. false
4. (List two:) Write a schedule showing when you need to do each meal preparation task. Make any advance preparations necessary. Prepare foods that require the longest cooking time first.
5. Microwaves enter food and cause tiny particles in the food to vibrate. This movement causes friction that creates the heat that cooks the food.
6. one-fourth
7. (List five:) saves time, saves energy, kitchen stays cool, easy cleanup, safe, saves nutrients (Students may justify other responses.)
8. Convection ovens have fans that move hot air around the food. Moving air cooks food faster than the still air in conventional ovens.
9. (List one:) Convenience foods often cost more than foods made from scratch. They may not taste as good as homemade foods. They may not be as nutritious as homemade foods.

■ Teacher's Resource Guide/Binder

Chapter 24 Quiz

1.	T	8.	F
2.	T	9.	F
3.	F	10.	T
4.	T	11.	A
5.	F	12.	D
6.	F	13.	B
7.	F		

14. A work triangle is the triangle formed by the movement between the food storage, cleanup, and cooking and serving areas of the kitchen. In a well-organized kitchen, the work triangle is small to save steps while working.
15. When purchasing convenience food products, you should compare the time savings with the cost. You should also consider taste, appearance, nutrition, and the need to add other ingredients.

Kitchen Work Triangle

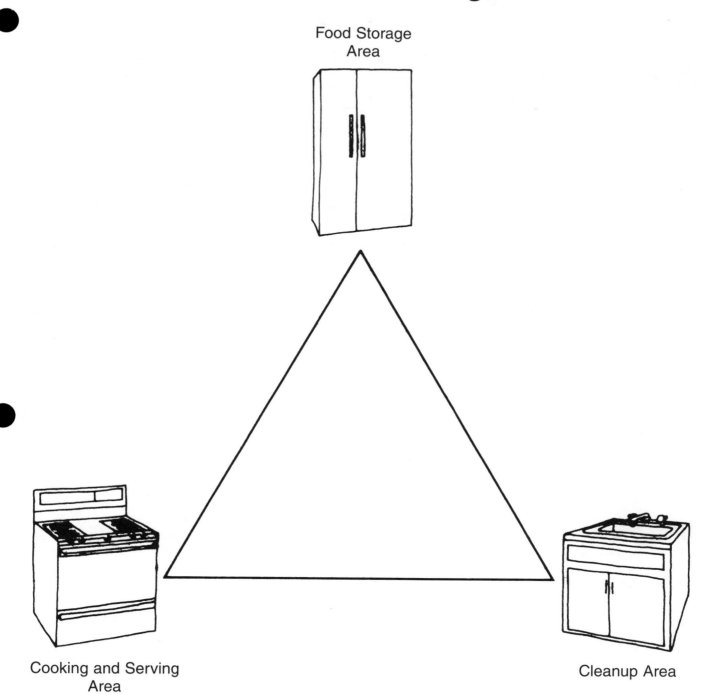

Food Storage
Area

Cooking and Serving
Area

Cleanup Area

My Personal Journal

Think of your experience using a microwave oven. What foods have you prepared using a microwave oven? Why did you use a microwave oven instead of a conventional range to prepare these foods? How could learning more about microwave cooking help you save time and effort in the kitchen?

Consider Convenience

Name _____ **Date** _____ **Period** _____

Interview an adult who is responsible for meal preparation. Record his or her responses to the questions below. Compile your findings with those of your classmates. Summarize them in an article for your school newspaper.

1. How often do you use convenience foods when preparing family meals? _____
   _____

2. How does your use of convenience products compare with your parents' use of convenience products when you were a child? Explain any differences. _____
   _____

3. What convenience food products do you use most? _____
   _____

4. What, if any, convenience products do you avoid using? Explain your response. _____
   _____

5. What do you see as the main advantage of using convenience products? _____
   _____

6. What do you see as the main disadvantage of using convenience products? _____
   _____

7. How do you think the taste of convenience foods compares with the taste of homemade foods?
   _____

8. How does the cost of convenience foods compare with the cost of homemade foods? _____
   _____

9. How do you think the nutritional value of convenience foods compares with the nutritional value of homemade foods? _____
   _____

10. What marketing technique would most likely persuade you to try a new convenience product? ___
    _____

Convenience in the Kitchen

Name _____

Date _____ **Period** _____ **Score** _____

CHAPTER 24 QUIZ

☐ True/False: Circle *T* if the statement is true or *F* if the statement is false.

T   F   1. Kitchens need to be designed to allow for activities other than cooking and eating.

T   F   2. Cabinets and counters may be found in all three kitchen work areas.

T   F   3. The size of a kitchen is more important than how the space is used.

T   F   4. Reading the recipe should be the first step in food preparation.

T   F   5. When preparing a recipe, it is best to get out ingredients one at a time as the recipe calls for them.

T   F   6. You should begin preparing foods that require the longest cooking time at the end of the meal preparation period.

T   F   7. Appliances provide the greatest time savings when you are preparing small amounts of food.

T   F   8. Although it is faster, microwave cooking is not as safe as conventional cooking.

T   F   9. Microwave cooking causes more nutrients to be lost from foods than conventional cooking.

T   F   10. Convection ovens are often found in combination with microwave ovens.

☐ Multiple Choice: Choose the best answer and write the corresponding letter in the blank.

_____ 11. In which work area of the kitchen is the refrigerator found?

    A. Food storage area.
    B. Cleanup area.
    C. Eating area.
    D. Cooking and serving area.

_____ 12. Which of the following statements does *not* apply to microwave cooking?

    A. Saves time.
    B. Saves energy.
    C. Keeps kitchen cool.
    D. Requires no special techniques.

_____ 13. Which of the following statements about convenience food products is *not* true?

    A. They often cost more than foods made from scratch.
    B. They often take more time to prepare than foods made from scratch.
    C. They may not taste as good as foods made from scratch.
    D. They may require the addition of other ingredients, such as eggs or meat.

☐ Essay Questions: Provide the answers you feel best show your understanding of the subject matter.

14. What is a work triangle and how does it relate to organizing space in the kitchen?

15. What factors should you consider when purchasing convenience food products?

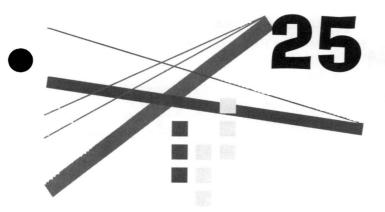

25 Getting Ready to Cook

Objectives

After studying this chapter, students will be able to
- list the types of information found in recipes.
- explain how to measure dry ingredients, liquid ingredients, and shortening.
- explain how to change recipe yield.
- define terms used in recipes.

Teaching Materials

Text, pages 271–277
  Words to Know
  Review It
  Apply It
  Think More About It
Student Activity Guide
  A. *Understanding Recipes*
  B. *Cooking Terms Crossword*
  C. *Measuring Ingredients*
Teacher's Resource Guide/Binder
  Recipe for Success, transparency master 25-1
  More or Less, reproducible master 25-2
  My Personal Journal, reproducible master 25-3
  Chapter 25 Quiz

Introductory Activities

1. Ask all students to stand. Then ask those students who have never made microwave popcorn to sit down. Ask students who have never made a sandwich to sit down. Ask students who have never baked cookies to sit down. Ask students who have never prepared a complete meal to sit down. Invite any students who remain standing to share their favorite cooking experience.
2. Ask students to complete the statement "The best thing about preparing your own food is . . ."

Strategies to Reteach, Reinforce, Enrich, and Extend Text Concepts

■ Understanding Recipes

3. **RT** *Recipe for Success,* transparency master 25-1. Use the transparency as you discuss with students tips for using recipes.
4. **RT** *Understanding Recipes,* Activity A, SAG. Have students write their answers to questions about the recipe on the worksheet.
5. **ER** Have students prepare a simple recipe at home. Have them describe the experience and the results of their food products in one-page written reports.

■ Measuring Ingredients

6. **RT** *Measuring Ingredients,* Activity C, SAG. Have students complete the charts to show their understanding of abbreviations and measurement equivalents used in recipes. Then have them describe the correct way to measure some common ingredients.
7. **RF** Have each student find a recipe in a cookbook, magazine, or newspaper that uses abbreviated measurements. Ask students to identify each of the abbreviations used. Then ask them to identify which ingredients should be measured in dry measuring cups, which should be measured in liquid measuring cups, and which should be measured in measuring spoons.
8. **RT** Have students practice measuring common dry and liquid ingredients and shortening.

Changing Recipe Yield

9. **RF** *More or Less,* reproducible master 25-2. Have students determine the amount of each listed ingredient needed to double and halve a recipe.
10. **RF** Bring in cookbooks with recipes designed to serve one or two and cookbooks with recipes designed to serve a crowd. Have students select appealing recipes and adjust them to serve a family of four.

Cooking Terms

11. **ER** Have students look through cookbooks to find cooking terms with which they are not familiar. Have them make a list of the terms and look up the definitions. Ask students to share their findings with the class.
12. **RT** Demonstrate for students the various preparation, cutting, and mixing techniques identified by the cooking terms defined in the chapter.
13. **RF** *Cooking Terms Crossword,* Activity B, SAG. Have students complete the crossword puzzle using cooking terms defined in the chapter.
14. **ER** *My Personal Journal,* reproducible master 25-3. Students are to describe the recipe preparation and measuring skills they have used as well as the skills they need to develop further. Students are also to explain how developing these skills will help them in the future.

Answer Key

Text

Review It, page 277
1. (List three:) list of ingredients, amounts of ingredients, directions for combining ingredients, oven temperature, length of cooking time, yield
2. (Student response.)
3. true
4. A. tsp. or t.
   B. tbsp. or T.
   C. c. or C.
   D. gal.
   E. lb. or #.
   F. oz.
5. Place liquid measuring cups on a flat, level surface before you begin to pour in the liquid. Check the amount of liquid at eye level.
6. true
7. 5⅓ tablespoons
8. A. mincing
   B. beating
   C. marinating
   D. shredding

Student Activity Guide

Understanding Recipes, Activity A
1. 375°F
2. butter or margarine, sugar, and brown sugar
3. flour, baking soda, and salt
4. the eggs and vanilla
5. one teaspoonful
6. Bake for 8 to 10 minutes or until light brown.
7. about 6 dozen 2½-inch cookies
8. (Student response.)
9. 1¼ cup
10. 1½ cups

Cooking Terms Crossword, Activity B

Measuring Ingredients, Activity C
(For abbreviations, see chart 25-2 in the text. For measurement equivalents, see chart 25-5 in the text. Explanations are student response.)

Teacher's Resource Guide/Binder

More or Less, reproducible master 25-2
1. 2 cups, ½ cup
2. 1½ cups, ⅜ cup (6 tablespoons)
3. 1½ cups, ⅜ cup (6 tablespoons)
4. 4 eggs, 1 egg
5. 2 teaspoons, ½ teaspoon.
6. 4½ cups, 1⅛ cups (1 cup plus 2 tablespoons)
7. 2 teaspoons, ½ teaspoon.
8. 1 teaspoon, ¼ teaspoon.
9. 2 cups, ½ cup
10. 4 cups, 1 cup
11. 12 dozen, 3 dozen

Chapter 25 Quiz

1. tsp. or t.
2. tbsp. or T.
3. cup
4. ounce
5. 3
6. ⅓

7. 16
8. 4
9. G
10. F
11. B
12. C

13. A
14. E
15. H
16. J
17. D
18. I

19. (Student response.)

20. Firmly press room-temperature shortening into ½ cup dry measuring cup. Overfill the measuring cup, being sure there are no air spaces. Level it with a narrow spatula or straight-edged knife. Remove the shortening from the cup with a rubber scraper.

Recipe for Success

Tips for Using Recipes
(Makes successful food products)

well-written recipe   correct equipment
required ingredients   adequate time

1. Measure accurately.

2. Mix ingredients in order.

3. Use correct pan size.

4. Follow cooking times and temperatures carefully.

More or Less

Name _____ **Date** _____ **Period** _____

Fill in the blanks on the left with the amount of each ingredient you would use if you were making a double batch of chocolate chip cookies. Fill in the blanks on the right with the amount of each ingredient you would use if you were making a half batch.

CHOCOLATE CHIP COOKIES

Double		**Half**
1. _____	1 cup butter	_____
2. _____	¾ cup sugar	_____
3. _____	¾ cup brown sugar	_____
4. _____	2 eggs	_____
5. _____	1 teaspoon vanilla	_____
6. _____	2¼ cups flour	_____
7. _____	1 teaspoon baking soda	_____
8. _____	½ teaspoon salt	_____
9. _____	1 cup chopped nuts	_____
10. _____	2 cups chocolate chips	_____
	Yield: 6 dozen cookies	

My Personal Journal

Think about your food preparation experiences. What skills in using recipes and measuring ingredients have you used? What skills do you feel you need to practice more? How will developing these skills help you in the future?

_____

_____

_____

_____

_____

_____

_____

_____

_____

_____

_____

_____

_____

_____

_____

_____

_____

_____

_____

_____

_____

_____

_____

_____

Getting Ready to Cook

Name _____

Date _____ **Period** _____ **Score** _____

CHAPTER 25 QUIZ

☐ Fill in the Blanks: Complete the following charts by filling in the blanks.

Abbreviations:

1. _____ teaspoon

2. _____ tablespoon

3. c. or C. _____

4. oz. _____

Measurement Equivalents:

5. _____ teaspoons = 1 tablespoon

6. 5⅓ tablespoons = _____ cup

7. _____ tablespoons = 1 cup

8. _____ cups = 1 quart

☐ Matching: Match the following cooking terms with their definitions.

_____ 9. Covering food with a seasoned liquid for a period of time.

_____ 10. Taking a rubber scraper down through a mixture, across the bottom of a bowl, up through the mixture, and over the top.

_____ 11. Dipping a food in liquid and then rolling it in crumbs.

_____ 12. Cutting food into small, uneven pieces.

_____ 13. Pouring liquid over a food while it is cooking.

_____ 14. Cutting through shortening to combine it with flour.

_____ 15. Cutting food into very tiny pieces.

_____ 16. Mixing ingredients by tumbling them lightly with a spoon and a fork.

_____ 17. Beating a mixture, such as shortening and sugar, until it is light and fluffy.

_____ 18. Removing the skin or outer covering from a food.

A. baste
B. bread
C. chop
D. cream
E. cut in
F. fold
G. marinate
H. mince
I. pare
J. toss

☐ Essay Questions: Provide the answers you feel best show your understanding of the subject matter.

19. Give three tips for using recipes.

20. Describe how to measure ½ cup of shortening.

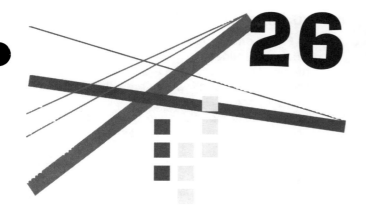

26 Fruits and Vegetables

Objectives

After studying this chapter, students will be able to
- give guidelines to follow when buying fresh, canned, frozen, and dried fruits and vegetables.
- explain how to store fruits and vegetables to maintain their quality.
- describe how to prepare fruits and vegetables to be eaten raw or cooked.

Teaching Materials

Text, pages 278–287
> *Words to Know*
> *Review It*
> *Apply It*
> *Think More About It*

Student Activity Guide
> A. *Buying Fruits and Vegetables*
> B. *Storing Fruits and Vegetables*
> C. *Preparing Fruits and Vegetables*
> D. *A "New" Fruit and Vegetable*

Teacher's Resource Guide/Binder
> *Getting the Pick of the Season,* transparency master 26-1
> *My Personal Journal,* reproducible master 26-2
> *Fruit and Vegetable Recipes,* reproducible master 26-3
> *Proper Storage Guards Against the Enemies of Freshness,* color transparency CT-26
> Chapter 26 Quiz

Introductory Activities

1. Go around the room asking each student to name his or her favorite fruit and vegetable. Write responses on the chalkboard. Comment on the variety or lack of variety the responses represent.
2. Allow students to sample fresh, frozen, canned, and dried peaches. Ask students why they think fruits and vegetables are sold in different forms.

Ask what they know about buying and preparing the various forms. Use their responses to help you determine which points you should emphasize as you go through the chapter.

Strategies to Reteach, Reinforce, Enrich, and Extend Text Concepts

■ Buying Fruits and Vegetables

3. **RT** *Getting the Pick of the Season,* transparency master 26-1. Use this master to discuss what to look for when buying fresh fruits and vegetables.
4. **RF** *Buying Fruits and Vegetables,* Activity A, SAG. Have students visit a supermarket to complete the chart and answer the questions about buying fruits and vegetables.
5. **RF** Have students compare the price per pound of different varieties of such fresh fruits and vegetables as apples and peppers. Discuss why prices might vary.
6. **RT** Have students compare the prices of generic, store brand, and national brand canned or frozen fruits and vegetables.

■ Storing Fruits and Vegetables

7. **RF** *Proper Storage Guards Against the Enemies of Freshness,* color transparency CT-26. Use this transparency to illustrate the various factors that can affect the freshness of food. Emphasize how proper storage can help keep food fresh.
8. **ER** Ask a produce manager from a grocery store to speak to your class about how to select different types of fresh fruits and vegetables.
9. **RT** *Storing Fruits and Vegetables,* Activity B, SAG. Have students describe how to store the fruits and vegetables listed on the worksheet.

Preparing Fruits and Vegetables

10. **RF** *Preparing Fruits and Vegetables*, Activity C, SAG. Have students answer the questions on the worksheet about preparing fruits and vegetables.

11. **ER** *My Personal Journal*, reproducible master 26-2. Students are to describe a time when a piece of produce spoiled in their homes. They are to describe how they could have prepared the produce before it spoiled and explain what they could do in the future to avoid spoiled produce.

12. **ER** Have students use their choice of fruits, spreads, and toppings to create fresh fruit snacks.

13. **ER** Divide the class into lab groups. Have each group prepare a cooked fruit using a different preparation method—simmering, baking, broiling, and microwaving. Have all students sample each type of fruit and compare the tastes and textures.

14. **ER** Have students prepare a salad or relish tray with fresh vegetables.

15. **EX** Have students cook a portion of a mild vegetable, such as green beans or corn, in a small amount of water until crisp-tender. Have them cook another portion in a large amount of water for a longer period of time. Then ask them to analyze the two portions and write a brief report comparing the color, taste, texture, and appearance.

16. **EX** *Fruit and Vegetable Recipes*, reproducible master 26-3. Have students prepare the recipes on the master. Then have them evaluate their lab experience and the food products.

17. **ER** *A "New" Fruit and Vegetable*, Activity D, SAG. Have each student draw and describe one fruit and one vegetable that he or she has never tried before. Then have students use cookbooks and other references to find out how to prepare the fruits and vegetables they have selected.

Answer Key

■ Text

Review It, Page 287

1. B
2. (List three:) Brussels sprouts, cauliflower, turnips, onions, broccoli, cabbage
3. produce
4. Produce costs less, is fresher, and offers a better selection when it is in season.
5. Foods in cans with dents, bulges, or leaks have a high risk of causing food poisoning.
6. time, light, heat, and moisture
7. Dip cut fruit in lemon, orange, grapefruit, or pineapple juice and serve it as soon after preparing it as possible.
8. add sugar
9. Soaking vegetables causes nutrient loss.
10. false

■ Student Activity Guide

Buying Fruits and Vegetables, Activity A

1. (Student response.)
2. Fruits and vegetables that are in season are often of better quality and lower in price than those that are out of season.
3. These are signs of old, over-ripe, low-quality produce. This produce has declined in flavor and nutrient value.
4. It is available year-round and sometimes frozen in mixes or with sauces.
5. Items that are partially thawed will not last as long. These items may not taste as good either.
6. Like frozen, canned fruits and vegetables are available year-round. However, the canning process can change the flavors of fruits and vegetables. Also, textures tend to become softer from the canning process.
7. Foods in these cans have a high risk of causing food poisoning.
8. The water in them has been removed.

Storing Fruits and Vegetables, Activity B
(See the section on storing fruits and vegetables pages 282–283 of the text.)

Preparing Fruits and Vegetables, Activity C

1. This washes off pesticides and dirt.
2. Dip the cut fruit in lemon, orange, grapefruit, or pineapple juice. Also, serve the fruit as soon after preparing as possible.
3. to help it hold its shape and add flavor
4. This will allow more even cooking.
5. (Student response.)
6. Soaking vegetables causes nutrient loss.
7. until they are tender, but slightly crisp
8. in a small amount of water for a short time
   The pan should be covered during cooking.
9. They should be cooked with water and cooked in an uncovered pan for a short time.
10. when a fork can easily be pushed into the center of them
11. For 10 to 20 minutes. This helps protect against food poisoning.
12. (Student response.)

■ Teacher's Resource Guide/Binder

Chapter 26 Quiz

1.	T	8.	F
2.	F	9.	F
3.	F	10.	T
4.	T	11.	A
5.	T	12.	C
6.	T	13.	D
7.	F		

14. (Student response.)
15. The cooking process changes the texture, flavor, and color of vegetables.

Getting the Pick of the Season

■ Choose medium size.

■ Check firmness.

■ Look for bright color.

■ Avoid bruises, cracks, and spots.

My Personal Journal

Think of a time when a piece of fresh produce spoiled in your home. Why did it spoil? How could you have prepared it before it spoiled? About how much money was wasted as a result of this spoilage? What could you do in the future to avoid spoiled produce?

Fruit and Vegetable Recipes

Granola Baked Apples
(Makes 4 servings)

4   cooking apples
¾   cup granola
2   tablespoons brown sugar

1. Core apples.

2. Cut out center of apples to leave ½-inch shell. Chop ½ cup apple from the center and reserve. Cut a strip of peel ½-inch wide around the top of the apple.

3. In a medium bowl, mix granola, reserved ½ cup chopped apple, and brown sugar.

4. Fill scooped out apples with granola mixture and place in a shallow baking dish. Pour water in baking dish to fill ¼-inch deep.

5. Cover apples and bake in 350°F oven for 45 minutes, or until apples are tender. Serve with sour cream, if desired.

Cherry Tomatoes Vinaigrette
(Makes 6 servings)

½   teaspoon salt
¼   cup lemon juice
¾   cup oil
1   clove garlic, crushed
½   teaspoon basil
½   teaspoon thyme
1   tablespoon parsley, chopped
2   pints cherry tomatoes

1. Mix all ingredients except tomatoes in a bowl.

2. Wash cherry tomatoes and remove stems.

3. Add tomatoes to dressing and chill 2 hours or overnight.

Fruits and Vegetables

Name _____

Date _____ **Period** _____ **Score** _____

CHAPTER 26 QUIZ

☐ True/False: Circle *T* if the statement is true or *F* if the statement is false.

T F 1. Fruits are good sources of vitamin A, vitamin C, and fiber.

T F 2. Oranges are a tropical fruit.

T F 3. Although they are high in nutrients, most vegetables are also high in calories.

T F 4. The strong-flavored vegetables tend to taste even stronger after cooking.

T F 5. Fresh fruits and vegetables cost less and are of higher quality when they are in season.

T F 6. Frozen fruits and vegetables may be less crisp than fresh produce.

T F 7. Dried vegetables have a soft, pliable texture.

T F 8. Frozen fruits should be thawed completely before serving.

T F 9. Fresh vegetables should be soaked in cool water to remove dirt and pesticides.

T F 10. Vegetables canned at home should be boiled for 10 to 20 minutes before they are eaten.

☐ Multiple Choice: Choose the best answer and write the corresponding letter in the blank.

_____ 11. Which of the following is *not* a mild flavored vegetable?

    A. Broccoli.
    B. Corn.
    C. Peas.
    D. Zucchini.

_____ 12. Which of the following is an indication that a canned fruit or vegetable may be harmful?

    A. The product is packed in heavy syrup.
    B. The label is marked Grade D (Substandard).
    C. The can is bulging.
    D. The can has a generic label.

_____ 13. Which of the following can destroy vitamins in fresh fruits and vegetables?

    A. Light.
    B. Heat.
    C. Moisture.
    D. All of the above.

☐ Essay Questions: Provide the answers you feel best show your understanding of the subject matter.

14. Give three guidelines to follow when buying fresh fruits and vegetables.

15. What effects does the cooking process have on fresh vegetables?

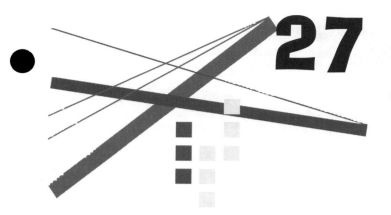

27 Cereal Products

Objectives

After studying this chapter, students will be able to
- list a variety of cereal products and discuss points to consider when buying and storing them.
- describe techniques used when cooking starches and cereals to obtain quality products.
- explain basic steps in preparing quick breads and yeast breads.

Teaching Materials

Text, pages 288–297
  Words to Know
  Review It
  Apply It
  Think More About It
Student Activity Guide
  A. *Breakfast Cereals*
  B. *Bread Comparisons*
  C. *Cooking Cereal Products*
  D. *Making Breads*
Teacher's Resource Guide/Binder
  Preventing Lumps, transparency master 27-1
  Cereal Product Recipes, reproducible master 27-2
  My Personal Journal, reproducible master 27-3
  Chapter 27 Quiz

Introductory Activities

1. Ask students to name all the cereal products they ate yesterday. List their responses on the chalkboard. Help students realize that cereal products include much more than breakfast foods.
2. Ask students to explain why they think bread has been called the "staff of life."

Strategies to Reteach, Reinforce, Enrich, and Extend Text Concepts

■ Buying and Storing Cereal Products

3. **ER** Have students use different types of flour to prepare a basic biscuit recipe. Have them compare the taste, texture, and appearance of the different biscuits.
4. **ER** Have students make a poster chart showing the different varieties of pasta. Have them glue samples of the various pastas on the chart and describe how they may be served.
5. **ER** Have students research the food customs of a culture that uses rice as a staple in the diet. Ask them to write brief reports explaining how rice is used in that culture.
6. **RF** *Breakfast Cereals,* Activity A, SAG. Have students look at cereal packages in a grocery store to compare the cost and nutritional value of 12 ready-to-eat and cooked cereals.
7. **ER** *Bread Comparisons,* Activity B, SAG. Have students compare biscuits made from refrigerated dough, muffins made from a mix, and prepackaged bread with their homemade counterparts.
8. **EX** Store a securely wrapped slice of bread in a cool, dry place. Sprinkle a second slice of bread with a small amount of water. Securely wrap this slice and store it in a warm, moist place. Loosely wrap a third slice of bread and store it in a cool, dry place. After one week, have students analyze all three slices to introduce a discussion on proper storage of bread and cereal products.

■ Cooking Starches and Cereals

9. **RT** *Preventing Lumps,* transparency master 27-1. Use the transparency as you discuss with students the three main techniques for keeping starch granules separated to prevent lumps from forming during cooking.

10. **RT** *Cooking Cereal Products,* Activity C, SAG. Have students answer the questions and complete the chart on the worksheet to demonstrate their understanding of cereal cookery.

11. **RF** Have students prepare a sample of medium white sauce using 2 tablespoons of fat, 2 tablespoons of flour, and 1 cup of milk. Have them prepare a second sample of white sauce substituting 2 tablespoons of cornstarch for the flour. Ask students to compare the two samples in terms of thickness and appearance.

12. **ER** Discuss with students the versatile nature of pasta and rice as filling, nutritious, inexpensive meat extenders. Then divide the class into lab groups. Have each group prepare a different main dish recipe made with pasta or rice.

13. **RF** Have students prepare two samples of cooked cereal—one on top of the range and the other in the microwave oven. Have them compare the ease of preparation and the quality of the two products.

■ Making Breads

14. **RT** *Making Breads,* Activity D, SAG. Have students answer the questions on the worksheet to demonstrate their understanding of bread making.

15. **EX** *Cereal Product Recipes,* reproducible master 27-2. Have students prepare the recipes on the master. Then have them evaluate their lab experience and the food products.

16. **ER** Have students plan and prepare a brunch for faculty members that includes a variety of quick breads.

17. **ER** Have students prepare a simple recipe using a yeast raised dough, such as sweet rolls or pizza.

18. **ER** *My Personal Journal,* reproducible master 27-3. Students are to identify the information from the chapter they think they will remember most and explain how they can use this information in the future.

Answer Key

■ Text

Review It, page 297
1. cereals—wheat, corn, rice, and oats
   cereal products—(List four:) flour, pasta, breakfast cereal, muffins, bread (Students may justify other responses.)

2. B
3. false
4. Cereal products should be stored in a cool, dry place in tightly closed containers.
5. gelatinization
6. Starch can be coated with fat before liquid is added. Starch can be combined with sugar. Starch can be mixed with a cold liquid to form a paste before heating.
7. (List one:) Cereal products are less likely to burn when prepared in a microwave oven. Cereal products can be prepared and served in the same dish when they are cooked in a microwave oven.
8. air, steam, and carbon dioxide formed and trapped in baked goods
9. the proportions of ingredients—batters contain more liquid than doughs
10. Push two fingers into the dough. If the dough stays indented, it has risen enough.

■ Student Activity Guide

Cooking Cereal Products, Activity C
1. packages
2. starch
3. gelatinization
4. thickeners
5. a. fat
   b. sugar
   c. liquid
6. pasta
7. two
8. rice
9. covered
10. stand

Volume Increases of Cereal Products

1 cup uncooked	Cooked equivalent
White rice	3 cups
Brown rice	4 cups
Pasta	2 cups
Oatmeal (old fashioned)	3 cups
Cream of wheat (quick)	6 cups
Hominy grits	6 cups
Farina	5 cups

Making Breads, Activity D
1. ingredients in baked products that produce carbon dioxide, causing the baked goods to rise
2. yeast breads, quick breads
3. (List six:) muffins, nut breads, waffles, pancakes, biscuits, popovers, cream puffs
4. baking soda, baking powder
5. A mixture is called a batter when you can pour the mixed ingredients. A stiff, thick mixture that cannot be poured is called a dough.

6. If you stir the batter until the lumps are gone, the muffins will become tough when baking.

7. The pancakes are ready to turn when bubbles appear on the surface. Waffles are done when steam no longer pours from the waffle iron.

8. They will become tough.

9. Yeast is a tiny plant that produces carbon dioxide when mixed with the right ingredients. This gas causes yeast breads to rise.

10. The steps for making yeast breads should be numbered in the following order: 7, 5, 1, 3, 9, 6, 8, 4, 2, 10.

11. Toppings are often added.

12. (List three:) Pancakes, waffles, popovers, cream puffs, yeast breads. These products cannot be browned in the microwave.

■ Teacher's Resource Guide/Binder

Chapter 27 Quiz

1. F
2. T
3. F
4. T
5. T
6. T
7. F
8. F
9. T
10. T
11. dough
12. starch
13. cereals
14. quick breads
15. enriched
16. batter
17. pasta
18. leavening agents
19. (Student response should mention that cereal products are inexpensive, easy to store, and nutritious.)
20. to prevent lumps

Preventing Lumps

Coat starch granules with fat.

Combine starch with sugar.

Mix starch with cold liquid.

Cereal Product Recipes

Souper Rice
(Serves 4 to 6)

1½ cups white rice
1   can (10½ ounces) condensed cream of mushroom soup
1½ cups water

1. Grease a 2-quart casserole.

2. Combine rice, soup, and water in the casserole and stir until well blended.

3. Cover and bake rice in 350°F oven for 30 to 45 minutes, or until liquid is absorbed and rice is tender and fluffy.

Cheddar Biscuits
(Makes 12 large biscuits)

2   cups flour
1   tablespoon baking powder
½ teaspoon salt
½ cup sharp Cheddar cheese, grated
⅓ cup shortening
⅔ to ¾ cup milk

1. Preheat oven to 425°F.

2. Combine flour, baking powder, salt, and cheese in a mixing bowl.

3. Cut in shortening with pastry blender, two knives, or fingers until particles are about the size of small peas.

4. Add milk; stir with a fork until mixture forms a soft ball.

5. Turn dough out onto a lightly floured surface. Knead gently 8 to 10 times.

6. Roll dough into a circle about ½ inch thick. Cut out biscuits with a round biscuit cutter and place on an ungreased baking sheet about 2 inches apart.

7. Bake until golden brown, about 12 to 15 minutes.

My Personal Journal

Think about what you have learned about cereal products. What information about cereal products do you think you will remember most? Why do you think this information will stick in your mind? How will you use this information in the future?

Cereal Products

Name _____

Date _____ Period _____ Score _____

CHAPTER 27 QUIZ

☐ True/False: Circle *T* if the statement is true or *F* if the statement is false.

T   F   1. Iron and B vitamins are added when a grain is refined.

T   F   2. Fresh pasta is more expensive than dried pasta.

T   F   3. Quick-cooking cereals can be prepared by simply adding hot water to them.

T   F   4. Refrigerated bread will keep longer than bread stored at room temperature.

T   F   5. When starch and water are heated, the starch granules soften and swell.

T   F   6. Properly cooked pasta is a little chewy, but not crunchy.

T   F   7. Cereal products cook much more quickly in a microwave oven than they do on top of the range.

T   F   8. Muffins should be stirred until all ingredients are mixed and the batter is free from lumps.

T   F   9. A common order of steps for preparing yeast bread is mix, knead, rise, punch down, shape, and bake.

T   F   10. Although most quick breads microwave well, popovers and cream puffs cannot be prepared in a microwave oven.

☐ Fill-in-the-Blank: Complete the following statements by filling in the blanks.

_____ 11. A stiff, thick mixture of ingredients that cannot be poured, such as that used to make biscuits, is called a _____.

_____ 12. The complex carbohydrate portion of plants is _____.

_____ 13. Wheat, corn, rice, oats, and other seeds from grasses are _____.

_____ 14. Muffins, waffles, and biscuits are all _____.

_____ 15. Cereal products that have missing B vitamins and iron added back to them are _____.

_____ 16. A pourable mixture of ingredients, such as that used to make pancakes and waffles, is called a _____.

_____ 17. Macaroni, spaghetti, and noodles are all types of _____.

_____ 18. Ingredients that make bread products rise are called _____.

☐ Essay Questions: Provide the answers you feel best show your understanding of the subject matter.

19. Explain why cereal products play a major role in the diets of people around the world.

20. Why is it important to keep starch granules separated when cooking starches and cereals?

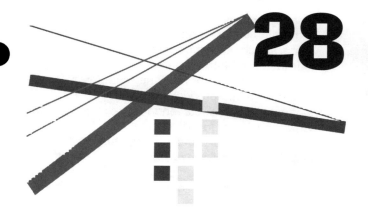

28 Milk and Milk Products

Objectives

After studying this chapter, students will be able to
■ describe a variety of dairy products and discuss points to consider when buying and storing them.
■ give tips for preparing dairy products and foods made with dairy products.

Teaching Materials

Text, pages 298–307
  Words to Know
  Review It
  Apply It
  Think More About It
Student Activity Guide
  A. *From Cow to Carton*
  B. *Cheese Tasting*
  C. *Dairy Products Facts*
Teacher's Resource Guide/Binder
  Tips for Preparing Dairy Products, transparency master 28-1
  My Personal Journal, reproducible master 28-2
  Dairy Products Recipes, reproducible master 28-3
  Chapter 28 Quiz

Introductory Activities

1. Mention a few sayings that contain references to dairy products, such as "peaches and cream complexion," "land flowing with milk and honey," "moon made of green cheese," and "like mother's milk." Ask students what they think these sayings mean. Invite them to think of others.
2. Tell students that some people have described milk as the closest thing to a perfect food. Ask students why they think milk may have been given

this description. Ask them to explain why they agree or disagree with this description.

Strategies to Reteach, Reinforce, Enrich, and Extend Text Concepts

■ Types of Dairy Products

3. **ER** *From Cow to Carton,* Activity A, SAG. Have students visit a dairy farm or interview a dairy owner or farmer. Students should ask about the steps milk goes through from the time the cow is milked until the milk is purchased by the consumer. Students should use the space provided to write a report on their findings.
4. **ER** Have students research how UHT processed milk is processed or how consumers are accepting and using UHT processed milk. Students should give an oral report on their findings.
5. **RF** Have students taste samples of fresh fluid milk, UHT processed milk, dry milk, and canned milk. Students should compare their flavors.
6. **RF** *Cheese Tasting,* Activity B, SAG. Prepare and label trays of up to eight types of cheese for students to sample. Have students use the chart provided to describe the appearance, texture, and flavor of each cheese. Students should then answer the questions that follow.
7. **RF** Have students examine the labels on various frozen milk products. Students should discuss which ingredients are probably added as stabilizers and which are added for flavor. If nutrition labeling is available, students should compare the calorie and fat content of various products.

8. **ER** Have students write a report on how yogurt is made.

■ Buying and Storing Dairy Products

9. **ER** Have students sample store brand, name brand, and gourmet Cheddar cheese. Provide students with prices for each type of cheese. Students should discuss whether the difference in cost is worth the difference in flavor.

10. **ER** Have students develop a public service announcement that gives tips for storing dairy products. The announcement may be for radio or television.

■ Preparing Dairy Products

11. **RT** *Tips for Preparing Dairy Products,* transparency master 28-1. Use the transparency as you discuss with students some of the key points to keep in mind when preparing dairy products.

12. **RF** *Dairy Products Facts,* Activity C, SAG. Have students complete the statements by writing terms related to milk and milk products in the blanks.

13. **EX** Divide the class into groups and have each group examine a different type of ice cream freezer. Each group should give a report on how their freezer works and what it costs. Advantages and disadvantages of the freezers should be pointed out.

14. **ER** *My Personal Journal,* reproducible master 28-2. Students are to describe their favorite dairy food and explain the points that are important to remember when cooking with or preparing it.

15. **ER** *Dairy Products Recipes,* reproducible master 28-3. Have students work in groups to prepare Microwave Nachos and Strawberry Yogurt Shakes. Students should sample the foods they prepare and evaluate the results.

Answer Key

Text

Review It, page 307
1. pasteurization
2. Whole milk contains three to four percent fat. Lowfat milk may have one or two percent fat. Skim milk has had most of the fat removed.
3. C

4. false
5. Buttermilk, yogurt, and sour cream are all made with a special type of bacteria that gives them a sour taste and thick texture.
6. because the government sets standards for the content of these products
7. because milk products tend to pick up flavors and odors from other foods
8. by using fresh milk and low temperatures and by thickening the milk before adding ingredients
9. Heating cheese at high power settings can cause it to become rubbery in the microwave oven.
10. Stirring prevents the formation of large ice crystals that give frozen desserts a grainy texture.

■ Student Activity Guide

Dairy Products Facts, Activity C
1. calcium
2. vitamin D
3. pasteurization
4. whole
5. lowfat
6. skim
7. buttermilk
8. UHT processed
9. dry
10. evaporated
11. sweetened condensed
12. curds
13. whey
14. cheese
15. unripened
16. ripened
17. processed
18. lowfat ice cream
19. stabilizers
20. sherbet
21. custard
22. yogurt
23. cream
24. heavy whipping
25. light
26. half-and-half
27. sour
28. imitation
29. butter
30. margarine
31. perishable
32. scorch
33. curdling
34. scalding

Teacher's Resource Guide/Binder

Chapter 28 Quiz
1. F
2. T
3. F
4. F
5. F
6. T
7. F
8. F
9. T
10. F
11. A
12. D
13. B
14. (Student response.)
15. Cut cheese in small pieces so it will melt faster; wait until the last minutes of cooking time to add cheese to soups and casseroles; keep cooking time short; use medium to medium-high power settings in the microwave.

Tips for Preparing Dairy Products

Milk

- Use low temperatures.

- Thicken before adding ingredients high in acids, enzymes, or salts.

- Remove any film that forms on surface.

Cheese

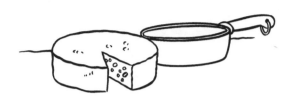

- Cut into small pieces.

- Add during last few minutes of cooking time.

- Use medium to medium-high microwave power setting.

Frozen Desserts

- Use temperatures below 32°F.

- Stir during freezing.

Whipping Cream

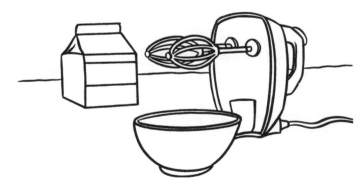

- Chill cream, bowl, and beaters before whipping.

- Do not overbeat.

My Personal Journal

Think of your favorite dairy food. What is this food? Why do you enjoy it? What points are important to remember when cooking with or preparing this food?

_____

_____

_____

_____

_____

_____

_____

_____

_____

_____

_____

_____

_____

_____

_____

_____

_____

_____

_____

_____

_____

_____

_____

_____

_____

Dairy Products Recipes

Microwave Nachos
(Serves 2)

24   Tortilla chips
½   cup Cheddar cheese, shredded
     dash chili powder

1. Arrange tortilla chips on a 10-inch dinner plate.

2. Sprinkle cheese and chili powder evenly over chips.

3. Microwave uncovered on medium power until cheese is melted, 1 to 1½ minutes.

Strawberry Yogurt Shake
(Serves 2)

1   cup fresh or frozen strawberries
1   cup strawberry yogurt
1   cup milk
1   teaspoon vanilla

1. Wash, hull, and quarter fresh strawberries. (Frozen strawberries should be thawed slightly.)

2. Combine strawberries, yogurt, milk, and vanilla in a blender container. Blend on high speed for 20 seconds or until mixture is smooth.

Milk and Milk Products

Name _____

Date _____ **Period** _____ **Score** _____

CHAPTER 28 QUIZ

☐ True/False: Circle *T* if the statement is true or *F* if the statement is false.

T   F   1. Pasteurization destroys all the harmful bacteria in milk.

T   F   2. UHT processed milk is sterilized by heating it to a very high temperature for a few seconds.

T   F   3. Dry milk is usually more expensive than fluid milk.

T   F   4. Sweetened condensed milk and evaporated milk can be interchanged in recipes.

T   F   5. Processed cheese is made with vegetable oil instead of milkfat.

T   F   6. Stabilizers are added to ice cream to help it keep a smooth, creamy texture.

T   F   7. Sweet butter has salt added to it.

T   F   8. Scalding means boiling milk.

T   F   9. Frozen desserts should be stirred constantly to prevent large ice crystals from forming.

T   F 10. For best results when whipping cream, you should make sure the cream, bowl, and beaters are at room temperature.

☐ Multiple Choice: Choose the best answer and write the corresponding letter in the blank.

_____ 11. Which of the following milk products contains three to four percent fat?

      A. Whole milk.
      B. Lowfat milk.
      C. Skim milk.
      D. Half-and-half.

_____ 12. Which of the following is an unripened cheese?

      A. American cheese.
      B. Cheddar cheese.
      C. Colby cheese.
      D. Cottage cheese.

_____ 13. Which of the following does *not* cause curdling?

      A. Enzymes.
      B. Low temperatures.
      C. Tomatoes.
      D. Salt-cured meats.

☐ Essay Questions: Provide the answers you feel best show your understanding of the subject matter.

14. List four tips for storing dairy products.

15. How can you avoid making cheese tough when you cook it?

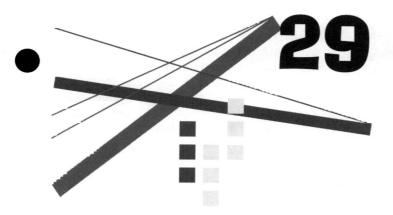

29 Protein Foods

Objectives

After studying this chapter, students will be able to
- discuss points to consider when buying meat, poultry, fish, and eggs.
- explain how to properly store meat, poultry, fish, and eggs.
- describe the various cooking methods that are used to prepare protein foods.

Teaching Materials

Text, pages 308–318
Words to Know
Review It
Apply It
Think More About It
Student Activity Guide
A. *Choosing Cuts of Meat*
B. *Buying Protein Foods*
C. *Storing Protein Foods*
D. *Preparing Protein Foods*
Teacher's Resource Guide/Binder
My Personal Journal, reproducible master 29-1
Tips for Storing Meat, Poultry, and Fish, transparency master 29-2
Protein Food Recipes, reproducible master 29-3
Chapter 29 Quiz

Introductory Activities

1. *My Personal Journal,* reproducible master 29-1. Students are to describe the main dish of their favorite meal. Then they are to explain why many people center their meals around protein foods. They are also to state why they think a meal without a protein food for the main course is or is not complete.
2. Tell students that protein foods are costly compared to many other foods. Ask students to explain whether they think protein foods are worth their high cost.

Strategies to Reteach, Reinforce, Enrich, and Extend Text Concepts

■ Buying Protein Foods

3. **RT** *Choosing Cuts of Meat,* Activity A, SAG. Have students label the drawing to indicate sections of the animal that are less tender, fairly tender, very tender, or most tender. Students should then match the beef cuts listed with their location on the animal.
4. **RF** *Buying Protein Foods,* Activity B, SAG. Have students list signs of quality for each of the protein foods given.
5. **ER** Have students prepare a demonstration on how to choose a type of protein food. Students should prepare and use visual aids in their demonstration.
6. **RF** Have students visit a grocery store and record prices for various types of protein foods. Students should determine which protein foods are the best buys.

■ Storing Protein Foods

7. **RT** *Tips for Storing Meat, Poultry, and Fish,* transparency master 29-2. Use the transparency as you discuss with students proper techniques for storing protein foods.
8. **RF** Have students practice wrapping meat using freezer paper or foil. (Any nonperishable item about the size of a piece of meat can be wrapped instead of meat.)
9. **RF** *Storing Protein Foods,* Activity C, SAG. Have students read the given situations involving

storage of protein foods. Students should then answer the question following each situation.

■ Preparing Protein Foods

10. **ER** Have students browse through recipes for protein foods in cookbooks or magazines. Students should determine what cooking method is being used in each recipe.
11. **RF** *Preparing Protein Foods*, Activity D, SAG. Have students match the given phrases and preparation terms or internal temperatures. Students should then describe how they would cook each of the protein foods listed.
12. **RT** Prepare a thick piece of meat using an appropriate cooking method. Have students practice using and reading a meat thermometer as the meat cooks. Allow students to sample the meat when it is done.
13. **ER** Invite a chef or seafood store owner to talk to the class about preparing different types of fish. The guest should describe flavors of different fish and provide recipes. If possible, have the guest prepare a seafood recipe and allow the class to try samples.
14. **ER** *Protein Food Recipes*, reproducible master 29-3. Have students work in groups to prepare Fiesta Burgers and Easy Egg Scramble, following the steps in the recipes. Students should sample the food they prepare and evaluate the results.

Answer Key

■ Text

Review It, page 318
1. B
2. marbling
3. Prime, Choice, Select, and Standard
4. (List three:) flesh that is not slimy; tight scales; red gills; bright, bulging eyes; no strong odor
5. to prevent freezer burn
6. one or two days
7. because eggs may pick up flavors and odors from strong smelling foods like onions
8. (List four of each:) dry heat—roasting, baking, broiling, grilling, frying; moist heat—boiling, simmering, poaching, braising, stewing
9. true
10. The eggs will continue to cook and become overcooked, and a greenish ring will form around the yolk.

■ Student Activity Guide

Choosing Cuts of Meat, Activity A
1. less tender
2. very tender
3. most tender
4. very tender
5. fairly tender
6. less tender
7. fairly tender

Examples of beef cuts from these areas:
- 7   Skirt steak, flank steak
- 1   Chuck roast, pot roast, blade roast, short ribs
- 6   Shank, brisket, corned brisket
- 2   Rib roast, rib eye roast, rib eye steak, back ribs
- 3   Top loin steak, T-bone steak, porterhouse steak, tenderloin steak (filet mignon), tenderloin roast
- 5   Round steak, rump roast, bottom round roast, tip steak
- 4   Sirloin steak, top sirloin steak

Buying Protein Foods, Activity B
(See "Buying Protein Foods" section of the text.)

Storing Protein Foods, Activity C
1. in the coldest part of the refrigerator
2. three to four days
3. one or two days
4. one or two days
5. She should remove the store wrapper and rewrap it in a freezer bag, freezer paper, or heavy aluminum foil. She can then freeze it and thaw it when it is needed.
6. She should separate the package into smaller portions, wrap them, and store them in the freezer.
7. No. He should cook them within a day or two. He could refreeze them after cooking them.
8. one to two days
9. No. It should not be refrozen.
10. The eggs should be stored in the refrigerator in their original carton. The eggs will stay fresh longer.

Preparing Protein Foods, Activity D
1. H
2. A
3. D
4. G
5. K
6. B
7. O
8. P
9. Q
10. C
11. J
12. E
13. F
14. I
15. L
16. N
17. M

(Preparation chart: Student response. Responses should reflect a proper preparation method for each food.)

■ Teacher's Resource Guide/Binder

Chapter 29 Quiz
1. F
2. T
3. F
4. T
5. T
6. F
7. T
8. F
9. T
10. F
11. F
12. F
13. C
14. D
15. B
16. E
17. A
18. F
19. Muscles of the animal that are used more tend to be tougher and have less fat in them. Muscles that are not used as much tend to be more tender and have more fat.
20. Place the thermometer in the thickest part of the muscle without touching bone or fat. Leave it in until the temperature indicator stops moving. Then read the internal temperature.

My Personal Journal

Think of your favorite meal. What is the main dish? Why do you think many people center their meals around protein foods? Do you think a meal without a protein food for the main course is complete? Why or why not?

_____
_____
_____
_____
_____
_____
_____
_____
_____
_____
_____
_____
_____
_____
_____
_____
_____
_____
_____
_____
_____
_____
_____
_____

Tips for Storing Meat, Poultry, and Fish

■ Wrap tightly.

■ Store in coldest part of the refrigerator.

■ Follow recommended storage times.

■ Freeze for longer storage.

■ Do not refreeze.

Protein Food Recipes

Fiesta Burgers
(Serves 4)

1   pound lean ground beef
½   package (1.25 ounces) taco seasoning mix
1   tomato, sliced
2   ounces Cheddar cheese, shredded
½   cup sour cream
4   hamburger buns

1. In a medium bowl, thoroughly mix ground beef and taco seasoning mix.

2. Divide beef mixture into 4 equal portions and shape into patties about ½ inch thick.

3. Place patties in a skillet and cook over medium heat until both sides are brown, turning a few times during cooking.

4. Place burgers on buns and top with tomato slices, Cheddar cheese, and sour cream.

Easy Egg Scramble
(Serves 2)

1   tablespoon butter or margarine
1   tablespoon chives
4   eggs
2   tablespoons bacon bits
¼   cup milk

1. Place butter or margarine in a round, 1-quart casserole dish and microwave on high until melted, 45 seconds to 1½ minutes.

2. Add remaining ingredients and beat them together with a fork.

3. Microwave egg mixture uncovered, stirring every minute, until eggs are set but still moist, 2 to 4 minutes.

4. Stir eggs before serving.

Protein Foods

Name _____

Date _____ **Period** _____ **Score** _____

CHAPTER 29 QUIZ

☐ True/False: Circle *T* if the statement is true or *F* if the statement is false.

T F 1. Fat makes meat more dry and tough.

T F 2. Select cuts of meat are good choices if you want to cut down on fat and cholesterol.

T F 3. In poultry, white meat contains more fat than dark meat.

T F 4. When you buy fresh fish, you should make sure it has firm flesh that is not slimy.

T F 5. The price per pound does not always give you a true picture of the cost of protein foods.

T F 6. Ground beef stays fresh longer than other cuts of beef such as roasts or steaks.

T F 7. Meat and poultry can be refrozen after cooking.

T F 8. Properly stored eggs are safe to use for up to two months.

T F 9. Fresh pork should be cooked to an internal temperature of 160°F.

T F 10. When poultry is done cooking, the drumstick should be firmly attached to the bird.

T F 11. Fish takes longer to cook than meat or poultry.

T F 12. When starting with simmering water, soft-cooked eggs should be cooked for 13 to 15 minutes.

☐ Matching: Match the following statements with the appropriate terms.

_____ 13. Fat that is mixed in with the muscle portion of meat.

_____ 14. Grade of meat that is mainly found in restaurants.

_____ 15. A type of drying that happens when frozen food is exposed to air.

_____ 16. A type of cooking method appropriate for young poultry.

_____ 17. A type of cooking method appropriate for less tender cuts of beef.

_____ 18. A type of cooking method appropriate for fish, especially lean fish.

A. braising
B. freezer burn
C. marbling
D. prime
E. roasting
F. steaming

☐ Essay Questions: Provide the answers you feel best show your understanding of the subject matter.

19. Why does the location on the animal affect the flavor and tenderness of beef?

20. Explain how to use a meat thermometer to test the internal temperature of meat.

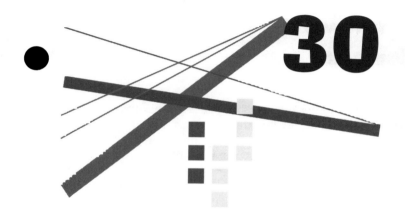

30 Desserts

Objectives

After studying this chapter, students will be able to
- describe the two basic types of cakes and the six basic types of cookies.
- give some tips for preparing a high-quality pastry.

Teaching Materials

Text, pages 319–328
  Words to Know
  Review It
  Apply It
  Think More About It
Student Activity Guide
  A. *Cakes and Cookies*
  B. *Pie Facts*
Teacher's Resource Guide/Binder
  Types of Cakes, transparency master 30-1
  Dessert Recipes, reproducible master 30-2
  My Personal Journal, reproducible master 30-3
  Types of Cookies, color transparency CT-30
  Chapter 30 Quiz

Introductory Activities

1. Ask students why they think some people feel a meal is not complete if it does not end with dessert.
2. Ask students to name their favorite desserts. Write their responses on the chalkboard. Note how many of the desserts listed are cakes, cookies, or pies.

Strategies to Reteach, Reinforce, Enrich, and Extend Text Concepts

■ Cakes

3. **RT** *Types of Cakes,* transparency master 30-1. Use the transparency to introduce students to the basic differences among the three main types of cakes.
4. **RT** Have students examine recipes for different types of cakes and determine whether they are shortened or unshortened cakes.
5. **RF** Have students examine different types of bakeware used to prepare cakes. Students should note possible advantages and disadvantages of each type of bakeware.
6. **ER** Select two students to prepare cakes while the rest of the class observes. One student should make a cake from a mix, and the other should make a comparable cake from scratch. Have the class observe the amount of time and effort involved in making each cake. Supply students with prices for ingredients so they can determine the cost of each cake. When the cakes are finished, have students try a sample from each cake and write down their observations on flavor. Have students discuss which type of cake they would prefer to eat or make and why.
7. **RF** Have students discuss how the preparation method for making shortened cakes differs from the preparation method for making unshortened cakes.
8. **ER** Invite a cake decorator to class to demonstrate how to make frosting and decorate cakes. If possible, allow students to try some decorating.

Cookies

9. **RT** *Types of Cookies,* color transparency CT-30. Use the transparency to introduce students to the six basic types of cookies. Ask students to give other examples of each type.

10. **ER** Have students make a bulletin board depicting how to properly store cookies.

11. **RF** Have students bring in favorite cookie recipes and compile them into a classroom cookie cookbook. Students should group the recipes into the following sections: dropped cookies, bar cookies, molded cookies, rolled cookies, pressed cookies, and refrigerator cookies.

12. **ER** Divide the class into six lab groups. Assign each group a different type of cookie. Have groups choose and prepare a recipe for their assigned type of cookie. Then have each group explain to the class what type of cookie they made and what was involved in making it. Each group should distribute samples of their cookie to the class.

13. **RF** Have students compare cookies in a blind taste test. Choose one type of cookie, such as chocolate chip. Provide samples of the cookie prepared in the following different ways: from scratch, from mix, and from frozen or refrigerated dough. Label the samples with letters and let students determine which sample they prefer and why. Then let students know how each sample was prepared.

14. **RF** *Cakes and Cookies,* Activity A, SAG. Have students fill in the word puzzle using the terms described. Students should also match each cake and cookie listed with the type of cake or cookie described.

Pies

15. **ER** Have students try making pastry and placing it in a pie plate. Then have students evaluate their results.

16. **RT** Have students list types of pies that are usually made with one crust, two crusts, or a non-pastry crust.

17. **RT** *Pie Facts,* Activity B, SAG. Have students read the statements about making pie and determine whether they are true or false.

18. **ER** *Dessert Recipes,* reproducible master 30-2. Have students work in groups to prepare Microwave Caramel Treats and Fudge Crunch Pie. Students should sample the foods they prepare and evaluate the results.

19. **ER** *My Personal Journal,* reproducible master 30-3. Students are to describe their favorite desserts. Then they are to explain nutritional considerations they should keep in mind when including dessert in their diets.

Answer Key

Text

Review It, page 328

1. shortened cakes
2. (Describe two:) If the cake springs back when it has been lightly touched in the center, it is done. If a toothpick inserted in the center of the cake comes out with no batter on it, the cake is done. If the edges of a shortened cake have pulled away from the sides of the pan, the cake is done.
3. to keep the cake from shrinking as it cools
4. true
5. The crisp cookies will become soft.
6. D
7. overmixing or too much handling of the dough
8. by flouring the rolling surface and the rolling pin
9. to allow steam to escape so humps and blisters will not form in the crust during baking
10. (Student response. Examples might include graham cracker crust and chocolate cookie crumb crust.)

Student Activity Guide

Cakes and Cookies, Activity A

1								M	O	L	D	E	D				
2							D	R	O	P	P	E	D				
3							P	R	E	S	S	E	D				
4									S	H	O	R	T	E	N	E	D
5							R	O	L	L	E	D					
6							B	A	R								
7	R	E	F	R	I	G	E	R	A	T	O	R				
8								U	N	S	H	O	R	T	E	N	E	D

Pie Facts, Activity B

1. T	6. T	11. T	16. T
2. T	7. T	12. T	17. F
3. T	8. F	13. F	18. T
4. F	9. T	14. F	19. T
5. F	10. F	15. T	20. T

(Description of favorite kind of pie is student response.)

Teacher's Resource Guide/Binder

Chapter 30 Quiz

1. T	6. T	11. G	16. F
2. F	7. F	12. H	17. D
3. T	8. T	13. B	18. E
4. F	9. T	14. A	
5. T	10. F	15. C	

19. (List three:) dropped cookies, bar cookies, molded cookies, rolled cookies, pressed cookies, refrigerator cookies, no-bake cookies. (Examples are student response.)
20. (Student response.)

Types of Cakes

Shortened

- contain fat

- layer cakes, pound cakes

Unshortened

- contain no fat

- angel food cakes, sponge cakes

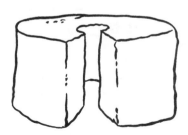

Chiffon

- contain fat

- beaten egg whites make them rise

Dessert Recipes

Microwave Caramel Treats
(Makes about 3 dozen cookies)

36 caramels
 2 tablespoons milk
 1 cup crisp rice cereal
 1 cup coconut
 1 cup chopped walnuts
   powdered sugar

1. Place caramels and milk in medium-sized glass bowl and microwave on high power for 1 minute.

2. Remove mixture from microwave and stir. Continue to microwave on high power until caramels are melted, removing the bowl from the microwave and stirring the mixture every 30 seconds.

3. Add crisp rice cereal, coconut, and chopped walnuts to mixture and mix well.

4. Grease hands and form caramel mixture into 1-inch balls.

5. Roll balls in powdered sugar.

Fudge Crunch Pie
(Makes one 9-inch pie)

1   cup sour cream
1   cup milk
1   package (3¾ ounces) chocolate fudge instant pudding
 ¾ cup chopped walnuts
1   tub (9 ounces) nondairy whipped topping
1   commercially prepared 9-inch graham cracker crust

1. In a large bowl, mix together sour cream, milk, and pudding mix with an electric mixer.

2. Stir chopped walnuts into pudding mixture.

3. Pour mixture into commercially prepared graham cracker crust.

4. Spread nondairy whipped topping evenly over top of pie.

5. Refrigerate pie until serving time.

My Personal Journal

Think about your favorite dessert. What type of dessert is it? How often do you eat this dessert? What nutritional considerations should you keep in mind when including dessert in your diet?

_____
_____
_____
_____
_____
_____
_____
_____
_____
_____
_____
_____
_____
_____
_____
_____
_____
_____
_____
_____
_____
_____
_____
_____
_____

Desserts

Name _____

Date _____ **Period** _____ **Score** _____

CHAPTER 30 QUIZ

☐ True/False: Circle *T* if the statement is true or *F* if the statement is false.

T F 1. Desserts should not be eaten as substitutes for healthy food choices from the Food Guide Pyramid.

T F 2. When baking a cake, cake pans should be filled to the top with batter.

T F 3. A cake is done if it springs back when you lightly touch the cake in the center.

T F 4. A cake should be removed from the pan as soon as it is taken out of the oven.

T F 5. Unshortened cakes should be cooled in their pans upside down.

T F 6. Cakes should be completely cooled before they are frosted.

T F 7. Crisp cookies should be stored in a container with a tight-fitting lid.

T F 8. Soft cookies should not be stored with crisp cookies.

T F 9. Some ingredients in no-bake cookies are cooked on top of the range.

T F 10. Pastry needs to be mixed and worked very much so it will be tender.

☐ Matching: Match the following terms with their definitions.

_____ 11. Cakes that contain fat.

_____ 12. Cakes that contain no fat and rely on air and steam to make them rise.

_____ 13. Cookies made from a soft dough that is dropped from a spoon onto a cookie sheet.

_____ 14. Cookies made from a soft dough that is spread evenly into a pan.

_____ 15. Cookies made from a stiff dough that is shaped with the hands.

_____ 16. Cookies made from a stiff dough that is rolled into a thin layer and cut with cookie cutters or a knife.

_____ 17. Cookies made by pushing a stiff dough through a cookie press.

_____ 18. Cookies made by shaping a stiff dough into a long roll, chilling the dough, and slicing the roll.

A. bar cookies
B. dropped cookies
C. molded cookies
D. pressed cookies
E. refrigerator cookies
F. rolled cookies
G. shortened cakes
H. unshortened cakes

☐ Essay Questions: Provide the answers you feel best show your understanding of the subject matter.

19. List three types of cookies and give an example of each type.

20. Describe the steps involved in making pastry for a pie.

31 Foods of Different Cultures

Objectives

After studying this chapter, students will be able to
- explain how geography, tradition, and religion can influence food customs.
- list foods that are typical of different regions of the United States.
- discuss food customs of Mexico, China, and Italy.

Teaching Materials

Text, pages 329–338
  Words to Know
  Review It
  Apply It
  Think More About It
Student Activity Guide
  A. *Culture and Its Food*
  B. *Foods of Other Countries*
Teacher's Resource Guide/Binder
  My Personal Journal, reproducible master 31-1
  Staples of Other Lands, transparency master 31-2
  Recipes from Other Countries, reproducible master 31-3
  Regions of the United States, color transparency CT-31
  Chapter 31 Quiz

Introductory Activities

1. Name some local ethnic restaurants. Ask students why they think these restaurants are popular.
2. Ask students why they think seafood restaurants are more common in coastal regions than in inland regions. Ask why bread and wine are served during some Christian church services. Ask why many families in the United States eat turkey on Thanksgiving day. Explain that geography, religion, and tradition are all cultural factors that affect food customs.

Strategies to Reteach, Reinforce, Enrich, and Extend Text Concepts

■ Influences on Food Customs

3. **RF** Have students write a short essay on how their food customs would be different if two aspects of their geography were different.
4. **ER** Ask students to choose a country or region of a country. Have them do research to find out what the geography of that country or region is like. Students should also find out what foods are plentiful in that country or region. Have students discuss their findings in class.
5. **ER** Invite a religious leader to discuss the symbolism of certain foods in his or her religion.
6. **RF** Arrange with the editor of your school newspaper for your class to write a "food page" article about traditional food customs for an upcoming holiday. Show students some sample food pages from your local newspaper to help generate ideas. Divide students into four groups. Have one group research the origins of the food customs and write introductory copy for the article. Have another group find traditional recipes to include in the article. This group should write creative descriptions and preparation tips for each recipe. Have a third group create sketches of the food and other artwork to illustrate the article. Have the fourth group research the origins of traditional nonfood customs for celebrating the holiday and write concluding copy for the article.
7. **ER** Have each student research a religion other than his or her own or a holiday that is not celebrated in his or her family. Students should find out as much as they can about food customs related

to their subject. Have students give oral reports on their findings.

8. **ER** *My Personal Journal*, reproducible master 31-1. Students are to write about traditional foods their families eat for holiday meals and explain how those food traditions were started.

9. **RT** *A Culture and Its Food*, Activity A, SAG. Have students choose a country or a region of the United States and use the form provided to report on the geography, cultural aspects, and food customs of the country or region.

■ Food Customs of the United States

10. **RT** *Regions of the United States,* color transparency CT-31. Use the transparency to introduce students to the regions of the United States whose food customs they will be studying.

11. **RF** Bring in some foods that are common in regions of the United States other than your own for students to try. Have students discuss their reactions to these foods.

12. **ER** Have students research food customs of Native American tribes and discuss their findings in class.

13. **RT** Place an outline of the United States on a bulletin board and divide it into the seven regions discussed in the text. As you study the chapter, have students place pictures of foods typical of each region on the board.

14. **ER** As a class, have students choose a region other than their own. Have them research the foods of that region and plan a meal typical of that region. Have students work in groups to prepare foods for the meal. Students may also plan decorations and entertainment typical of that region.

■ Food Customs of Other Countries

15. **RT** *Staples of Other Lands,* transparency master 31-2. Use the transparency to introduce students to basic staple foods of Mexico (tortilla), China (rice), and Italy (pasta). Ask students to give examples of how these staples are used in the cuisine of each country. Ask them what foods would be considered staples in the United States.

16. **RT** *Foods of Other Countries*, Activity B, SAG. Have students match the listed foods to their countries of origin. Then have them complete the given statements by filling in the blanks.

17. **RF** Have students divide into groups of three. Students should visit a supermarket and make a list of foods they do not commonly use at home. Students should try to match as many foods as possible with the countries in which they are typically eaten.

18. **ER** Invite a person from another country to speak on the food customs of that country. Have

the person demonstrate how to make one or two foods from that country. Recipes for those foods should be available to the class.

19. **ER** *Recipes from Other Countries*, reproducible master 31-3. Have students work in groups to prepare Burritos and Chicken Stir-Fry. Students should sample the foods they prepare and evaluate the results.

Answer Key

■ Text

Review It, page 338
1. because people in most cultures make dishes from foods that can be easily found in their region
2. (Student response.)
3. true
4. (List eight:) English, Spanish, French, Native Americans, Africans, Germans, Irish, Italians, Slavs, European Jews, Asians
5. B
6. potluck
7. Aztec and Spanish
8. (Describe two:) Tortillas can be rolled around foods and served as enchiladas. Tortillas can be folded in half, filled, and served as tacos. Tortillas can be fried and topped and served as tostadas.
9. stir-frying, steaming, and deep-frying
10. (List three:) Parmesan, Romano, mozzarella, ricotta

■ Student Activity Guide

Foods of Other Countries, Activity B

1. M	11. M	21. American
2. I	12. C	22. Mexico
3. C	13. M	23. Aztec
4. M	14. I	24. Spanish
5. I	15. M	25. China
6. I	16. M	26. chopsticks
7. M	17. C	27. stir-fried
8. C	18. I	28. Italy
9. M	19. M	29. Greeks
10. I	20. I	30. seasonings

■ Teacher's Resource Guide/Binder

Chapter 31 Quiz

1. F	7. T	13. H
2. T	8. F	14. A
3. T	9. F	15. D
4. T	10. T	16. G
5. F	11. E	17. B
6. F	12. C	18. F
19. (Student response.)		
20. (Student response.)		

My Personal Journal

Think about some of the traditional foods your family eats for holiday meals. What are these foods? How long has your family been eating these traditional foods? How were these food traditions started?

_____

_____

_____

_____

_____

_____

_____

_____

_____

_____

_____

_____

_____

_____

_____

_____

_____

_____

_____

_____

_____

_____

_____

Staples of Other Lands

Mexico – tortillas

China – rice

Italy – pasta

Recipes from Other Countries

Burritos
(Serves 8)

8 flour tortillas
1 can (15 ounces) refried beans
½ cup sliced black olives

4 ounces Monterey Jack cheese, shredded
1 cup salsa

1. Preheat a skillet over high heat, and preheat oven to 325°F.
2. Heat tortillas in the skillet for 30 seconds on each side, dampening each tortilla slightly with water before heating.
3. Place beans, olives, and cheese on the tortilla and fold as shown:

4. Place tortillas in a baking pan and heat in oven until cheese is melted, 15 to 20 minutes.
5. Top with salsa before serving.

Chicken Stir-Fry
(Serves 4)

½ teaspoon garlic powder
½ teaspoon onion powder
¼ teaspoon ground ginger
1 tablespoon brown sugar
2 tablespoons soy sauce
1 tablespoon cornstarch
⅔ cup cold water
1 pound boneless, skinless chicken breasts, slightly frozen

2 tablespoons sesame oil or vegetable oil
1 green pepper, cut into thin strips
1 red pepper, cut into thin strips
1 cup fresh snow peas
1 can (8 ounces) whole water chestnuts, drained and sliced
4 cups hot, cooked rice

1. Combine garlic powder, onion powder, ginger, brown sugar, soy sauce, cornstarch, and water in a small bowl and set aside.
2. Thinly slice chicken breasts.
3. Preheat oil in a wok or large skillet over medium heat.
4. Add green pepper, red pepper, and snow peas to wok or skillet. Cook until vegetables are crisp-tender, 3 minutes, stirring constantly.
5. Push vegetables to the side of the wok or skillet. Add chicken and cook until chicken is lightly browned, 3 minutes, stirring constantly.
6. Add water chestnuts and stir vegetables and chicken together.
7. Stir in seasoning mixture from step 1. Bring to a boil and cook until mixture thickens slightly, 1 to 2 minutes, stirring constantly.
8. Serve over hot rice.

Foods of Different Cultures

Name _____

Date _____ Period _____ Score _____

CHAPTER 31 QUIZ

☐ True/False: Circle *T* if the statement is true or *F* if the statement is false.

T F 1. Food customs of a desert country would probably include many fish dishes.

T F 2. Some religions restrict the eating of certain foods.

T F 3. In some cultures, food is considered an art form.

T F 4. Foods native to North America include cranberries and peanuts.

T F 5. Okra was brought to the United States by French colonists.

T F 6. Immigrants to the United States tended to settle with people from cultures other than their own.

T F 7. Soul food is based on the food customs of African slaves, Native Americans, and less wealthy Europeans.

T F 8. Creole foods have roots in the English and Chinese cultures.

T F 9. At potluck dinners, one family makes a dinner to share with several families.

T F 10. Stir-frying is cooking small pieces of food over high heat with very little oil.

☐ Matching: Match the following foods with their appropriate countries or regions of the United States.

_____ 11. Huckleberry pie, cranberry catsup, and salmon.

_____ 12. Barbecued beef, thick stews, and tamales.

_____ 13. Fried rice, sweet and sour pork, and wontons.

_____ 14. Baked beans, pumpkin pie, and clam chowder.

_____ 15. Beef, pork, chicken, mashed potatoes, and vegetables.

_____ 16. Enchiladas, refried beans, and flan.

_____ 17. Fried chicken, smoked ham, and pecan pie.

_____ 18. Teriyaki, coconut bread, and poi.

A. Northeast and Middle Atlantic states
B. South
C. West and Southwest
D. Midwest
E. Alaska
F. Hawaii
G. Mexico
H. China

☐ Essay Questions: Provide the answers you feel best show your understanding of the subject matter.

19. Give three examples of how religion influences the foods of cultures.

20. What factors in Italy's culture affected Italy's cuisine?

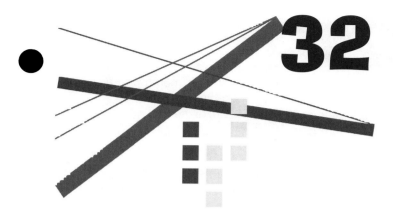

32 At the Table

Objectives

After studying this chapter, students will be able to
- set a table correctly and identify different types of meal service.
- demonstrate proper mealtime etiquette to be used both at home and in restaurants.
- describe the different types of restaurants.

Teaching Materials

Text, pages 339–349
  Words to Know
  Review It
  Apply It
  Think More About It
Student Activity Guide
  A. *Eating Etiquette*
  B. *Tipping*
Teacher's Resource Guide/Binder
  Setting the Table, transparency master 32-1
  My Personal Journal, reproducible master 32-2
  Planning a Party, reproducible master 32-3
  Chapter 32 Quiz

Introductory Activities

1. Ask students what functions meals serve other than to provide people with nourishment. Write their responses on the chalkboard. Note how many of the functions listed are social. With this in mind, ask students why what they do at a meal can be as important as what they eat.
2. Ask each student to think of a special occasion he or she celebrated over a meal, either in someone's home or in a restaurant. Ask students to think about how the atmosphere—the way the table was set and the way the food was served—contributed to the celebratory mood.

Strategies to Reteach, Reinforce, Enrich, and Extend Text Concepts

■ Eating at Home

3. **RT** *Setting the Table*, transparency master 32-1. Use the transparency to show students step-by-step how to place items on the cover.
4. **ER** Have students try setting a creative table at home using items around the house. Students should have family members evaluate the table setting. Then they should write a report on the activity and include photos or sketches of the finished table.
5. **RF** Have students practice different types of meal service using empty tableware and serving dishes.
6. **ER** *My Personal Journal*, reproducible master 32-2. Students are to describe a time when they felt uncomfortable eating with others. Then they are to explain how using mealtime etiquette would have made the situation more comfortable.
7. **RF** Have students write an article about what table manners reflect about a person.
8. **ER** *Planning a Party*, reproducible master 32-3. Students are to write a plan for a dinner party, including the type of party, theme, number of guests, menu, and service style.

■ Eating Out

9. **ER** Invite a restaurant owner or manager to talk to your class about restaurant management and the responsibilities of the employees.
10. **EX** Have students collect menus from several restaurants in the community. (Students should be sure to get permission before taking menus.)

Students should group the menus according to type of restaurant. Then have students compare the types of food choices and prices for the different restaurants.

11. **ER** Have students write a one-page report on what they think restaurants will be like 50 years from now.

12. **ER** Using collected menus, have students write down nutritious meal choices at various types of restaurants. Students should discuss the choices they made with the class.

13. **RF** *Eating Etiquette*, Activity A, SAG. Have students read about the given situations and describe how they should be handled.

14. **EX** Have students role-play a restaurant setting portraying acceptable and unacceptable restaurant manners. Have the class discuss the role-play situations.

15. **RF** *Tipping*, Activity B, SAG. Have students answer the given questions about tipping. Then have them figure the appropriate tips for the given checks.

Answer Key

■ Text

Review It, page 349

1. cover
2. just above the tips of the knives
3. A
4. place it on the edge of the saucer
5. Invitations should include date, time, place, and other information guests should know. R.S.V.P. and a telephone number should also be included if you want guests to let you know if they are coming.
6. (Student response.)
7. Look for vegetables, fruits, soups, and nonfried items on the menu.
8. false
9. Quietly call the problem to your server's attention.
10. 15 to 20 percent of the total bill

■ Student Activity Guide

Eating Etiquette, Activity A

1. serving utensils
2. Ask to have it passed to you.

3. They should be eaten with the fingers.
4. with a fork and a knife
5. with your fingers
6. Watch the host or hostess.
7. Use a napkin to cover your mouth and turn your head away from the table.
8. Place them on a plate or saucer without letting them touch the table.
9. Excuse yourself.
10. 6:00 P.M.
11. Excuse yourself and go to the restroom.
12. Call him or her in a clear but soft voice as he or she goes by your table, or use eye contact and/or a little hand wave.
13. Let your server know so he or she can clean it up. Apologize briefly and thank the server for cleaning up the mess.
14. Let your server know. Explain the problem quietly without accusations or threats.

Tipping, Activity B

1. A tip is something given for the service you receive.
2. 15 to 20 percent
3. before tax
4. when the service was very good
5. when the service was poor
   A. 15% tip is $3.30
      20% tip is $4.40
   B. (The amount is rounded off to $12.00 before figuring the tip.)
      15% tip is $1.80
      20% tip is $2.40

■ Teacher's Resource Guide/Binder

Chapter 32 Quiz

1.	F	8.	T
2.	F	9.	F
3.	T	10.	C
4.	T	11.	A
5.	F	12.	C
6.	F	13.	B
7.	T		

14. (Student response. For diagram, see *Setting the Table,* transparency master 32-1.)
15. (Student response.)

Setting the Table

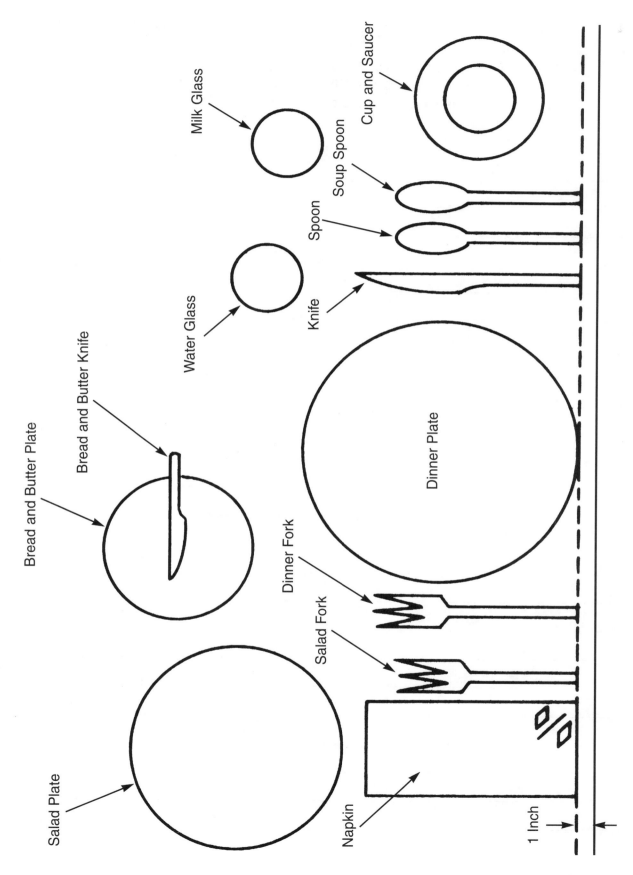

My Personal Journal

Think of a time when you felt uncomfortable eating with others. Where did the meal take place? Who was there? Why did you feel uncomfortable? How could using meal-time etiquette have made the situation more comfortable?

_____

_____

_____

_____

_____

_____

_____

_____

_____

_____

_____

_____

_____

_____

_____

_____

_____

_____

_____

_____

_____

_____

Planning a Party

Name _____ **Date** _____ **Period** _____

Complete the following activity to help you plan a dinner party.

1. What occasion will this party be celebrating? _____

2. What will be the theme of the party? _____

3. When will you hold the party? Give the date and time. _____

4. Where will you hold the party? _____

5. Whom will you invite to the party? _____

   _____

   _____

   _____

6. Write a menu that reflects your theme. Remember to keep the menu simple. Choose recipes that you have made before and can prepare ahead of time.

   _____

   _____

   _____

   _____

   _____

   _____

7. What style of meal service will you use? Explain your choice. _____

   _____

8. What type of dinnerware will you use? _____

9. What type of flatware will you use? _____

10. What type of beverageware will you use? _____

11. What type of table linens will you use? _____

12. What type of centerpiece will you use? _____

13. What other decorations will you use? _____

14. Other than eating dinner, what activities will your party include? _____

   _____

At the Table

Name _____

Date _____ Period _____ Score _____

CHAPTER 32 QUIZ

☐ True/False: Circle *T* if the statement is true or *F* if the statement is false.

T   F   1. Centerpieces must contain flowers.

T   F   2. Family service is a very formal type of meal service.

T   F   3. Plate service saves the trouble of getting serving dishes and utensils ready for a meal.

T   F   4. Keeping foods at the proper temperature is a major concern with buffet service meals.

T   F   5. When you invite dinner guests, trying a recipe that you've never prepared before is a good idea.

T   F   6. If you want guests to let you know in advance whether they are coming to your party, you should write "V.S.R.T." on the invitation.

T   F   7. Barbecues are more fun if you keep the menu simple.

T   F   8. Fast-food restaurant menus often include mainly fried or grilled menu items.

T   F   9. Chicken au gratin would be a good menu choice for a person who doesn't like cheese.

☐ Multiple Choice: Choose the best answer and write the corresponding letter in the blank.

_____ 10. If you want some more potatoes and they are across the table from you, you should _____.
A. reach across the table to get them
B. get up and walk to the other side of the table to get them
C. ask someone to pass them to you
D. pass your plate to someone and ask the person to serve you some more potatoes

_____ 11. As a dinner guest, when you are finished eating, you should _____.
A. place your knife and fork across the center of your plate
B. fold your napkin and put it on the table
C. leave the table right away
D. take your dirty dishes to the kitchen right away

_____ 12. If you are eating at a full-service restaurant and you want more water, you should _____.
A. get up and get some more
B. shout at your server to bring more water
C. call your server in a clear but soft voice as he or she goes by your table
D. get up and find the server and ask him or her to bring you more water

_____ 13. If you order a well-done hamburger and your server brings you a rare one, you should _____.
A. eat it without saying anything so you don't embarrass your dinner companions
B. call your server and calmly let him or her know your hamburger is not done as you ordered it
C. call the manager and say you will never eat in the restaurant again unless your burger is replaced
D. walk out without eating or paying for the meal

☐ Essay Questions: Provide the answers you feel best show your understanding of the subject matter.

14. Explain or draw a diagram with labels of how to set a table.

15. Why do menu prices vary among different types of restaurants?

Part Six

The Clothes You Wear

Part goal: Students will learn about clothing design, selection, construction, and care.

Bulletin Board

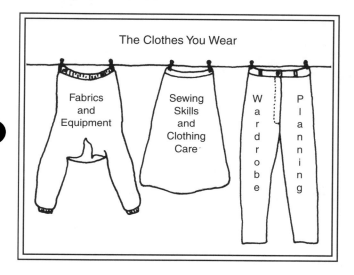

The Clothes You Wear

Fabrics and Equipment

Sewing Skills and Clothing Care

Wardrobe Planning

Title: "The Clothes You Wear"

Attach a clothesline across the bulletin board. Cut out shapes of clothing from construction paper. Label the clothing shapes as shown. Hang the clothing shapes on the clothesline with clothespins.

Teaching Materials

Text
Chapters 33–39, pages 350–442
Student Activity Guide
Chapters 33–39
Teacher's Resource Guide/Binder
You and Your Clothes, reproducible master

Introductory Activities

1. *You and Your Clothes*, reproducible master. Have students answer the questions provided to help them think about various aspects of clothing. This activity can also give you ideas about projects in which students might be interested in making.
2. Ask students to complete the following statement: "When I want to make a good impression, I wear . . ."
3. Invite a panel of "experts" in the clothing field to class. Panelists may include a clothing store manager, dry cleaner, textile worker, tailor, fashion writer, etc. Have each panelist give an overview of his or her work. Then have students ask any questions they may have.
4. Have students debate the issue of buying clothes versus making clothes.

You and Your Clothes

Name _____ **Date** _____ **Period** _____

Complete the following statements.

1. My favorite colors to wear are _____

   because _____

2. The styles I enjoy wearing the most are _____

   _____

3. These are the clothes I would wear for:

   A school day— _____

   _____

   A day at the beach— _____

   _____

   A job interview— _____

   _____

   A religious service— _____

   _____

   A hike in the woods— _____

   _____

4. If I had $500 to spend on clothes, I would _____

   _____

   _____

5. The greatest advantage of learning how to sew would be _____

   _____

6. If I could choose anything I wanted to make for my first sewing project, I would choose _____

   _____

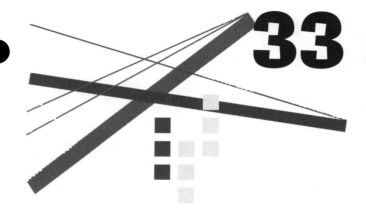

33 Clothing Design

Objectives

After studying this chapter, students will be able to
■ list and describe the elements and principles of design.
■ apply the elements and principles of design as you select clothes and accessories.

Teaching Materials

Text, pages 351–362
  Words to Know
  Review It
  Apply It
  Think More About It
Student Activity Guide
  A. *The Elements of Design and You*
  B. *Color*
  C. *The Principles of Design and You*
  D. *Design Crossword*
Teacher's Resource Guide/Binder
  A World Without Color, transparency master 33-1
  My Personal Journal, reproducible master 33-2
  Visual Effects of Design, reproducible master 33-3
  Color Wheel, color transparencies CT-33A, CT-33B, CT-33C
  Chapter 33 Quiz

Introductory Activities

1. Have each student bring in a picture from a magazine or catalog showing someone wearing an outfit the student finds attractive. Ask students to explain why they find the outfits in their pictures appealing. Note the responses that relate to the elements and principles of design. Explain that students will be learning more about these elements and principles and how to use them to enhance their appearance when choosing clothing.

2. Ask students the following questions relating their responses to chapter information: What do clothing designers do? What do you think clothing designers consider when designing new clothes?

Strategies to Reteach, Reinforce, Enrich, and Extend Text Concepts

■ The Elements of Design

3. **RF** *A World Without Color,* transparency master 33-1. Use the transparency to generate discussion about what the world would be like without color. Ask students why they think color is one of the main factors people consider when choosing clothes.
4. **RT** *Color Wheel,* color transparencies CT-33A, CT-33B, CT-33C. Use these transparencies to illustrate the primary, secondary, and intermediate colors on the color wheel.
5. **RT** *Color,* Activity B, SAG. Students are asked to complete statements related to color, fill in a color wheel, create color schemes, distinguish between warm and cool colors, and identify neutrals.
6. **RF** Have students each select one hue from the color wheel. Ask them to find as many values and intensities of the hue as possible. Display these in class.
7. **ER** Ask students to make a list of all the colors in their wardrobes. Have them decide which colors they wear most often. Which do they wear least often? Have them explain why.
8. **RF** Have students bring pictures to class showing different kinds of lines in garments and outfits.

Ask them to describe the effects created by the lines in the outfits.

9. **ER** Ask students to design a display illustrating lines, textures, forms, and colors in outfits.

10. **EX** *The Elements of Design and You,* Activity A, SAG. Students are asked to analyze their features and identify those they would like to play up and those they would like to conceal. Then after each element of design listed in the activity, they are to describe how they could use each element to play up their good features and conceal the ones that are not as good.

11. **ER** *My Personal Journal,* reproducible master 33-2. Each student is to describe one of his or her favorite outfits. The student is to explain why he or she likes wearing the outfit. Then the student is to describe how the colors, lines, textures, and forms of the outfit enhance his or her appearance.

■ The Principles of Design

12. **RT** Have students draw or collect pictures of clothing showing formal and informal balance. Have them distinguish between formal and informal balance.

13. **RT** Using a catalog, have students select pictures of outfits and accessories that would be in proportion to their body types.

14. **RF** Have students illustrate the principle of emphasis in clothing by using pictures or by identifying an item of emphasis on outfits they are wearing.

15. **RF** *The Principles of Design and You,* Activity C, SAG. Students are asked to mount pictures from a magazine or catalog or to sketch outfits that represent each of the principles of design. They are to choose outfits they think would look good on them and briefly describe how the principle was used in each outfit. They are then asked how harmony is achieved in a design.

■ The Overall Design

16. **RF** Have a student try a black shoe on one foot and a white shoe of the same style on the other foot. Ask the class to decide which looks larger and explain why. (Gloves may be used in place of shoes.)

17. **ER** Have students design a bulletin board entitled "What Your Clothing Can Do for You." Have students caption each illustration with their reasons for the selection.

18. **EX** *Visual Effects of Design,* reproducible master 33-3. Students are to cut pictures from magazines or catalogs to illustrate specified visual effects. Then they are to answer questions based on the pictures they choose.

19. **RF** *Design Crossword,* Activity D, SAG. Students are asked to complete a crossword puzzle using terms related to design. This can be used as a review of concepts presented in the chapter.

Answer Key

■ Text

Review It, page 362
1. You will be able to play up your good features and hide ones that aren't as good.
2. color, line, texture, form
3. When white is added to a color, the color is a tint. When black is added to a color, the color is a shade.
4. C
5. skin tone, eye color, hair color, body shape, personality
6. B
7. true
8. balance, proportion, rhythm, emphasis
9. through repetition, gradation, and radiation
10. harmony

■ Student Activity Guide

Color, Activity B
1. primary
2. secondary
3. intermediate

The Principles of Design and You, Activity C
(Descriptions are student response.)
Harmony is achieved in a design when the principles of design are used correctly.

Design Crossword, Activity D

Crossword solution — across and down answers:
- FORM
- RHYTHM
- PROPORTION
- EMPHASIS
- HARMONY
- BALANCE
- COLOR
- PRINCIPLES
- ELEMENTS
- LINE
- DESIGN
- TEXTURE

■ Teacher's Resource Guide/Binder

Chapter 33 Quiz

1. T	6. F	11. E	16. C
2. F	7. T	12. G	17. D
3. F	8. F	13. B	18. F
4. T	9. F	14. H	
5. T	10. T	15. A	

19. (Student response.)
20. (Student response.)

A World Without Color

My Personal Journal

Think of one of your favorite outfits. What does this outfit look like? Why do you like to wear this outfit? How do the colors, lines, textures, and form of this outfit enhance your appearance?

_____

_____

_____

_____

_____

_____

_____

_____

_____

_____

_____

_____

_____

_____

_____

_____

_____

_____

_____

_____

_____

_____

_____

Visual Effects of Design

Name _____ **Date** _____ **Period** _____

Cut pictures from a magazine or catalog to illustrate the specified visual effects. Answer the questions based on the pictures you choose.

1. Attach a picture that uses one or more of the following clothing designs to make the model look taller and thinner:
   - vertically striped fabrics with narrow stripes
   - fabrics with dull textures
   - one-color outfit
   - slacks or pants with slim rather than full legs
   - matching pants and sweater
   - narrow belt in the same color as the outfit or no belt at all
   - less intense or cool colors
   - garments that are not too tight

   a. Which of the above designs does this picture illustrate? _____
   _____

   b. How do these designs make the model look taller and thinner?_____
   _____

   c. Is this a visual effect you would try to create when choosing an outfit for yourself? Explain why or why not. _____
   _____

2. Attach a picture that uses one or more of the following clothing designs to make the model look shorter and heavier:
   - Shirt or blouse that contrasts with slacks or skirt
   - Horizontal design or plaid
   - Wide belt and/or large pockets
   - Medium to large prints
   - Bulky, nubby textures
   - White, light, bright, and/or warm colors
   - Padded shoulders
   - Shiny fabrics

   a. Which of the above designs does this picture illustrate? _____
   _____

   b. How do these designs make the model look shorter and heavier? _____
   _____

   c. Is this a visual effect you would try to create when choosing an outfit for yourself? Explain why or why not. _____
   _____

Clothing Design

Name _____

Date _____ **Period** _____ **Score** _____

CHAPTER 33 QUIZ

☐ True/False: Circle *T* if the statement is true or *F* if the statement is false.

T F 1. By clever use of design, you can play up your good features and hide features that aren't as good.

T F 2. Color, line, texture, and form are the principles of design.

T F 3. If you were wearing blue jeans and an orange sweater, you would be wearing an analogous color scheme.

T F 4. You can look thinner in a blue outfit than in a red one.

T F 5. White, gray, and black are called *neutrals*.

T F 6. Horizontal lines have a slimming effect and can make you look tall and slender.

T F 7. The principles of design are guides that tell you how the elements of design are combined.

T F 8. A large plaid would look in proportion on a small person.

T F 9. If you want to draw attention away from your waistline, wear a colorful belt.

T F 10. Harmony is achieved when all parts of a design look as if they belong together.

☐ Matching: Match the following terms with their definitions.

_____ 11. Gives direction to a design.

_____ 12. How something feels when you touch it and how it looks on the surface.

_____ 13. Hues that can reflect your moods, looks, and feelings.

_____ 14. The shape of an object.

_____ 15. Equal weight on both sides of an imaginary center line.

_____ 16. Refers to how the size of one part relates to the size of another part and how the size of one part relates to the size of the whole item.

_____ 17. A feeling of movement.

_____ 18. The center of interest in a design.

A. balance
B. color
C. proportion
D. rhythm
E. line
F. emphasis
G. texture
H. form

☐ Essay Questions: Provide the answers you feel best show your understanding of the subject matter.

19. Explain how knowing about design can help you select garments and outfits that will enhance your appearance.

20. Describe a feature you would like to play up. Then describe a feature you would like to conceal. Explain how you can do this through the use of elements and principles of design.

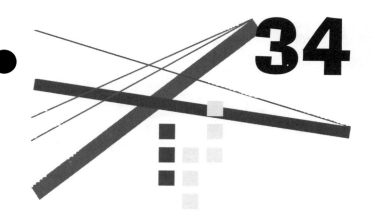

34 Building a Wardrobe

Objectives

After studying this chapter, students will be able to
- identify styles, fashions, classics, and fads.
- choose appropriate clothing for various activities and climates.
- make a wardrobe inventory.
- discuss the types of information they can use to make wise clothing purchases.

Teaching Materials

Text, pages 363–375
  Words to Know
  Review It
  Apply It
  Think More About It
Student Activity Guide
  A. *A Wardrobe Inventory*
  B. *Expanding Your Present Wardrobe*
Teacher's Resource Guide/Binder
  Clothes to Match Your Activities, reproducible master 34-1
  Clothing Quality Guidelines, reproducible master 34-2
  My Personal Journal, reproducible master 34-3
  Chapter 34 Quiz

Introductory Activities

1. Define the term *wardrobe* for students. Then go around the room asking each student to complete one of the following statements: "I am happy with my wardrobe because . . ." "I am unhappy with my wardrobe because . . ." Explain that by studying this chapter, students will learn how to select a wardrobe that meets their needs.
2. Bring in the most recent annual list of Blackwell's best- and worst-dressed celebrities, which can be found in *People* magazine. Ask students if they agree or disagree with Blackwell's assessments. Ask them what they think makes a well-dressed person.

Strategies to Reteach, Reinforce, Enrich, and Extend Text Concepts

■ Fashion Sense

3. **ER** Have students identify styles, fashions, classics, and fads that are currently popular. Have them create a bulletin board display labeling each illustration as a style, fashion, classic, or fad.
4. **RF** Ask students to list as many past fads as they can. Ask them why they think the fads didn't last. Then have them list and discuss current fads.

■ Clothes to Match Your Activities

5. **RF** *Clothes to Match Your Activities,* reproducible master 34-1. Students are to list 10 of their activities. Next to each activity, have them describe the types of clothes that would be appropriate to wear.
6. **RF** Ask students to discuss standards of dress that are expected at a variety of places such as at school, place of worship, wedding, fancy restaurant, etc.
7. **ER** Have students pretend they have a set amount of money to spend on their wardrobes. Using catalogs, ask them to plan a wardrobe for themselves within this budget. Have students keep in mind their activities as they select clothes for their wardrobes.

■ Your Wardrobe Inventory

8. **RT** *A Wardrobe Inventory*, Activity A, SAG. Students are asked to complete a wardrobe inventory.

9. **ER**   Have students interview two people they feel are well dressed. Have them ask these people how they plan their wardrobes.

■ Expanding Your Present Wardrobe

10. **RF**   *Expanding Your Present Wardrobe*, Activity B, SAG. Students are asked to list clothes and accessories they feel they need to add to their wardrobes and estimate the costs. (A catalog may be used to help in estimating prices.) Students are then asked to answer questions about their lists.

11. **RF**   Have students cut out pictures of six garments from magazines and catalogs and mount them on paper. Have students list all the possible outfits they could make by mixing and matching.

12. **RF**   Have students each select a basic garment. Then have them demonstrate the different looks they can achieve by using different accessories with this outfit.

13. **ER**   Ask someone who knows how to sew to discuss the advantages of knowing how to sew in relation to expanding his or her wardrobe. Ask him or her to model items he or she has made.

■ Shopping for Clothes

14. **RF**   Have students list local stores where they shop for clothes. Have them describe each store and the advantages and disadvantages of each.

15. **EX**   Have students select a garment and comparison shop for it at three different stores. Ask them to set up guidelines they want to consider as they shop. In a report, have students share their experiences with the class.

16. **ER**   Ask a manager or salesclerk from a department store to talk to the class about advertising, sales, returned merchandise, etc. Have students prepare a list of questions in advance.

17. **ER**   Have students write an advertisement about their favorite place to shop for clothes. Ask them to explain why they chose this particular place to shop.

18. **EX**   Divide the class into groups. Have them produce a TV commercial to sell a garment or accessory. (These may be videotaped.) Then have the students present their commercials to the class. Class members can evaluate the commercials in terms of effectiveness.

19. **ER**   Have students create a bulletin board display of different advertisements for clothing sales. Discuss terms often used to urge consumers to buy.

20. **RT**   Have students search for care labels in several garments. Ask them to note the location of care labels in garments such as coats, shirts or blouses, dresses, pants, undergarments, etc.

21. **RF**   Have students design a hangtag and label for a garment they might buy, such as blue jeans.

Check to see that information required by law is included on the labels.

22. **RT**   Ask students to collect hangtags and labels for a bulletin board display.

23. **RT**   Have students distinguish between labels and hangtags.

24. **RT**   *Clothing Quality Guidelines*, reproducible master 34-2. Use this master as a basis for discussion about judging quality in clothes. Encourage students to take this list of guidelines with them the next time they go shopping for clothes.

25. **RF**   Have students bring to class garments they think are well made and garments they feel are not well made. Explain the points to consider when looking for quality clothing.

26. **ER**   Have students arrange a display of garments. Have them analyze the garments and rate them in terms of quality from best to worst. Have them provide explanations with each rating.

27. **ER**   *My Personal Journal,* reproducible master 34-3. Students are to describe garment purchases with which they were unhappy. Then they are to explain how they could avoid making unsatisfactory garment purchases in the future.

Answer Key

■ Text

Review It, page 375
1. fashion
2. Air is trapped between the layers and becomes warm from the heat of the body.
3. a list of clothes and accessories; a description of the color and fabric of each item; an indication of whether each item should be kept, repaired, or discarded
4. Only a few garments are needed to create many outfits. Therefore, you seem to have more clothes than you really do.
5. (List five:) belts, jewelry, scarves, hats, neckties, handbags, shoes
6. (List three:) getting the color and style you want, getting better fit, saving money, expressing creativity and personality, helping you make wise decisions when selecting ready-made clothes
7. B
8. true
9. fiber content, name of manufacturer, country of origin, and care instructions
10. (List two:) have feet measured, wear the same type of socks or hose you plan to wear with the shoes, try on both shoes and walk in them

■ Teacher's Resource Guide/Binder

Chapter 34 Quiz

1. T	7. T	13. F
2. F	8. T	14. T
3. T	9. T	15. D
4. T	10. T	16. C
5. F	11. T	17. A
6. F	12. F	18. B

19. (List four:) Mixing and matching. Using accessories. Sewing your own clothes. Buying clothes. (Other appropriate responses can be considered.)
20. (Student response.)

Clothes to Match Your Activities

Name _____ **Date** _____ **Period** _____

In the chart below, list 10 of your activities. Next to each activity, describe the types of clothes that would be appropriate to wear.

Activity	Clothing Needs

Clothing Quality Guidelines

Name _____**Date** _____**Period** _____

Keeping the following guidelines in mind will help you find quality garments when shopping for clothes.

Shirts and Blouses

When shopping for a shirt or blouse, check to see that
- there is ample room across the chest or bust, back, and shoulders
- shoulder seams come to the end of the shoulder bone
- they are long enough to stay tucked in jeans, skirts, or slacks
- armholes are large enough for arms to move freely
- collars have even, sharp points
- topstitching is smooth
- buttons are sewn on securely and placed directly under buttonholes
- the buttonholes are well-made
- cuffs are neat, even, and fit comfortably around wrists
- pockets are securely sewn on flat without wrinkles

Jeans and Slacks

Before you buy jeans or slacks, be sure
- you can walk and sit comfortably in them
- the seat area fits smoothly without bagging or binding
- the crotch length is just right—not too long or too short
- the waistband has a double thickness of fabric
- there is reinforced stitching at bottom of zipper and corners of pockets
- the zipper has a locking pull tab so it will not unzip by itself
- seams are straight and not puckered
- you can follow the instructions given on the care label
- they fall straight without wrinkling

Dresses and Skirts

Before choosing a dress or skirt, see if
- it is cut with enough fabric so it does not look skimpy
- the garment feels good on your body
- it hangs straight from the waistband without cupping under the hips
- the waistline fits snugly at your natural waistline
- the waistline does not roll up. (It rolls if it is too tight in the hip area.)
- the bustline darts (if present) point toward the highest point of the bust
- zippers work smoothly and have a lock tab
- the seams are wide enough to alter, if needed

Jackets and Suits

When choosing a jacket or suit, make sure
- it fits across the back shoulders smoothly, with no wrinkles or bunching
- the armholes are large enough for an undershirt, shirt, and sweater to be worn underneath
- the outside stitching is smooth
- the jacket fits smoothly across the chest area when buttoned
- the pocket corners are reinforced
- you see about one-half inch of shirt cuffs below jacket sleeves
- the collar fits closely around the neck without gaps
- any pattern in the fabric matches at center, side seams, and pockets
- the buttons are sewn on securely with a shank beneath so they button easily and smoothly
- linings and interfacings are used as needed to give strength, support, and better shape to the garment

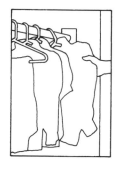

My Personal Journal

Think of a time when you bought a garment with which you were unhappy. What did this garment look like? Where did you buy it and how much did it cost? Why were you unhappy with it? How could you avoid making this type of unsatisfactory purchase in the future?

_____

_____

_____

_____

_____

_____

_____

_____

_____

_____

_____

_____

_____

_____

_____

_____

_____

_____

_____

_____

_____

_____

_____

_____

_____

_____

_____

_____

Building a Wardrobe

Name _____

Date _____ **Period** _____ **Score** _____

CHAPTER 34 QUIZ

☐ True/False: Circle *T* if the statement is true or *F* if the statement is false.

T F   1. Fashion sense is knowing how to achieve a well-dressed look.

T F   2. A wardrobe inventory should be completed after you shop for clothes.

T F   3. A wardrobe can seem larger than it really is by mixing and matching.

T F   4. Accessories can add variety to a wardrobe.

T F   5. Discount stores offer more customer services than department stores and specialty shops.

T F   6. When ordering from mail-order catalogs, be sure to send cash.

T F   7. In many cases, sale items cannot be returned.

T F   8. By law, garment labels must state the fiber content, name of the manufacturer, country of origin, and care instructions.

T F   9. Comparison shopping means comparing garments and prices in different stores before buying.

T F   10. For a good fit, it's a good idea to try clothes on with the other garments and accessories you plan to wear with them.

T F   11. Quality affects the fit, appearance, and wearability of a garment.

T F   12. Major alterations, such as changing a neckline or adjusting a garment for shoulder width, are worthwhile and will make the garment look great.

T F   13. Accessories are often more expensive than garments.

T F   14. The most important feature of shoes is good fit.

☐ Matching: Match the following terms with their definitions.

_____ 15. The design of a garment. It has features that make it unlike any others. Examples: jeans and slacks.

_____ 16. A style that is popular at a certain time. Examples: raised or lowered hemlines.

_____ 17. A style that stays in fashion for a long time. Examples: a tailored shirt or blazer.

_____ 18. A new style in clothing that is popular for only a short time. Examples: miniskirts and platform shoes.
　　　　　A. classic
　　　　　B. fad
　　　　　C. fashion
　　　　　D. style

☐ Essay Questions: Provide the answers you feel best show your understanding of the subject matter.

19. List four ways you can expand your present wardrobe.

20. Name two local stores where you can buy clothes. List advantages and disadvantages of shopping in each store.

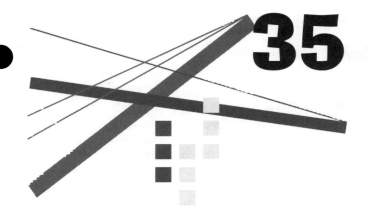

35 Fibers, Yarns, and Fabrics

Objectives

After studying this chapter, students will be able to
- classify fibers as natural or manufactured.
- explain how fibers are formed into yarns and then constructed into fabrics.
- discuss the functions of various finishes.
- describe various dyeing and printing techniques.

Teaching Materials

Text, pages 376–389
   Words to Know
   Review It
   Apply It
   Think More About It
Student Activity Guide
   A. *Fiber Facts*
   B. *From Fiber to Yarn to Fabric*
   C. *Fabric Construction*
   D. *Finishing, Dyeing, and Printing Match*
Teacher's Resource Guide/Binder
   Comparing Fibers, reproducible master 35-1
   My Personal Journal, reproducible master 35-2
   Direct Roller Printing, transparency master 35-3
   Fabric Construction, color transparencies CT-35A, CT-35B
   Chapter 35 Quiz

Introductory Activities

1. Show students pictures of a variety of items, other than apparel, made from textiles. Such items include upholstery, carpeting, umbrellas, conveyor belts, artificial turf, and surgical implant materials. Ask students to identify what these items have in common.

2. Pass samples of fibers around the room. Ask students what they think the hairlike material they are passing around has to do with the clothes they wear.

Strategies to Reteach, Reinforce, Enrich, and Extend Text Concepts

■ Natural and Manufactured Fibers

3. **RT**   *Fiber Facts*, Activity A, SAG. Students are asked to complete a chart about natural fibers and manufactured fibers.
4. **RF**   Have students check the care labels in six of their garments. Have them make a list of all the fibers used to produce each garment. Ask them how the fiber content relates to the use or performance of the garment.
5. **EX**   *Comparing Fibers,* reproducible master 35-1. Students are to read case studies about teens who are trying to decide between two garments, each made of a different fiber. Students are to give recommendations and supporting reasons for the garment each teen should choose.
6. **ER**   *My Personal Journal,* reproducible master 35-2. Students are to describe their most comfortable garments. Then they are to explain how the fiber content of the garments contributes to their comfort.

■ Yarns

7. **RT**   Ask students to distinguish between spun yarns, monofilament yarns, and multifilament yarns.

8. **RF**   Give students samples of various types of yarns. Have them identify the yarns as single yarns, ply yarns, or cord yarns.
9. **RT**   Ask students to describe how blends and combinations can be used to obtain fabric with better performance, better appearance, or lower prices.

■ Fabrics

10. **ER**   Ask someone who owns or manages a fabric store to speak to students about the advantages and disadvantages of various fibers and the construction of various types of fabrics.
11. **ER**   From a scrap of woven fabric, have students unravel a small section. From the yarns they collect, have them compare the filling yarns with the warp yarns. Compare the strength, twist, and stretch. Ask students to report their findings.
12. **RF**   Using small strips of different colored paper (one color for the warp and one color for the filling), have students make samples of the plain weave, twill weave, and satin weave. Ask students to mount their samples on a sheet of paper.
13. **EX**   *From Fiber to Yarn to Fabric*, Activity B, SAG. Students are asked to obtain a scrap of fabric. They are to analyze it to see how fibers, yarns, and fabrics are related.
14. **RF**   *Fabric Construction*, color transparencies CT-35A, CT-35B. Use these transparencies to illustrate how woven and knitted fabrics are constructed. Provide actual samples of each fabric weave and knit. Have students identify fabric characteristics and fabric names for each weave or knit. Write their responses on the chart provided.
15. **RF**   *Fabric Construction*, Activity C, SAG. Students are asked to identify various types of fabric constructions. Then they are to mount a fabric sample of the fabric construction. (Using a microscope may be helpful in identifying the fabric samples.)
16. **ER**   Have students compare a woven fabric and a knit fabric. Ask them to compare the fabrics in terms of stretch and resistance to wrinkles. Ask students to report their findings in class.
17. **ER**   Have students collect as many types of fabric samples as they can find. Make an attractive bulletin board display and have students name each type of fabric according to the fibers used and method of fabric construction.

■ Finishes

18. **ER**   Ask students to look through mail-order catalogs and magazines to find advertisements about clothing that has been given a special finish. Have them research the finish and find out how it enhances the performance or wearability of the garment.

19. **RF**   *Finishing, Dyeing, and Printing Match*, Activity D, SAG. Students are asked to match textile finishing, dyeing, and printing terms with their definitions.

■ Dyeing

20. **RT**   Have students explain the difference between fiber dyeing, yarn dyeing, and piece dyeing.
21. **ER**   Have students research primitive dyeing methods. Then conduct an experiment in dyeing with some of the items people used in dyeing many years ago. Use natural colored pieces of fabric, such as unbleached muslin. Display the finished products on the bulletin board. Label them according to the type of dye used.

■ Printing Fabrics

22. **RT**   Ask students to explain the difference between dyeing and printing. Have them identify samples of each.
23. **RT**   *Direct Roller Printing*, transparency master 35-3. Use the transparency to illustrate for students how direct roller printing is done. Explain that the color trough holds dye, which is picked up by the furnisher roller. The furnisher roller transfers the dye to an engraved printing roller. The printing roller uses the dye to print the engraved design directly onto the fabric. A separate color trough, furnisher roller, and printing roller are used for each color in a multicolor printed fabric.
24. **RT**   Have students describe direct roller printing and rotary screen printing. Ask them to identify examples of each.

Answer Key

■ Text

Review It, page 389

1. (List three:) cotton—cotton plant, flax—flax plant, ramie—China grass, wool—sheep fleece, silk—cocoon of the silkworm
2. (Student response.)
3. to hold fibers or filaments together and to increase the strength of the yarns
4. better performance, less expensive
5. weaving interlaces yarns at right angles to each other; knitting loops yarns together
6. true
7. (List three:) hats, handcrafts, diapers, operating gowns, bandages, cleaning cloths, garment interfacings (Students may justify other responses.)
8. A
9. colorfast
10. direct roller printing and rotary screen printing

■ Student Activity Guide

From Fiber to Yarn to Fabric, Activity B

4. Fibers, yarns.

Fabric Construction, Activity C

1. plain weave
2. twill weave
3. satin weave
4. weft knit
5. warp knit

Finishing, Dyeing, and Printing Match, Activity D

1.	F	11.	S
2.	K	12.	J
3.	A	13.	C
4.	Q	14.	E
5.	O	15.	L
6.	T	16.	M
7.	B	17.	P
8.	G	18.	R
9.	I	19.	D
10.	N	20.	H

■ Teacher's Resource Guide/Binder

Comparing Fibers, reproducible master 35-1

1. Connie should buy the polyester blouse. Acetate wrinkles easily, whereas polyester resists wrinkling.

2. Karl should choose the acrylic sweater. Some acrylic items can be machine washed, whereas wool fabrics must be dry-cleaned or hand washed.
3. Ramone should order the cotton jersey. Cotton is cool and comfortable in warm weather. Polyester does not absorb moisture, which makes it uncomfortable to wear in warm weather.
4. Janita should shop for an acetate dress. Acetate is inexpensive, whereas silk is expensive.
5. Calvin should choose the wool socks. Wool is the warmest of all fibers.

Chapter 35 Quiz

1.	T	10.	F
2.	F	11.	T
3.	T	12.	F
4.	F	13.	F
5.	F	14.	T
6.	T	15.	T
7.	T	16.	C
8.	F	17.	B
9.	F	18.	A

19. (Student response.)
20. Weaving is the process of interlacing yarns at right angles to produce a fabric. Knitting is done by looping yarns together.

Comparing Fibers

Name _____ **Date** _____ **Period** _____

A teen in each of the following cases is trying to decide between two garments, each made of a different fiber. Give your recommendation and supporting reasons for the garment each teen should choose.

1. Connie is trying to choose between two blouses. One is made of acetate; the other is made of polyester. She wants a blouse that will still look nice after wearing it all day. Which blouse do you think Connie should buy? Give reasons for your recommendation.

    _____

    _____

    _____

2. Karl is looking at two sweaters. One is made of wool; the other is made of acrylic. Karl likes his garments to require little special care. Which sweater would you recommend for Karl? Give reasons for your recommendation.

    _____

    _____

    _____

3. Ramone wants to get a new bicycling jersey. He sees two that he likes in his favorite cycling supplies catalog. One is made of cotton; the other is made of polyester. Ramone does a lot of riding in hot summer temperatures, and he tends to get warm easily. Which jersey do you think Ramone should order? Give reasons for your recommendation.

    _____

    _____

    _____

4. Janita wants to get a dress to wear to the prom. An article in her Teen Chic magazine said silk and acetate were the hottest fabrics for prom dresses this year. However, the article didn't give any pricing information, and Janita is on a tight budget. Which type of dress would you suggest Janita look for when she goes shopping? Give reasons for your recommendation.

    _____

    _____

    _____

5. Calvin wants to get a pair of socks to keep his feet warm when he goes cross country skiing. The sporting goods store had several styles of thick socks. Some were made of wool, and some were made of cotton. Which socks would you recommend that Calvin buy? Give reasons for your recommendation.

    _____

    _____

    _____

My Personal Journal

Think of your most comfortable garment. What type of garment is it? From what fiber(s) is the garment made? How does the fiber content of the garment contribute to its comfort?

_____

_____

_____

_____

_____

_____

_____

_____

_____

_____

_____

_____

_____

_____

_____

_____

_____

_____

_____

_____

_____

_____

Direct Roller Printing

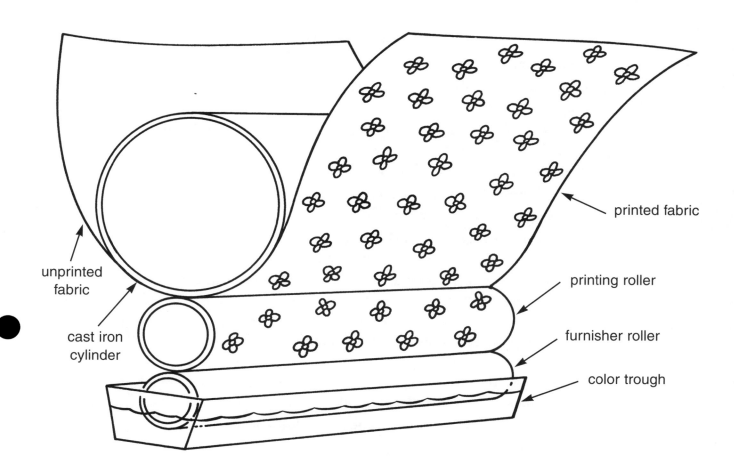

unprinted fabric

printed fabric

cast iron cylinder

printing roller

furnisher roller

color trough

Fibers, Yarns, and Fabrics

Name _____

Date _____ **Period** _____ **Score** _____

CHAPTER 35 QUIZ

☐ True/False: Circle *T* if the statement is true or *F* if the statement is false.

T   F   1.   Natural fibers come from plant, animal, and mineral sources.

T   F   2.   Cotton is not very absorbent.

T   F   3.   Wool comes from the fleece of sheep.

T   F   4.   Acetate is more resistant to wrinkling, shrinkage, and sunlight than triacetate.

T   F   5.   Nylon is a very weak fiber.

T   F   6.   Acrylic is often used as a substitute for wool.

T   F   7.   Fabrics made of both natural and manufactured fibers are called blends.

T   F   8.   Weaving is the process of looping yarns.

T   F   9.   Satin weave fabrics are very durable.

T   F   10.   Warp knitting can be done either by hand or machine.

T   F   11.   A finish is a treatment given to fibers, yarns, or fabrics that can improve the look, feel, or performance of the fabric.

T   F   12.   Mercerization is a chemical treatment used to give fabrics a stain-repellent finish.

T   F   13.   A water-repellent finish makes fabric waterproof.

T   F   14.   Yarn dyeing costs less than fiber dyeing, but more than piece dyeing.

T   F   15.   You can often tell that a fabric has been printed because the wrong side of the fabric is often much lighter than the right side.

☐ Multiple Choice: Choose the best answer and write the corresponding letter in the blank.

_____ 16. Which of the following is a natural fiber?
  A. Polyester.
  B. Spandex.
  C. Cotton.
  D. Nylon.

_____ 17. Which of the following is a twill weave fabric?
  A. Gingham.
  B. Denim.
  C. Satin.
  D. Percale.

_____ 18. Which of the following is a warp knit?
  A. Tricot.
  B. Rib-knit.
  C. Jersey.
  D. Velour.

☐ Essay Questions: Provide the answers you feel best show your understanding of the subject matter.

19. Choose one fiber. Indicate its source. Then list its advantages, disadvantages, and end uses.

20. Explain the difference between weaving and knitting.

         Reproducible Quiz

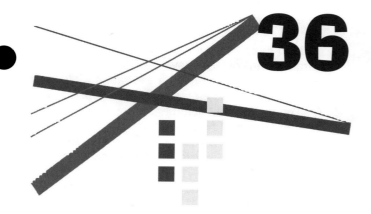

36 Sewing Tools and Notions

Objectives

After studying this chapter, students will be able to
- identify the various pieces of sewing equipment they will be using in class.
- discuss points to consider when choosing notions.

Teaching Materials

Text, pages 390–400
   Words to Know
   Review It
   Apply It
   Think More About It
Student Activity Guide
   A. *Sewing Tools*
   B. *Notes on Notions*
   C. *The Sewing Machine*
Teacher's Resource Guide/Binder
   My Personal Journal, reproducible master 36-1
   Minor Problems and Cures for Sewing Machines, reproducible master 36-2
   Tips for Choosing Notions, transparency master 36-3
   Chapter 36 Quiz

Introductory Activities

1. Ask students to name all the tools and supplies they think would be needed to make a garment. Write their responses on the chalkboard. Hold up objects discussed in the chapter they did not name. See how many of these objects they can identify by name and function.
2. Ask students to complete the statement "Learning about the parts of a sewing machine before using the machine is important because . . ."

Strategies to Reteach, Reinforce, Enrich, and Extend Text Concepts

■ Sewing Equipment

3. **RF** Have students demonstrate how to use marking tools.
4. **RT** Have students describe the difference between scissors and shears.
5. **RT** Ask students to explain the uses of various types of needles: sharps, betweens, and crewels.
6. **RF** Have students demonstrate the use of the emery bag.
7. **RF** Ask students to demonstrate the use of a thimble.
8. **ER** *My Personal Journal,* reproducible master 36-1. Students are to describe their greatest concern about their first experience using a sewing machine. They are to explain what they will do to ease this concern and what value knowing how to operate a sewing machine has for them.
9. **RF** *The Sewing Machine,* Activity C, SAG. Students are asked to identify various parts of the sewing machine and describe the purpose of each part.
10. **ER** Ask a representative from a sewing machine company to speak to the class about sewing machines. Discussion topics might include use and care of a sewing machine, features of various models, etc. Prepare a list of questions in advance.
11. **RF** Demonstrate to the class how to correctly use a sewing machine. Then have students practice using the machine.
12. **ER** List several requirements such as being able to thread the sewing machine, properly controlling the speed of the sewing machine, following lines by stitching on paper using an unthreaded machine,

etc. When students have met these requirements, issue them a "Sewing Machine Operator's License."

13. **RT** *Minor Problems and Cures for Sewing Machines*, reproducible master 36-2. Use this transparency master as a basis of discussion about how to keep a sewing machine running properly.

14. **RF** Have students discuss the importance of using pressing equipment as they sew.

15. **RF** Prepare a display of various types of sewing equipment. Have students describe the purpose of each.

16. **ER** Have students choose one piece of sewing equipment. Have them compare the prices of the item in various stores and share this information with the class. Then have them demonstrate how to properly use this piece of sewing equipment. Demonstrations may be videotaped.

17. **RT** *Sewing Tools*, Activity A, SAG. Students are asked to identify sewing tools and describe how they are used.

■ Notions

18. **RT** *Tips for Choosing Notions*, transparency master 36-3. Use the transparency as you discuss with students points they should keep in mind when choosing sewing notions for their projects.

19. **RT** Prepare a display of various sewing notions. Have students identify them by labeling them.

20. **RF** *Notes on Notions*, Activity B, SAG. Students are asked questions about notions. Then they are asked to visit a fabric store and complete a chart describing various notions and their cost.

■ Your Sewing Box

21. **RF** Have students prepare a sewing box they can use to keep their small sewing equipment organized.

22. **RF** Have students list items they would keep in a sewing box.

Answer Key

■ Text

Review It, page 400

1. A
2. The ink can soak through to the right side of the fabric. Ink is difficult, if not impossible, to remove from fabric.
3. false
4. sharps
5. Ballpoint pins are recommended for use with knits because they have rounded points that slip between yarns and help prevent cutting and snagging.

6. An emery bag is used to remove rough spots or dull points from needles and pins. You do this by pushing the pins into the bag several times.
7. Sergers can join two layers of fabric to form a seam, trim away extra seam allowance width, and overcast the fabric edges all in one step.
8. A. The handwheel controls the movement of the take-up lever and needle.
   B. The spool pin holds the spool of thread.
   C. The take-up lever controls the flow of needle thread.
   D. The presser foot holds fabric against the feed system teeth.
9. notions
10. polyester or polyester/cotton thread

■ Student Activity Guide

Sewing Tools, Activity A

1. thimble
2. tailor's pencil
3. shears
4. seam ripper
5. skirt marker
6. tailor's ham
7. pins
8. tailor's chalk
9. scissors
10. sleeve board
11. needles
12. tracing wheel
13. dressmaker's carbon paper
14. seam gauge
15. tape measure
16. clippers
17. pinking shears
18. steam iron and press cloth
19. needle threader
20. pin cushion

(Descriptions are student response. Information can be found in Chapter 36 of the text.)

Notes on Notions, Activity B

1. items that become part of a garment or project, such as thread, buttons, snaps, zippers, tapes, trims, elastic, and interfacing
2. so they can be cared for in the same manner
3. This is so you can match colors, and you will be able to finish your project without stopping to run to the store for a needed item.
4. Thread usually looks lighter when it is stitched into fabric.
5. according to the type and length specified on your pattern and the color of the fabric
6. Sew-through buttons have holes in them through which you sew with thread. Shank buttons have a loop behind the button through which the thread is stitched.
7. black, silver
8. Read the package directions.
9. It is used to prevent stretching and provides shape to a garment.
10. (Student response.)

The Sewing Machine, Activity C

1. head
2. handwheel
3. bobbin winder
4. spool cap
5. spool pin
6. needle position selector
7. stitch width lever

8. bobbin winder
   tension disc
9. take-up lever
10. face plate
11. needle thread
    tension dial
12. thread guides
13. presser foot
14. feed system
15. needle plate
16. needle clamp
17. removable extension
    table

18. stitch length dial
19. reverse-stitch button
20. presser foot lifter
21. thread cutter
22. slide plate
23. speed controller
24. electrical power cord
25. machine plug
26. power and light
    switch
27. bobbin winding indent

(Descriptions can be found in the Sewing Machine section in Chapter 36 of the text.)

■ Teacher's Resource Guide/Binder

Chapter 36 Quiz

1.	F	10.	F
2.	F	11.	T
3.	F	12.	F
4.	T	13.	F
5.	T	14.	A
6.	T	15.	D
7.	T	16.	C
8.	T	17.	E
9.	T	18.	B

19. (Student response.)
20. (Student response.)

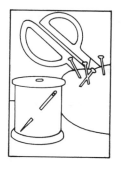

My Personal Journal

Think about your first experience using a sewing machine. What is (was) your greatest concern about using the machine? How can (did) you ease this concern? What value will (does) knowing how to operate a sewing machine have for you?

_____

_____

_____

_____

_____

_____

_____

_____

_____

_____

_____

_____

_____

_____

_____

_____

_____

_____

_____

_____

_____

_____

_____

_____

_____

Minor Problems and Cures for Sewing Machines

Name _____ Date _____ Period _____

Problem	Cause	Cure
1. Loud noise as you start to sew and matted threads in seamline.	Machine threaded wrong.	Thread machine again.
2. Lower thread breaks.	Lower tension too tight. Knot in bobbin thread.	Adjust tension screw. Check thread.
3. Puckered seamline.	Tension too tight. Thread too heavy or too light for fabric. Pulling on fabric.	Check by sewing on different weight fabric.
4. Machine locks. Needle will not go up and down.	Thread caught in bobbin.	Turn handwheel backward to release thread.
5. Skipping stitches.	Needle bent, blunt, too long or short. Needle threaded wrong.	Check needle. Thread needle again.
6. Looped stitches. Top line Bottom line.	Top tension adjusted wrong. Bottom tension adjusted wrong.	Check tension.
7. Needle picks or pulls thread in line of stitching.	Point of needle bent when it hit a pin.	Insert new needle.
8. Needle breaks.	Presser foot loose and needle hit it. Pulling fabric while stitching.	Tighten presser foot. Do not pull fabric.
9. Machine runs "hard."	Needs cleaning and oiling.	Clean and oil according to instruction booklet.
10. Machine will not run at all.	Machine may be unplugged. Cord or outlet may be defective.	Check to see if plugged in tightly. Check another outlet to see if cord is okay.

Tips for Choosing Notions

● **Thread**
    color should be slightly
    darker than fabric

Fasteners
    zippers
    choose type and length
    specified on pattern

    hooks and eyes, snaps
    choose black for dark fabrics; silver for light fabrics

    buttons
● choose size and number
    listed on pattern

    hook and loop tape
    choose precut shapes or
    by the yard

Tapes, Trims, Elastic
    choose type, width, and
    color according to decorative or functional use

Interfacing
● choose same weight or
    slightly lighter than fabric

Sewing Tools and Notions

Name _____

Date _____ Period _____ Score _____

CHAPTER 36 QUIZ

☐ True/False: Circle *T* if the statement is true or *F* if the statement is false.

T F 1. A sewing gauge is 60 inches long.

T F 2. When transferring pattern markings to fabric, use a ballpoint pen to mark the fabric.

T F 3. Shears and scissors are the same.

T F 4. A size 1 needle is larger than a size 12 needle.

T F 5. Ballpoint pins are recommended for use with knit fabrics.

T F 6. An emery bag is used to remove rough spots or a dull point from a needle or pin.

T F 7. When using the sewing machine, the fabric, stitch, and thread will determine the tension setting needed.

T F 8. Sewing machines use two threads: the needle thread and the bobbin thread.

T F 9. Sergers join two layers of fabric to form a seam, trim away extra seam allowance width, and overcast the fabric edges.

T F 10. A press cloth creates "iron shine" on fabrics.

T F 11. The notions you select should require the same care as your fabric.

T F 12. Choose interfacing that is heavier than the garment fabric.

☐ Matching: Match the following terms with their definitions.

_____ 13. A steam iron, ironing board, press cloth, sleeve board, and pressing ham.

_____ 14. Items such as a tape measure, skirt marker, and seam gauge.

_____ 15. Items used as you stitch a garment or project together, such as needles, pins, pin cushions, and thimbles.

_____ 16. Items such as shears, scissors, clippers, and seam rippers.

_____ 17. Items that become a part of a garment or project, such as thread, buttons, snaps, zippers, tapes, trims, elastic, and interfacings.

_____ 18. Items such as tracing wheels, dressmaker's carbon paper, tailor's chalk, and pencils.

A. measuring tools
B. marking tools
C. cutting tools
D. sewing tools
E. notions
F. pressing equipment

☐ Essay Questions: Provide the answers you feel best show your understanding of the subject matter.

19. List and describe four pieces of sewing equipment.

20. Describe three sewing notions and points to consider when choosing them.

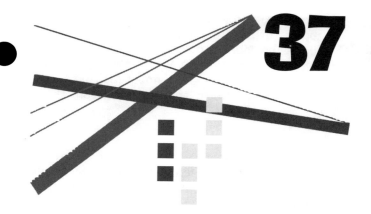

37 Getting Ready to Sew

Objectives

After studying this chapter, students will be able to
- choose patterns and fabrics to match their interests and skills.
- prepare patterns and fabrics for sewing.

Teaching Materials

Text, pages 401–415
  Words to Know
  Review It
  Apply It
  Think More About It
Student Activity Guide
  A. *Choosing a Pattern*
  B. *Your Measurements*
  C. *The Pattern Envelope Back*
  D. *Pattern Symbols*
  E. *Fabric Grain*
  F. *Cutting Layouts*
Teacher's Resource Guide/Binder
  Evaluating Your Sewing Skills, reproducible master 37-1
  Taking Body Measurements, transparency master 37-2
  My Personal Journal, reproducible master 37-3
  Chapter 37 Quiz

Introductory Activities

1. Have students collect pictures of garments or items that would be easy first projects to sew. Display them on the bulletin board.
2. Discuss with students the following statement: "The basic skills you learn are more important than the items you make when making your first sewing project."

Strategies to Reteach, Reinforce, Enrich, and Extend Text Concepts

■ Planning Your Project

3. **RF** *Evaluating Your Sewing Skills*, reproducible master 37-1. Students are to complete an evaluation to help them choose a sewing project that would match their skill level.
4. **RF** Have students select patterns from pattern books. Have them explain whether the pattern is for a beginner or a more experienced sewer.
5. **ER** Have students bring articles of clothing to class they no longer wear. Ask them to discuss ways the garments could be redesigned or recycled.

■ Body Measurements

6. **RT** *Taking Body Measurements*, transparency master 37-2. Use the transparency as you explain where and how to take various body measurements.
7. **RT** *Choosing a Pattern*, Activity A, SAG. Students are asked to choose the body measurement that is most important when choosing a pattern for various garments described in the activity. Then in class, students can discuss why these measurements are most important.
8. **RF** *Your Measurements*, Activity B, SAG. Ask students to choose a partner and measure each other. Have them record their measurements in the appropriate measurement chart. Then have them use these measurements to determine their figure types and pattern sizes. A pattern catalog can be used in determining figure type and pattern size.

■ Exploring Patterns

9. **RF** Ask salespersons or department managers to save old pattern catalogs for use in the classroom as new ones arrive. Divide the class into groups according to the number of pattern catalogs available to allow students to become familiar with the format and various sections.

10. **RT** *The Pattern Envelope Back*, Activity C, SAG. Students are asked to study a sample pattern envelope back and identify each item indicated.

11. **RT** *Pattern Symbols*, Activity D, SAG. Students are asked to identify pattern symbols on a sample pattern piece and to briefly describe the meaning of each symbol.

■ Preparing the Pattern and Fabric

12. **RF** *Fabric Grain*, Activity E, SAG. Students are asked to define *grain*, identify items related to fabric grain, describe the results of making a garment from fabric that was off-grain, and describe how they would check the grain of the fabric.

13. **RF** Have students demonstrate how to straighten the grain of fabric and lay pattern pieces on the straight grain.

14. **RF** *Cutting Layouts*, Activity F, SAG. Students are asked to respond to statements and questions about pattern guide sheet cutting layouts.

15. **ER** Have students lay out and pin their pattern pieces according to the correct layout on the guide sheet. Check students' pattern layouts before they cut out their patterns.

16. **ER** Have students test three different ways of transferring pattern markings to fabric on fabric scraps. Have them compare the results.

17. **ER** *My Personal Journal*, reproducible master 37-3. Students are to describe their current sewing skills. Then they are to list skills they feel they need to develop further and explain how these skills will help them in the future.

Answer Key

■ Text

Review It, page 415

1. (List two:) few pattern pieces; loose fit; no collars, cuffs, pockets, or pleats; label such as Jiffy, Simple-to-Sew, Very Easy, Step-by-Step, or For Beginners

2. A. bust measurement
   B. hip measurement
   C. waist measurement
   D. chest measurement

3. If you already know your pattern number, the pattern index can tell you the page on which your pattern is illustrated in the catalog.

4. (List 10:) brand or company name, pattern number, figure type, size, a sketch or photograph of the garment or project, amount of fabric needed, number of pattern pieces, garment description, suggested fabrics, notions needed, back view, body measurements, amount of lining or interfacing needed, finished garment measurements, nap indication, foreign language translation

5. C

6. true

7. selvages

8. project or view, fabric width, and pattern size

9. These symbols indicate the direction in which you should cut. By cutting in this direction (with the grain), you will avoid stretching or raveling your fabric.

10. Place the colored side of the carbon paper next to the wrong side of the fabric. Then roll the tracing wheel along the markings to be transferred.

■ Student Activity Guide

Choosing a Pattern, Activity A

1. hip	4. bust	7. bust
2. waist	5. shirt neck	8. bust
3. chest	6. chest	9. hip

Pattern Symbols, Activity D

1. cutting line	7. adjustment lines
2. seam allowance	8. fold line for dart
3. stitching line	9. dart stitching line
4. center front	10. directions for stitching
5. buttonhole placement	11. dot
6. grain line	12. notch

(Descriptions are student response.)

Fabric Grain, Activity E

1. the direction yarns run in a fabric
2. a. selvages
   b. crosswise grain
   c. lengthwise grain
3. lengthwise
4. The fabric would not be easy to handle. The finished garment would twist, pull to one side, and hang unevenly.
5. (Student response.)

Cutting Layouts, Activity F

1. The third layout should be circled.
2. 1, 3, 6, 7, 8
3. 2, 4, 5
4. 4, 5

■ Teacher's Resource Guide/Binder

Chapter 37 Quiz

1. F	5. T	9. H	13. J	17. I
2. T	6. T	10. E	14. A	18. G
3. T	7. F	11. D	15. F	
4. F	8. F	12. B	16. C	

19. The fabric would not be easy to handle. The finished garment would twist, pull to one side, and hang unevenly.

20. Find the one that matches your project or view, fabric width, and pattern size.

Evaluating Your Sewing Skills

Name _____**Date** _____**Period** _____

Complete the following evaluation to help you choose a sewing project that will match your skill level.

1. Check all the following sewing skills that you have done:
   _____ take body measurements
   _____ choose a garment pattern for your size and figure type
   _____ purchase fabric and notions listed on the back of a pattern envelope
   _____ adjust length of a garment pattern
   _____ check fabric grain
   _____ lay out pattern pieces according to a cutting layout on a pattern guide sheet
   _____ pin pattern pieces to fabric
   _____ cut out pattern pieces
   _____ mark pattern pieces
   _____ operate a sewing machine
   _____ use directional stitching
   _____ staystitch fabric pieces
   _____ hand or machine baste fabric pieces
   _____ ease or gather fabric pieces
   _____ make darts
   _____ stitch a seam
   _____ finish a seam
   _____ trim or grade a seam
   _____ clip or notch a seam
   _____ attach a facing to a garment
   _____ apply interfacing
   _____ insert a zipper
   _____ mark a hem
   _____ finish a hem
   _____ secure a hem with hand stitching
   _____ sew on buttons, hooks and eyes, and/or snaps

2. How would you rate your level of sewing experience? (Check one.)
   _____ beginner   _____ intermediate   _____ advanced

3. What type of sewing project would match your current skill level?_____
   _____

Taking Body Measurements

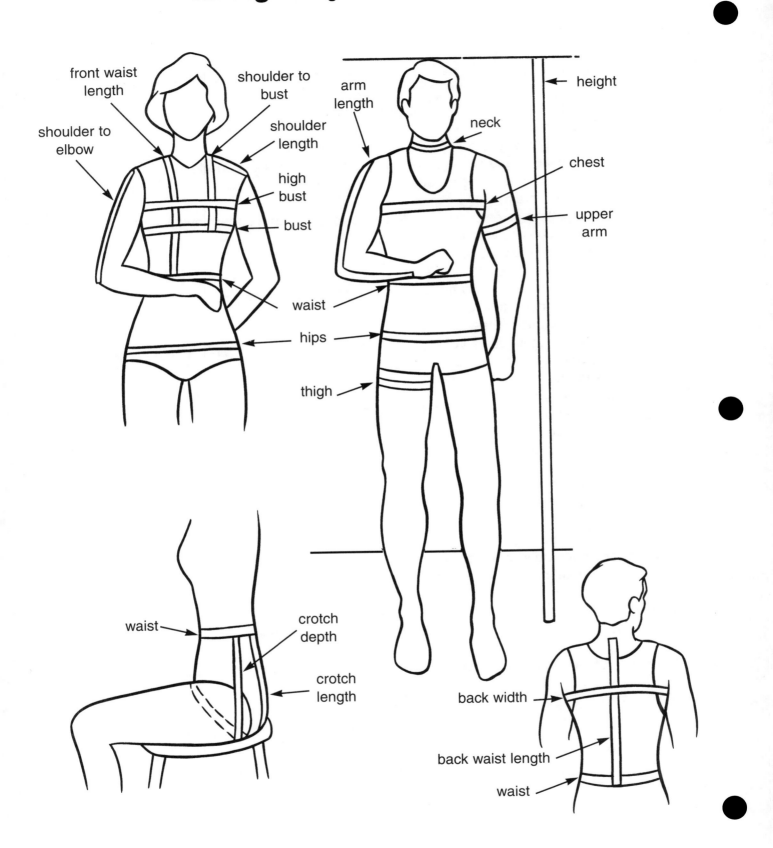

front waist length

shoulder to bust

shoulder to elbow

shoulder length

high bust

bust

arm length

neck

height

chest

upper arm

waist

hips

thigh

waist

crotch depth

crotch length

back width

back waist length

waist

My Personal Journal

Think about your sewing skills. What skills do you currently have? What skills do you feel you need to develop further? How will learning sewing skills help you in the future?

_____

_____

_____

_____

_____

_____

_____

_____

_____

_____

_____

_____

_____

_____

_____

_____

_____

_____

_____

_____

_____

_____

_____

_____

Getting Ready to Sew

Name _____

Date _____ **Period** _____ **Score** _____

CHAPTER 37 QUIZ

☐ True/False: Circle *T* if the statement is true or *F* if the statement is false.

T F 1. If you are allowed to select a pattern for your first project, select one that is difficult.

T F 2. Through redesigning and recycling, you can transform an old garment into something new and exciting.

T F 3. Body measurements should be taken over undergarments.

T F 4. Most stores will let you return or exchange patterns.

T F 5. The most common pattern adjustment is for length.

T F 6. When pinning the pattern to the fabric, pins should be placed at right angles to the cutting lines.

T F 7. As you cut out a garment, pull the fabric toward you instead of walking around the table.

T F 8. When transferring pattern markings to fabric, use dark-colored carbon paper on light-colored fabrics.

☐ Matching: Match the following terms with their definitions.

_____ 9. A basic plan that helps you put together a garment.

_____ 10. Found inside the pattern envelope, it gives you detailed, step-by-step directions on how to cut and sew your garment. It also suggests fabric and cutting layouts, has explanations of marking symbols, and has a few basic sewing instructions.

_____ 11. On a pattern piece, the heavy line with arrows on both ends.

_____ 12. The bold outline around each pattern piece.

_____ 13. The broken line just inside the cutting line on a pattern piece.

_____ 14. These two parallel lines show you where to lengthen or shorten a pattern piece to change the fit of the garment.

_____ 15. The diamond-shaped symbols along and beyond the cutting line used to help join pieces together at the right place.

_____ 16. They aid you in matching seams and other construction details.

_____ 17. The smooth, closely-woven edges of fabric that do not ravel.

_____ 18. When the crosswise and lengthwise yarns of a fabric are at right angles to each other.

A. adjustment lines
B. cutting line
C. dots
D. grain line
E. guide sheet
F. notches
G. on-grain
H. pattern
I. selvages
J. stitching line

☐ Essay Questions: Provide the answers you feel best show your understanding of the subject matter.

19. Describe what would happen if you made a garment from fabric that was off-grain or crooked.

20. Explain how you know which cutting layout to use when using a pattern.

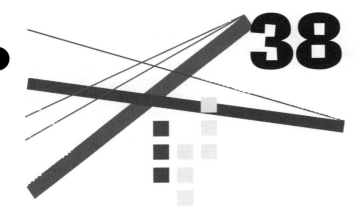

38 Sewing Skills

Objectives

After studying this chapter, students will be able to
■ perform basic construction steps using a sewing machine.
■ identify basic seam finishes.
■ demonstrate how to mark, finish, and hand stitch a hem.

Teaching Materials

Text, pages 416–427
  Words to Know
  Review It
  Apply It
  Think More About It
Student Activity Guide
  A. *Directional Stitching*
  B. *Seam Finishes*
  C. *Hem Finishes*
  D. *Securing Hems*
  E. *Darts, Clipping and Notching, and Zippers*
  F. *Sewing Skills Match*
Teacher's Resource Guide/Binder
  My Personal Journal, reproducible master 38-1
  Why Press as You Sew? transparency master 38-2
  Project Evaluation, reproducible master 38-3
  Chapter 38 Quiz

Introductory Activities

1. Read to students the dictionary definition for the word *construct*. Ask them how they think that term applies to a sewing project.
2. *My Personal Journal,* reproducible master 38-1. Students are to describe what interests them most about constructing a sewing project. Then they are to describe any concerns they have about constructing a project and explain what they can do to ease their concerns.

Strategies to Reteach, Reinforce, Enrich, and Extend Text Concepts

■ Machine Sewing

3. **RF** *Directional Stitching,* Activity A, SAG. Students are asked to study sample pattern pieces and arrows showing directional stitching and indicate whether the arrows are pointing in the correct direction. Students are also asked to describe the purpose of directional stitching.
4. **ER** Have students test directional stitching. Cut diagonally across a square fabric scrap. Have students sew up one of the cut edges and sew down the other cut edge. Ask them to compare the edges of each.
5. **RF** Have students make samples of darts on scraps of fabric and press them correctly. Display them on the bulletin board.

■ Making a Seam

6. **RT** *Why Press as You Sew?* transparency master 38-2. Use the transparency to emphasize the value of pressing throughout the sewing process. Remind students they should press wrinkled pattern pieces, wrinkled fabric, darts, all seams and garment details, zipper tapes, hems, and the completed garment.
7. **ER** Have students test three types of seams and seam finishes on the same fabric. Ask them to compare the results and determine which seams and finishes work best for that particular fabric. (Students should be given various types of fabrics to try.)
8. **RF** *Seam Finishes,* Activity B, SAG. Students are asked to identify seam finishes and explain when each would be used and how each would be produced.

■ Facing and Interfacing

9. **RT** Ask students to distinguish between extended facings and fitted facings. Ask them to show examples of each to the class.

10. **RT** Demonstrate understitching. Then ask students to produce samples of understitching or to do it on the garments on which they are working.

■ Zippers

11. **RT** Discuss with students areas of a garment where a centered zipper application would be used versus where a lapped zipper application would be used.

12. **RT** Demonstrate to the class how to apply a centered zipper and a lapped zipper. Have students produce samples of these two zipper applications.

13. **RF** *Darts, Clipping and Notching, and Zippers,* Activity E, SAG. Students are asked to complete an activity in which they demonstrate knowledge of darts, clipping and notching, and zipper applications.

■ Hems

14. **RT** Demonstrate how to properly mark a hem. (You may ask a student who is ready to hem his or her garment to volunteer as a model for the demonstration.)

15. **RF** *Hem Finishes,* Activity C, SAG. Students are asked to identify hem finishes and explain when each would be used and how it would be produced.

16. **RF** *Securing Hems,* Activity D, SAG. Students are asked to identify hem stitches and explain when each would be used and how it would be produced.

17. **ER** Have students test three types of hem finishes and hemming stitches on the same fabric. Ask them to compare the results and determine which hem finish and hem would work best for that particular fabric. (Students should be given various types of fabrics to try.)

18. **RF** *Sewing Skills Match,* Activity F, SAG. Students are asked to complete a matching exercise about sewing skills.

19. **EX** *Project Evaluation,* reproducible master 38-3. This reproducible master can be used by both you and your students as you evaluate their projects.

Answer Key

■ Text

Review It, page 427

1. A
2. one-half inch from the cut edge of the fabric on curved and bias edges of loosely woven or less sturdy fabric pieces
3. to check the fit of a garment, to transfer pattern markings, and to ease and gather
4. true
5. seam allowance

---

6. a pinked seam finish
7. Clipping is done on seams that form an inward curve, such as armhole, neckline, and waistline seams. Notching is done on seams that form an outward curve, such as collars and pockets.
8. An extended facing is cut as part of the garment pattern piece. A fitted facing is cut as a separate pattern piece.
9. A zipper foot allows you to stitch closer to the zipper coils.
10. so it will have time to stretch to its final shape

■ Student Activity Guide

Directional Stitching, Activity A
1. correct, incorrect   3. incorrect, correct
2. incorrect, correct   4. correct, incorrect
   Directional stitching is done to prevent the fabric from stretching and puckering.

Seam Finishes, Activity B
1. pinked finish
2. turned and stitched finish
3. zigzag finish
(Explanations are student response.)

Hem Finishes, Activity C
1. pinked hem finish
2. zigzag hem finish
3. turned and stitched hem finish
4. seam binding hem finish
5. bias binding hem finish
(Explanations are student response.)

Securing Hems, Activity D
1. hemming stitch
2. slip stitch
3. blind stitch
(Explanations are student response.)

Darts, Clipping and Notching, and Zippers, Activity E
1. B
2. A. clipped   B. notched
3. A. centered   B. lapped

Sewing Skills Match, Activity F

1. A	5. B	9. K	13. H	17. N
2. D	6. E	10. R	14. I	18. Q
3. L	7. O	11. P	15. C	
4. G	8. F	12. M	16. J	

■ Teacher's Resource Guide/Binder

Chapter 38 Quiz

1. T	5. T	9. I	13. J	17. K
2. T	6. T	10. B	14. E	18. A
3. F	7. T	11. G	15. C	
4. F	8. D	12. H	16. F	

19. Stitch to within ⅝ inch of the corner. Stop. Be sure the needle is down into the fabric. Lift the presser foot. Turn the fabric. Lower the presser foot, and continue to sew.
20. (Student response.)

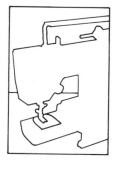

My Personal Journal

Think about making a sewing project. What interests you most about constructing a project? What is your greatest concern about constructing the project? What can you do to ease your concerns?

_____

_____

_____

_____

_____

_____

_____

_____

_____

_____

_____

_____

_____

_____

_____

_____

_____

_____

_____

_____

_____

_____

_____

_____

Why Press as You Sew?

Pressing

- improves grain lines of fabric

- removes creases and wrinkles, which eases cutting and assembling garment pieces

- decreases need for pinning and basting

- creates garment shaping

- gives garment a professional appearance

Project Evaluation

Name _____ **Date** _____ **Period** _____

Pattern: Company name _____ Number _____ Size _____

Fabric: Name of fabric _____ Fabric sample: (Attach here.)

Fiber content _____

Care instructions _____

_____

Cost: Pattern: _____

Fabric: _____

Interfacing: _____

Thread: _____

Fasteners: _____

Hem tape: _____

Other: _____

_____

_____

_____

Total $ _____

Cost of a comparable ready-made item: $

Evaluate your project. Then ask your teacher to evaluate it.
Scoring: 5 = Excellent   4 = Good   3 = Fair   2 = Below average   1 = Poor

	Student	Teacher
1. General appearance: Well-pressed and clean. No loose threads. Appropriate selection of notions and fabric. Fits properly. Appropriate selection of style for body type.		
2. Seams: Stitching straight and correct width. Correct tension, correct size stitches. Staystitching even. Seams finished properly and pressed open.		
3. Facings, collar, sleeves, waistband, and/or pockets: Neat in appearance.		
4. Fasteners (hooks, eyes, snaps, buttons, buttonholes, zippers): Applied neatly and correctly.		
5. Hem: Correct and even width. Edge finished properly. Stitches correctly done. Stitches do not show on right side.		

Additional comments: _____

_____

_____

_____

Sewing Skills

Name _____

Date _____ **Period** _____ **Score** _____

CHAPTER 38 QUIZ

☐ True/False: Circle *T* if the statement is true or *F* if the statement is false.

T F 1. The take-up lever of the sewing machine should be at its highest point to prevent the thread from being pulled out of the needle as you begin to sew.

T F 2. Easing and gathering are used to make extra fabric fit into a smaller space.

T F 3. Darts are made after the seams in a garment are sewn.

T F 4. A pinked seam finish should be used on fabrics that ravel.

T F 5. The purpose of interfacing is to add support, shape, and stability to garments.

T F 6. Most openings in side seams are closed with lapped zippers.

T F 7. When having a hem marked, try on the garment with the shoes and undergarments you plan to wear with it.

☐ Matching: Match the following terms with their definitions.

_____ 8. Stitching in the direction of the grain.

_____ 9. A line of regular machine stitches on a single thickness of fabric to prevent garment pieces from stretching out of shape.

_____ 10. Long, loose stitches.

_____ 11. A row of stitches used to hold two pieces of fabric together.

_____ 12. The fabric from the stitching to the edge of the fabric.

_____ 13. Cutting away part of the seam allowance.

_____ 14. To cut each seam allowance to a different width.

_____ 15. Done to allow seams that form inward curves to lie flat.

_____ 16. Done to allow seams that form outward curves to lie flat.

_____ 17. A row of stitches on the facing as close to the seam as possible through both seam allowances to prevent the facing from rolling to the outside of the garment.

_____ 18. To sew backward and forward in the same place for a few stitches to secure thread ends.

A. backstitching
B. basting
C. clipping
D. directional stitching
E. grading
F. notching
G. seam
H. seam allowance
I. staystitching
J. trimming
K. understitching

☐ Essay Questions: Provide the answers you feel best show your understanding of the subject matter.

19. Explain how to turn a corner while stitching with the sewing machine.

20. Describe the best way to mark an even hem.

Reproducible Quiz

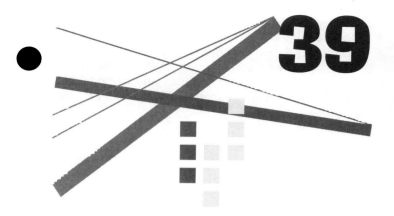

39 Caring for Clothes

Objectives

After studying this chapter, students will be able to
- discuss important points to remember when doing laundry, pressing and ironing, and storing clothes.
- demonstrate how to do simple clothing repairs and alterations.

Teaching Materials

Text, pages 428–442
   Words to Know
   Review It
   Apply It
   Think More About It
Student Activity Guide
   A. *Laundry Day*
   B. *Dry Cleaning Basics*
Teacher's Resource Guide/Binder
   Clothing Care Symbols, transparency master 39-1
   Stain Removal Guide, reproducible master 39-2
   My Personal Journal, reproducible master 39-3
   Guide for Sorting Clothes, color transparency CT-39
   Chapter 39 Quiz

Introductory Activities

1. Locate a garment that has not been cared for properly. Display it with a garment that has received proper care. Ask students which garment they would rather wear.
2. Ask students to explain how clothing care can affect clothing wear.

Strategies to Reteach, Reinforce, Enrich, and Extend Text Concepts

■ Routine Clothing Care

3. **RF** Ask students to explain the statement "Taking a few extra minutes for routine clothing care can save lots of time."
4. **RT** Prepare a bulletin board entitled "Steps in Clothing Care." Include daily, weekly, and seasonal care concepts.

■ Laundry Basics

5. **RT** *Clothing Care Symbols,* transparency master 39-1. Use the transparency as you explain to students the meanings of the various symbols used on clothing care labels. You may also wish to use the transparency as a review activity after students have studied Figure 39-2 in the text. Point to various symbols and see if students can correctly identify them.
6. **RT** *Stain Removal Guide,* reproducible master 39-2. Use the master to make student handouts. Review the listed stain removal methods with students. Then encourage them to post the handouts in the laundry areas of their homes.
7. **ER** *My Personal Journal,* reproducible master 39-3. Students are to describe a stain they got on a garment, explain how they treated the stain, and note whether they were able to remove it.
8. **RF** Have students bring empty bottles and boxes of laundry products to class. Have them

study the information on the labels and make an attractive display.

9. **ER** Have students visit a local appliance store. Have them compare features of different washers and dryers. Also have them study the prices and decide which ones would be the better buys.

10. **RT** *Guide for Sorting Clothes*, color transparency CT-39. Use this transparency as a basis of discussion about how to sort clothes. If possible, bring a large basket of clean clothes to class and let students practice sorting them into wash loads.

11. **ER** Have students compare the cost of owning laundry equipment versus doing their laundry at a commercial establishment. Have students discuss the advantages and disadvantages of each.

12. **RF** *Laundry Day*, Activity A, SAG. Students are asked to obtain permission from their families to wash a load of laundry at home. They are then to report their results to class by answering questions about the experience.

13. **ER** *Dry Cleaning Basics*, Activity B, SAG. Students are asked to interview a dry cleaner about dry cleaning and find out the answers to a list of questions.

14. **ER** As a class, visit a dry cleaning plant. Have students take notes on what they see and write a report about their experience.

■ Pressing and Ironing

15. **RF** Ask students to list safety practices to follow when using the iron.

16. **RT** Demonstrate the difference between ironing and pressing.

17. **RF** Have students demonstrate how to iron a shirt or blouse.

■ Storing Clothes

18. **RT** Discuss the following statement: "The most important thing to remember about storing clothes is to store only clean clothes."

19. **RF** Have students describe good and bad storage areas for clothes. Then have them list some appropriate storage containers in which to store clothes.

■ Repairing and Altering Your Clothes

20. **RT** Demonstrate various clothing repair techniques to the class such as repairing rips and tears, fixing fasteners, and repairing snags.

21. **ER** Hold a "Fix-It Day." Allow students to bring clean clothes in need of repair to class (along with any necessary thread, buttons, hooks, etc.). Have

a "before" session where needed repairs are discussed and an "after" session where students can display the results of the repairs.

22. **ER** Ask a person who works in an alterations shop or department to discuss and demonstrate alteration techniques that students would be able to do.

Answer Key

■ Text

Review It, page 442

1. (List two:) Check chairs for dirt, spills, and gum before sitting down; use a napkin when eating; watch what you lean against; use an umbrella when needed (Students may justify other responses.)
2. true
3. Fresh stains are easier to remove than old ones.
4. D
5. (List two:) loosely woven or knitted garments, wool garments, garments that have delicate trims, garments that have colors that run when washed
6. by removing clothes as soon as the dryer stops
7. Stains are removed before a garment is cleaned, and the method of removal depends on the type of stain. Also, light-colored stains can turn dark during the dry-cleaning process if they are overlooked.
8. pressing
9. Dampness in a basement can cause mildew and musty odors that are difficult to remove.
10. Pin the seam together and sew with short stitches. Extend the line of stitching a little past the rip in both directions.

■ Teacher's Resource Guide/Binder

Chapter 39 Quiz

1. F	8. F
2. T	9. F
3. F	10. F
4. F	11. D
5. T	12. C
6. T	13. D
7. T	

14. (Student response.)
15. Sometimes you can't see all the soiled spots in a garment. Some spots may turn yellow or brown during storage and be impossible to remove later. If insects find the spot, they will eat it as well as some of the fabric.

Clothing Care Symbols

Wash	Bleach

Dry	Iron

	Dryclean

Stain Removal Guide

Name _____**Date** _____**Period** _____

Post this chart in the laundry area of your home. Use it as a handy reference to help you remove stains from clothing.

Stain	Removal Method
Ballpoint ink	Laundering will remove some types of ballpoint ink, but sets other types. To see if the stain will wash out, find a similar scrap of fabric. Mark it with the ink and wash it. Acetone (nail polish remover) will usually remove fresh stains, but do not use acetone on synthetics. Old stains may require bleaching. Rubbing alcohol will remove some types of ink. Then wash as usual.
Blood	Soak stain in cold water. Rinse. Rub a heavy-duty detergent into the spot, then launder as usual. If the stain remains, use a few drops of ammonia and launder again.
Car grease	Most of these stains can be removed by rubbing a heavy-duty detergent into the stain. Let it stand for several hours or overnight. Wash in warm water. If the stain remains, put cleaning fluid on it and wash it again.
Chewing gum	Make the gum hard by putting ice on it. Remove as much as you can with a dull knife. Put cleaning fluid on the remaining spots. Then launder in hot, soapy water.
Chocolate	Soak stain in cool water for at least 30 minutes. Rinse. If stain remains, work heavy-duty detergent into the stain. Then rinse thoroughly. If the stain looks greasy, apply cleaning fluid.
Cosmetics (eyeshadow, lipstick, liquid makeup, mascara, blush)	Apply undiluted, heavy-duty, liquid detergent to stain. Work with your fingers to form suds. Rinse well. A second application may be needed. If the garment is not washable, use a spot remover. Rub the edges of the stain lightly with a cloth. This will prevent a circle from forming.
Deodorants and antiperspirants	Rub liquid detergent on stain. Wash in the hottest water that is safe for the fabric. Short-time soaking is needed if stain is heavy.
Grass and foliage	Dampen spot. Rub detergent in well. Wash garment as usual. If stain remains, use bleach according to manufacturer's directions.
Ice cream or milk	Sponge with dry-cleaning solvent or a prewash soil and stain remover. Rub stain between fingers to help remove it. Launder. Repeat if necessary.
Nail polish	Use nail polish remover. Before using, test a scrap or small area to be sure it will not cause damage. Do not use remover on furniture surfaces or acetate fabrics.
Fruit (fruit juices, soft drinks, punches)	If possible, sponge with cool water as soon as it happens. Do not use soap. Some fruit juices, especially citrus ones, are invisible after they dry. They turn brown or yellow on aging or when ironed. If stain remains, bleach the garment if possible. Apply white vinegar if bleach cannot be used. Launder again.
Perspiration	Presoak by wetting the area and applying heavy-duty detergent. Wait one hour. Then wash in hot water. If odor remains, soak garment in 2 tablespoons of baking soda to one gallon of water overnight. Wash as usual.

My Personal Journal

Think of a time when you got a stain on a garment. What type of stain was it? How long did you wait to treat the stain? How did you treat it? Were you able to remove the stain? Why or why not?

_____

_____

_____

_____

_____

_____

_____

_____

_____

_____

_____

_____

_____

_____

_____

_____

_____

_____

_____

_____

_____

_____

_____

_____

_____

Caring for Clothes

Name _____

Date _____ **Period** _____ **Score** _____

CHAPTER 39 QUIZ

☐ True/False: Circle *T* if the statement is true or *F* if the statement is false.

T   F   1. Sweaters should be hung on hangers.

T   F   2. If a care label does not say that you cannot do something, it is safe to assume that you can do it as long as you follow normal practices.

T   F   3. Oil-based stains include soft drinks, tea, coffee, and fruit juice.

T   F   4. Soaps work best in hard water.

T   F   5. Clothes should be sorted by fabric weight, color, degree of soil, and surface texture.

T   F   6. It is better to underload than to overload a washer.

T   F   7. Wool and silk garments are usually dry cleaned instead of laundered.

T   F   8. Ironing and pressing are the same process.

T   F   9. Rips in areas that receive a lot of stress should be repaired with a single row of basting stitches.

T   F   10. When altering a garment, if you let it out, you are making it smaller.

☐ Multiple Choice: Choose the best answer and write the corresponding letter in the blank.

_____ 11. To avoid damaging clothes _____.

    A. make sure your deodorant is completely dry before you dress
    B. put jewelry on after your clothes
    C. apply medicated cream, sunscreen, or makeup before you dress
    D. All of the above.

_____ 12. The first step in laundering your clothes is to _____.

    A. add bleach
    B. sort the clothes
    C. read the care labels
    D. add soap

_____ 13. Overloading the dryer can _____.

    A. cause clothes to become wrinkled
    B. add to the drying time
    C. be more efficient than underloading
    D. Both A and B.

☐ Essay Questions: Provide the answers you feel best show your understanding of the subject matter.

14. Describe two garments and explain how you would care for them.

15. Explain why it is important to launder or dry clean garments before storing them.

Part Seven The Place You Call Home

Part goal: Students will learn how homes fulfill needs and how they can help improve their homes through design and cleaning.

Bulletin Board

Title: "The Place You Call Home"

Draw the outline of a house divided into three areas on the board. Divide the class into three groups. Assign each group to one of three topics: "Housing Needs," "Room Arrangement," and "Cleaning." Have each group find and cut out magazine pictures they think represent their topic and arrange them in collage fashion on their sections of the bulletin board. Then write the appropriate label over each section of the board.

Teaching Materials

Text
Chapters 40–42, pages 443–476
Student Activity Guide
Chapters 40–42
Teacher's Resource Guide/Binder
My Home, reproducible master

Introductory Activities

1. *My Home*, reproducible master. Have students answer the questions provided to help them think of their homes in terms of places to fulfill needs, places with personal space, and places that need care. Have students discuss their responses as a class.
2. Have students complete the phrase "Home is . . ." in one sentence. Have students turn in their responses anonymously. Read some of the responses to the class.
3. Invite a person from another culture to discuss what housing is like in his or her culture. If possible, have the guest bring slides of homes in his or her culture.

My Home

Name _____ **Date** _____ **Period** _____

Answer the questions about your home in the space below. Discuss your responses with the class.

How does your home fulfill your physical needs? _____
_____
_____
_____

How does your home fulfill your emotional needs? _____
_____
_____
_____

How does your home fulfill your social needs? _____
_____
_____
_____

If you could have any kind of home, what would it look like? _____
_____
_____
_____

Are you satisfied with your personal space at home? If so, why? If not, how would you change it?
_____
_____
_____
_____
_____

How do you help out with cleaning at home? _____
_____
_____
_____

Which cleaning tasks do you wish were easier for you to do? _____
_____
_____
_____

Do you help conserve energy at home? If so, how? _____
_____
_____
_____

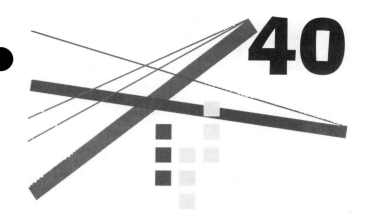

40 The Comforts of Home

Objectives

After studying this chapter, students will be able to
- explain how homes fulfill physical, emotional, and social needs.
- describe four main types of homes.
- list factors involved in choosing, paying for, and changing homes.

Teaching Materials

Text, pages 443–452
Words to Know
Review It
Apply It
Think More About It
Student Activity Guide
A. *Homes Fulfill Needs*
B. *Types of Homes Crossword*
C. *Choosing a Home*
D. *Buying vs. Renting*
E. *Your Dream Home*
Teacher's Resource Guide/Binder
My Personal Journal, reproducible master 40-1
Types of Homes, transparency master 40-2
Home Sweet Home, transparency master 40-3
Home Is Where the Heart Is, color transparency CT-40
Chapter 40 Quiz

Introductory Activities

1. *Home Is Where the Heart Is,* color transparency CT-40. Use this transparency to introduce housing. Discuss various types of housing and the advantages and disadvantages of each.

2. Go around the room and have each student tell what kind of home he or she lives in (house, apartment, condominium, etc.). Discuss the differences among the types of homes.

Strategies to Reteach, Reinforce, Enrich, and Extend Text Concepts

■ Homes Fulfill Needs

3. **ER** *My Personal Journal,* reproducible master 40-1. Students are asked to write about their homes and explain what makes a place a home.
4. **RF** *Homes Fulfill Needs,* Activity A, SAG. Have students list examples of physical, emotional, and social needs met by a home. Students should give examples of each need.
5. **RT** *Home Sweet Home,* transparency master 40-2. Use this transparency on an overhead projector as a basis of discussion and/or review about the needs that housing fulfills. Ask students to name specific needs that a home fulfills as you write them on the transparency.

■ Types of Homes

6. **RT** *Types of Homes,* transparency master 40-3. Use this transparency to illustrate the various types of homes and as a basis of discussion about the advantages and disadvantages of each type.
7. **RF** *Types of Homes Crossword,* Activity B, SAG. Have students complete the statements about types of housing by filling in the appropriate spaces on the puzzle.

8. **ER** Have students collect pictures, drawings, and photographs of a variety of homes. Students should include apartments, duplexes, mobile homes, town houses, freestanding homes, and attached homes. Students should use the drawings to create a bulletin board.

■ Choosing a Home

9. **EX** *Choosing a Home*, Activity C, SAG. Have students pretend they are real estate agents and describe the types of houses they would find for the given clients. Students should discuss their choices in class.

10. **ER** *Your Dream Home*, Activity E, SAG. Have students sketch or mount a picture of their dream home in the space provided. Students should also describe the home and answer the given questions about the home.

■ Paying for a Home

11. **EX** *Buying vs. Renting*, Activity D, SAG. Have students use the form provided to list the pros and cons of buying and renting. Students should then debate the pros and cons as a class. Have students decide which they would rather do.

12. **ER** Have students write a report on renting or buying a home. Students who write on renting should contact a rental agency. They should report information on restrictions, rent costs, and various rental policies. Students who write on buying should contact a real estate agency. They should report on closing costs, monthly payments, taxes, and other responsibilities involved with owning a home.

■ Changing Homes

13. **RF** Have students list advantages and disadvantages of moving to a new home. Students should discuss ways to focus on the positive aspects of moving and lessen the negative feelings that may come with moving.

14. **ER** Invite two families who have moved within the last two years to speak to the class. The families should focus on how they were able to support each other through the move.

Answer Key

■ Text

Review It, page 452
1. shelter
2. (Student response.)
3. (Student response.)
4. The arrangement of furniture makes rooms suited to different types of interaction. For instance, chairs

that are close to each other encourage talking. Chairs that are far apart make talking more difficult. The type of atmosphere affects how people interact. More formal rooms are often used for entertaining guests. More cozy, informal rooms may encourage more intimate conversations.

5. true
6. (Student response.)
7. B
8. (Student response.)
9. Advantages (list one:) homes can be changed fairly easily; renter is not responsible for major repairs; no large down payment is needed. Disadvantages (list one:) lack of control over how the owner cares for the property; may need to wait for owner to have repairs done; may need permission to make changes; time and money spent on changes will be lost if renter moves
10. false

■ Student Activity Guide

Types of Homes Crossword, Activity B

				A	P	A	R	T	M	E	N	T			
T			M			T									
O			U		T	R	I	P	L	E	X				
W			L		A										
N			T		C	O	N	D	O	M	I	N	I	U	M
H			I		H										O
O			F	R	E	E	S	T	A	N	D	I	N	G	B
U			A		D										I
S			M												L
E			I								D	U	P	L	E	X
S	I	N	G	L	E	F	A	M	I	L	Y				
			Y												

■ Teacher's Resource Guide/Binder

Chapter 40 Quiz

1.	F	10.	F
2.	T	11.	T
3.	T	12	G
4.	F	13.	D
5.	F	14.	B
6.	T	15.	E
7.	T	16.	F
8.	F	17.	A
9.	T	18.	C

19. (Student response.)
20. Families need to realize that each member may have some problems adjusting to the move. They need to talk to each other about their feelings and support each other. Families should focus on the fact they still have each other and work together to make their new place as much of a home as their old place was.

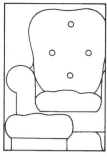

My Personal Journal

Write about your home. What makes a place a home?

_____

_____

_____

_____

_____

_____

_____

_____

_____

_____

_____

_____

_____

_____

_____

_____

_____

_____

_____

_____

_____

_____

_____

_____

_____

Types of Homes

Single Family Homes

Freestanding Home

Attached Homes
(town house or row house)

Mobile Home

Multifamily Homes

High-rise apartment building
or condominiums

Low-rise apartment building
or condominiums

Home Sweet Home

Homes
Fulfill Needs

Physical needs:

Emotional needs:

Social needs:

The Comforts of Home

CHAPTER 40 QUIZ

☐ True/False: Circle *T* if the statement is true or *F* if the statement is false.

T   F   1.   Only adults play a role in keeping a home safe and secure.

T   F   2.   A home does not have to be fancy to satisfy a person's need to belong.

T   F   3.   Having personal space in a home helps fill a person's need for self-confidence.

T   F   4.   The arrangement of a room does not affect how people interact in that room.

T   F   5.   A large area is needed for all forms of recreation.

T   F   6.   All family members need some privacy at home.

T   F   7.   A town house is a single-family home that is attached at the sides to other single-family homes.

T   F   8.   A good guideline for choosing an affordable home is to keep monthly housing costs to about one-half of the family income.

T   F   9.   A person's job affects that person's housing choices.

T   F   10.   People who own their homes cannot change their homes to suit their tastes.

T   F   11.   People who rent homes do not need to take care of major repairs to the rented property.

☐ Matching: Match the following terms with their definitions.

_____ 12. A home that is built for just one family.

_____ 13. A building that stands alone to house just one family.

_____ 14. A home built for just one family that is attached at the sides to other homes built for just one family.

_____ 15. A home that is completely built in a factory.

_____ 16. A home that is built to house more than one family.

_____ 17. A unit in a multifamily home that is rented.

_____ 18. A unit in a multifamily home that is owned.

A. apartment
B. attached home
C. condominium
D. freestanding home
E. mobile home
F. multifamily home
G. single-family home

☐ Essay Questions: Provide the answers you feel best show your understanding of the subject matter.

19. How does a home help you meet your social needs?

20. How can families make adjusting to changing homes easier for each other?

Reproducible Quiz

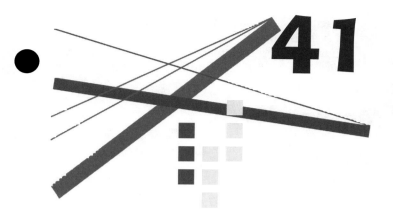

41 Your Personal Space

Objectives

After studying this chapter, students will be able to
- apply the elements and principles of design to the decoration and organization of their personal space.
- use a floor plan to choose a good arrangement for their bedroom furniture.
- discuss tips for sharing a room.

Teaching Materials

Text, pages 453–462
- *Words to Know*
- *Review It*
- *Apply It*
- *Think More About It*

Student Activity Guide
- A. *Decorating Your Room*
- B. *Your Bedroom*

Teacher's Resource Guide/Binder
- *My Personal Journal*, reproducible master 41-1
- *Roommate Rights and Responsibilities*, reproducible master 41-2
- *Dividing a Bedroom*, reproducible master 41-3
- *Coloring Your Personal Space*, color transparency CT-41
- Chapter 41 Quiz

Introductory Activities

1. Have each student make a poster using housing materials to form a color scheme. As a class, have students discuss how the different color schemes would make them feel if the color schemes were used in a bedroom.
2. Have students discuss their personal space at home. Ask if they have their own rooms or if they share with someone else. Ask how they make this space personal.

Strategies to Reteach, Reinforce, Enrich, and Extend Text Concepts

■ Making the Most of Your Room

3. **ER** *My Personal Journal,* reproducible master 41-1. Students are asked to write about their rooms. They are asked what they like most about their rooms and what they would change about their rooms.
4. **RF** Have students look through magazines or catalogs to find pictures of rooms they like. Have each student explain how the elements and principles of design are used in the rooms chosen.
5. **RT** *Coloring Your Personal Space,* color transparency CT-41. Use this transparency as an introduction to how colors can be used to achieve various effects and convey various moods. Have students describe how this information could be used widely in their rooms at home.
6. **ER** Have students visit a hardware store to look at the home decorating supplies. Students should write a description of at least one product they did not know about before their visit. The descriptions should include how the product should be used, cost of the product, and other factors.
7. **ER** Invite an interior designer to speak to your class about different furniture styles. The speaker should bring pictures or models of different types of furniture and discuss how the different styles can be combined attractively in rooms. (The main focus should be on bedroom furniture.)
8. **EX** Have students analyze their storage space at home. Students should list three to five ways they could improve the organization of their storage space. Have volunteers share their ideas for improvement with the class.

9. **ER** Divide the class into small groups. Have the groups develop plans for a do-it-yourself storage unit for a bedroom. Students should describe the materials that would be used, cost of the materials, and time involved in building the unit.

10. **RF** Have students list five ways they could use accessories to personalize their rooms.

11. **RF** *Decorating Your Room*, Activity A, SAG. Have students work through the exercises in the activity to find how they can make the most of their rooms.

■ Putting it all Together

12. **RF** *Your Bedroom*, Activity B, SAG. Have students draw a bedroom on the graph paper provided and then arrange furniture in it using the templates provided. Students should evaluate their arrangements using the questions provided.

13. **EX** Have students brainstorm ways to include a guest area in a bedroom, even if the room is fairly small.

14. **RF** Have students clip pictures of bedrooms designed for teens from magazines or catalogs. Students should try to identify furniture placement that organizes the room into different areas.

15. **RF** As a conversation starter, place your desk so that students must walk around it to get from the classroom door to their desks. Then have students discuss the importance of having good traffic patterns.

■ Sharing a Room

16. **RF** *Roommate Rights and Responsibilities*, reproducible master 41-2. Students are asked to pretend they will be acquiring a roommate and to indicate what they believe are the rights and responsibilities of roommates. They can share and compare their responses with the class.

17. **ER** Have students write an essay on what privacy means to them and how they find privacy at home. Students should also write about times when they do not have enough privacy.

18. **EX** Divide the class into two groups. Have one group make up questions about problems that two people who share a room might have. They should write the questions as if they are writing to an advice columnist. Have the other group write replies to the questions. Read the questions and answers aloud and have the class discuss them.

19. **RF** *Dividing a Bedroom*, reproducible master 41-3. Have students determine ways to divide a bedroom using the floor plan and templates

provided. Students should cut out the templates and try arranging them in different ways on the floor plan. Students may draw in other items that are not provided as templates.

Answer Key

■ Text

Review It, page 462
1. true
2. (Student response.)
3. B
4. (List three:) whether or not the furniture meets the buyer's needs; whether or not the buyer likes the style and appearance; quality; sturdiness; whether or not furniture is flawed or scratched; price
5. (Student response.)
6. accessories
7. Measure the dimensions of the room; draw the outline of the room to scale on paper; mark the location of doors, windows, heating vents, and electrical outlets.
8. (Student response.)
9. false
10. (List four:) book cases, shelves, folding screens, curtains, rolling shades, desks, plants (Students may justify other responses.)

■ Teacher's Resource Guide/Binder

Chapter 41 Quiz

1.	F	10.	F
2.	F	11.	T
3.	F	12.	C
4.	T	13.	B
5.	F	14.	A
6.	T	15.	E
7.	F	16.	F
8.	T	17.	D
9.	T		

18. (Student response.)
19. (List three:) only replace pieces that need to be replaced; use paint or new accessories to change the appearance of furniture; shop at garage sales, flea markets, or used furniture stores; find furniture through newspaper classified ads; buy inexpensive types of furniture such as director's chairs; buy flawed furniture that is reduced in price
20. (List two:) mount two rods, one under the other, for hanging clothes; mount hooks on closet walls; hang a shoe bag on the wall or door; add shelves, boxes, or closet organizing units to the closet

My Personal Journal

Write about your room. What do you like most about it? What would you change?

_____

_____

_____

_____

_____

_____

_____

_____

_____

_____

_____

_____

_____

_____

_____

_____

_____

_____

_____

_____

_____

_____

_____

_____

Roommate Rights and Responsibilities

Name _____ **Date** _____ **Period**

Pretend you will be acquiring a roommate. In the spaces below, indicate what you think are the rights and responsibilities of roommates. Share and compare your responses with the class.

Roommate Rights:

_____

_____

_____

_____

_____

_____

_____

_____

_____

_____

_____

_____

_____

Roommate Responsibilities:

_____

_____

_____

_____

_____

_____

_____

_____

_____

_____

_____

_____

Dividing a Bedroom

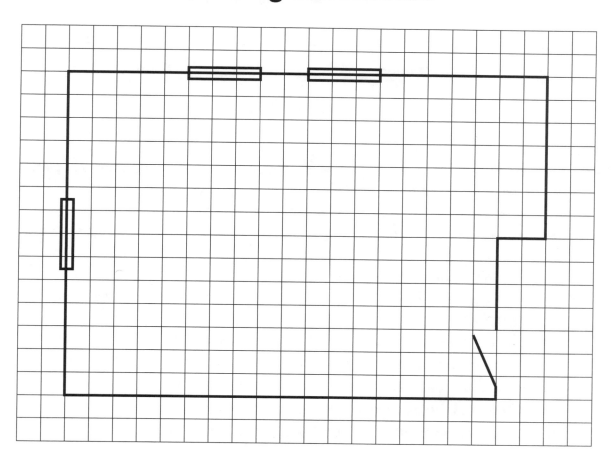

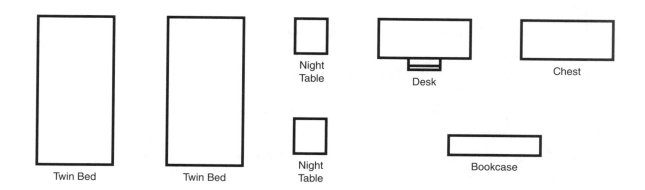

Twin Bed Twin Bed Night Table Desk Chest Night Table Bookcase

Your Personal Space

Name _____

Date _____ **Period** _____ **Score** _____

CHAPTER 41 QUIZ

☐ True/False: Circle *T* if the statement is true or *F* if the statement is false.

T F 1. You should not worry about how much money you can spend when you plan changes for your room.

T F 2. Cool, pale colors make a room seem more exciting.

T F 3. Using many different colors in your room is one way to achieve rhythm in the room's design.

T F 4. Painting is one of the least expensive, easiest ways to change your walls.

T F 5. To change the appearance of a room, all the furniture will most likely need to be replaced.

T F 6. Items that are used often should be stored where they can be easily reached.

T F 7. Bedroom storage should be limited to closets and drawers.

T F 8. Patterned sheets can be used as curtains in bedrooms.

T F 9. A floor plan can be used to help you find the best arrangement for furniture in a room.

T F 10. Since roommates share a room, they do not need to allow each other time alone in the room.

T F 11. Roommates do not need to agree on all the accessories used in their room.

☐ Matching: Match the following terms with their definitions.

_____ 12. The area of a home that belongs more to you than to anyone else in your home.

_____ 13. Areas of a room that set the stage for the room's furnishings and accessories.

_____ 14. The accents that make a room more attractive, comfortable, and convenient.

_____ 15. A drawing that shows the size and shape of a room.

_____ 16. The paths people take to get to different parts of a room.

_____ 17. Having time alone and personal belongings.

A. accessories
B. backgrounds
C. personal space
D. privacy
E. scale floor plan
F. traffic patterns

☐ Essay Questions: Provide the answers you feel best show your understanding of the subject matter.

18. Explain how the elements and principles of design can be used to give harmony to a room's design.

19. Give three ways to save money on furniture for a bedroom.

20. Give two ways to increase the amount of usable space in a closet.

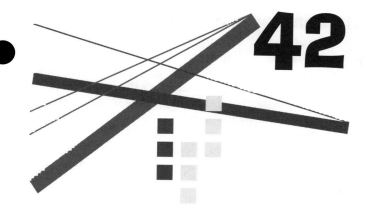

42 Keeping Your Home Clean and Safe

Objectives

After studying this chapter, students will be able to
- plan a cleaning schedule for their families or for themselves.
- help choose, organize, and use cleaning supplies that are appropriate for their homes.
- describe ways to make their homes safe.
- help conserve resources in their homes.

Teaching Materials

Text, pages 403–476
Words to Know
Review It
Apply It
Think More About It
Student Activity Guide
A. *Cleaning Agents and Equipment*
B. *Comparing Cleaning Products*
C. *Cleaning the House*
D. *Protecting Your Home from Fire*
Teacher's Resource Guide/Binder
My Personal Journal, reproducible master 42-1
The Safe Home, transparency master 42-2
Energy Conservation, transparency master 42-3
Conserving Energy in the Home, color transparency CT-42
Chapter 42 Quiz

Introductory Activities

1. Have students complete the following sentence: "A clean house is . . ." Discuss how important living in a clean house is to students.
2. *Conserving Energy in the Home*, color transparency CT-42. Ask students to identify ways to save energy in each room of the home. Write their responses in the rooms illustrated on the transparency.

Strategies to Reteach, Reinforce, Enrich, and Extend Text Concepts

■ A Cleaning Schedule

3. **ER** *My Personal Journal,* reproducible master 42-1. Students are asked to write about tasks they do to keep their homes clean and safe. They are also asked whether they believe they do their share of the housework.
4. **EX** Have students role-play a situation in which family members are trying to agree on cleaning standards. Some family members should want things to be extremely neat, and others should not care about mess. Have the class discuss the role-play when it is finished.
5. **ER** Have students list cleaning tasks they dislike and cleaning tasks they don't mind doing. Have students compare their lists and find tasks that most students dislike or don't mind. Students should discuss why they might sometimes have to do tasks they dislike. Students should also discuss ways to make the disliked tasks seem more tolerable.
6. **RF** Have students ask a parent with a small child what chores they assign to the child. Students should share their findings with the class.
7. **RF** Have each student write a personal cleaning schedule and try it at home for a few weeks. Have students discuss as a class how the schedules worked.

■ Getting Ready to Clean

8. **RF** *Cleaning Agents and Equipment*, Activity A, SAG. Have students match the cleaning agents and equipment listed with the appropriate purposes.

9. **ER** *Comparing Cleaning Products*, Activity B, SAG. Have students select two brands of cleaning products designed to do the same cleaning job, or select cleaning products to assign to students for comparison. Then have students compare the products using the chart provided. Students should present their results to the class.

10. **RF** Have students bring a cleaning tool to class or borrow one from the family and consumer sciences department. Students should demonstrate how to use the tool, including any special features that might be helpful.

11. **EX** Divide the class into groups of three or four. Have students brainstorm to create a cleaning product that is not on the market. Students should report to the class on the type of product they developed and try to "sell" the class on the product.

12. **ER** Have students plan a cleaning kit to be used in the home. Students should write a report on why each item is included in the kit and on the cost of each item.

■ Doing the Cleaning

13. **ER** Have students experiment with using different cleaning methods to remove different kinds of dirt. Students should keep records of the types of dirt tested, the methods used to clean up the dirt, and the effectiveness of the methods. For adhesive dirt, students may try cleaning adhesive dirt that has been left for one hour, two hours, five hours, one day, etc.

14. **ER** Invite a local commercial cleaning representative to discuss time and energy saving techniques used in their business. Students should note how these techniques could be adapted to home cleaning. Students should also compare commercial cleaning agents and equipment to home products.

15. **ER** Have students interview one to three adults to find out what methods they use to make home care easier. Students should report their results in class and discuss the ideas presented.

16. **RF** *Cleaning the House*, Activity C, SAG. Have students use the chart provided to plan how they would clean various areas of the house. Students should discuss their plans in class.

■ Safety in the Home

17. **ER** *Protecting Your Home from Fire*, Activity D, SAG. Have students interview a firefighter on how to protect a home from fire. Students should use information from the interview to write an article giving fire safety tips and precautions.

18. **RT** *The Safe Home*, transparency master 42-2. Review the safety precautions listed with the class. Have students discuss why each precaution is important. Have students list other steps that can be taken to keep a home safe and secure.

■ Conserving Resources

19. Have students research different heating methods for the home and write a short report on their findings.

20. *Energy Conservation*, transparency master 42-3. Have the class discuss each of the tips suggested on the chart. Have students suggest other ways of saving energy in the home.

21. Have students use their creativity to produce a bulletin board titled "Reducing Waste Products."

Answer Key

■ Text

Review It, page 476
1. true
2. Rotating jobs prevents family members from always getting stuck with cleaning jobs they don't like. It also helps assure that people spend equal amounts of time and effort on cleaning. This way, family members are less likely to resent doing unwanted jobs.
3. false
4. A
5. manufacturer's directions
6. Loose dirt is dry and does not bind to surfaces; using mainly dry methods of cleaning loose dirt works best. Adhesive dirt sticks to surfaces; scrubbing with water and mild detergent or a special cleaner works best for cleaning.
7. (Student response.)
8. adhesive
9. (List two:) pollution, space, expense
10. true

■ Student Activity Guide

Cleaning Agents and Equipment, Activity A

1. D	5. L	9. C	13. M
2. I	6. O	10. K	14. F
3. B	7. A	11. G	15. H
4. E	8. N	12. J	

■ Teacher's Resource Guide/Binder

Chapter 42 Quiz

1. F	5. T	9. T	13. G
2. F	6. F	10. D	14. A
3. T	7. F	11. B	15. F
4. T	8. T	12. C	16. E

17. Use mainly dry methods. A good method would be to sweep most of the dirt into a dust pan. When as much has been removed by sweeping as possible, a slightly damp cloth can be used to pick up the rest.
18. (Student response.)

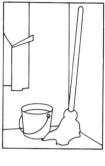

My Personal Journal

Write about tasks you do to keep your home clean and safe. Do you believe you do your share? Why?

_____

_____

_____

_____

_____

_____

_____

_____

_____

_____

_____

_____

_____

_____

_____

_____

_____

_____

_____

_____

_____

_____

_____

_____

The Safe Home

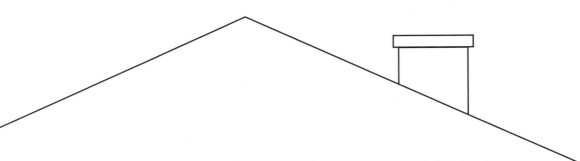

Preventing Falls

- Put all objects in their proper storage places when they are not being used.
- Do not leave any objects on stairs.
- Make sure stair steps are skid-proof. (If steps are carpeted, make sure carpet is secure.)
- Use rugs with nonskid backing.
- Place night lights in hallways and bathrooms.
- Place nonskid strips in bathtubs and on shower floors.
- Make sure outdoor walkways are clear. Keep them free of snow and ice in the winter.

Preventing Electrical Problems

- Make sure electrical cords are not frayed or cracked.
- Do not place cords where people may walk or trip over them. (Do not run cords under rugs.)
- Keep appliances away from bathtubs, showers, and sinks.
- Unplug and properly store electrical appliances when they are not in use.
- Cover unused electrical outlets, especially if there are young children in the family.

Preventing Fires

- Keep working smoke detectors in bedrooms, hallways, and attics.
- Keep a fire extinguisher in the kitchen. Learn how to use it.
- Store matches where children cannot reach them.
- Store oily rags in covered, metal containers.

Handling Home Security

- When you leave the house, check that all doors and windows are closed and locked.
- If you come home and find an opened door or broken window, don't go inside. Go to a neighbor's home and call your parents. If you can't reach them, then call the police. The police will check the house for you.
- If a stranger calls or comes to the door, don't tell the person you are home alone. Tell the person your parents are busy and can't come to the phone or door.

Handling Home Emergencies

- Keep emergency numbers next to the telephone.
- Plan fire escape routes. Practice using them.
- Learn safety procedures for emergencies such as tornadoes, hurricanes, storms, and earthquakes. Find out where the safest places in the home are during emergencies.

Energy Conservation

- Keep the furnace thermostat set at 65°F in winter and 78°F in summer.

- Adjust curtains or shades to prevent or allow sunlight to enter a room.

- Keep unused rooms cut off from heat or air conditioning by closing ducts and keeping doors closed.

- Securely shut doors and windows when heat or air conditioning is in use.

- Turn off lights in vacant rooms or when leaving a room.

- Keep the refrigerator clean. Avoid leaving the door open for any length of time and close it tightly.

- When cooking, use pans with tight-fitting lids and flat bottoms that fit the surface unit.

- Run dishwasher and laundry machine with full loads. Air-dry dishes or line-dry clothes when possible.

- Use water wisely. Take short showers. Use small amounts of water for baths and brushing teeth.

- Shut off faucet completely when finished.

- Repair leaky faucets.

- Keep all household appliances clean. Turn off irons, electric dryers, ovens, etc., when finished using.

- Use heat-drawing appliances wisely. For example, iron a full load of clothes at one time or cook several items in the oven at one time.

- Arrange drapes and furniture so they do not cover heat registers.

- Weatherstrip (place narrow plastic, fiber, or metal strips around the doors and windows) to prevent air leaks.

- When not using the fireplace, keep the damper closed to prevent outside air from entering the house.

Keeping Your Home Clean and Safe

Name _____

Date _____ **Period** _____ **Score** _____

CHAPTER 42 QUIZ

☐ True/False: Circle *T* if the statement is true or *F* if the statement is false.

T F 1. All members of the same family usually have the same cleaning standards.

T F 2. For most families, cleaning out closets is a weekly cleaning job.

T F 3. Ability and schedules should be considered when assigning cleaning jobs to family members.

T F 4. Cleaning together is more enjoyable when people have positive, helpful attitudes.

T F 5. A used cloth should be cleaned before it is used again for cleaning.

T F 6. Although dirt looks unpleasant, it never carries germs.

T F 7. Liquid spills should be allowed to dry before they are cleaned up.

T F 8. The best way to help keep the bathroom sanitary is to have family members clean up after themselves whenever they use the bathroom.

T F 9. Dirt can reduce the efficiency of many appliances.

☐ Matching: Match the following terms with their definitions.

_____ 10. A plan for organizing work.

_____ 11. Waste from man-made products that makes the environment unclean.

_____ 12. A chemical that is used to clean household surfaces.

_____ 13. Dust, crumbs, and other dry particles that are not bound to a surface.

_____ 14. Substances such as food and drinks that stick to surfaces.

_____ 15. An agent that kills germs and makes surfaces look nicer.

_____ 16. To use as little energy as possible to get a job done.

A. adhesive dirt
B. pollution
C. cleaning agent
D. cleaning schedule
E. conserve
F. disinfectant cleaner
G. loose dirt

☐ Essay Questions: Provide the answers you feel best show your understanding of the subject matter.

17. Describe how to remove a lot of loose dirt from a smooth surface.

18. List five ways to help conserve resources in the home.

Part Eight

Reaching New Heights

Part goal: Students will be able to develop leadership, teamwork, and job skills and will become acquainted with various careers in family and consumer sciences.

Bulletin Board

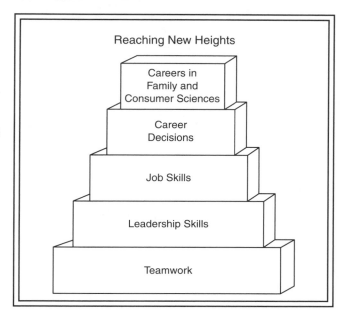

Title: "Reaching New Heights"

Using construction paper, cut out building blocks of various sizes. Label them as shown above. Ask students to discuss how each of these building blocks can lead to a successful career.

Teaching Materials

Text
Chapters 43–47, pages 447–528
Student Activity Guide
Chapters 43–47
Teacher's Resource Guide/Binder
Career Priorities, reproducible master

Introductory Activities

1. Have students complete the following statements: "The qualities I admire most in a leader are . . ." "The qualities I dislike most in a leader are . . ."
2. *Career Priorities*, reproducible master. Students are asked to consider various aspects about a career and indicate their opinions about each aspect. They are then asked to rank the aspects in order of importance to them.
3. Have students complete the following statement: "The ideal career for me would be . . ."
4. Team up with a guidance counselor to host an Education/Career Fair at your school. Invite representatives from various colleges, trade schools, vocational schools, etc. to be available to answer students' questions. Also invite people from various types of careers to talk with students about their careers and answer any questions students may have.

Career Priorities

Name _____ **Date** _____ **Period** _____

Consider various aspects about a career and indicate your opinions about each aspect. Then rank the aspects in order of importance to you. (There are no right or wrong answers.)

Aspects of a career	Very important	Somewhat important	Not important	I don't know	Rank
A variety of responsibilities					
Having a regular routine					
Like the type of work					
Nice surroundings					
A high salary					
Good benefits					
The chance to be creative					
Friendly coworkers					
A chance to help others					
Job security					
Traveling					
Making decisions					
Independence					
Leading others					
Being outdoors					
Others:					

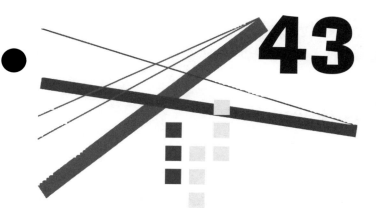

43 Working with a Group

Objectives

After studying this chapter, students will be able to
- describe the characteristics of a good leader.
- discuss opportunities for leadership.
- describe ways to reach group goals.
- describe characteristics of effective group members.
- explain what it means to be a good citizen.
- explain parliamentary procedure.

Teaching Materials

Text, pages 478–487
Words to Know
Review It
Apply It
Think More About It
Student Activity Guide
A. *Leaders and Group Members*
B. *Participating in Meetings*
Teacher's Resource Guide/Binder
A Good Leader, transparency master 43-1
My Personal Journal, reproducible master 43-2
Parliamentary Procedure, transparency master 43-3
Chapter 43 Quiz

Introductory Activities

1. Ask students to make a list of groups to which they belong. How do they demonstrate leadership abilities in these groups?
2. Ask students to define *citizen* and have them give examples of citizenship.

Strategies to Reteach, Reinforce, Enrich, and Extend Text Concepts

■ Being a Good Leader

3. **ER** Ask students to identify a leader they admire. Ask them to write a report describing the qualities that make this person a good leader.
4. **RF** *Leaders and Group Members*, Activity A, SAG. Students are asked to read statements that describe leaders and group members. They are to place a check near descriptions of positive qualities of leaders and group members.
5. **EX** Have students take turns role-playing various leadership situations. Ask other students to evaluate how the leaders handled the situations.
6. **ER** Invite employers to class to discuss with students the importance of developing leadership skills.
7. **ER** Have students interview an adult in a leadership role (president of a civic club, the PTA president, religious leader, sports coach, etc.). Have students give a report on this person's ideas about what skills are needed for effective leadership.
8. **RF** Have students write an essay on how developing leadership skills could help them now and in the future.

■ Opportunities for Leadership

9. **ER** Invite a panel of leaders of various clubs at school to speak to the class. Have each person outline the purpose of his or her club and discuss

committees, money-making functions, club meetings, etc.

10. **ER** Ask students to choose a school or community club to which they belong or to which they would like to belong. Ask them to prepare a report about the organization and describe opportunities for leadership within the organization.

11. **RT** *A Good Leader,* transparency master 43-1. Use this transparency to review the qualities of a good leader. Using an overhead projector, jot down examples of how leaders demonstrate these qualities.

■ Being a Part of a Group

12. **ER** Ask students to design posters to encourage membership in various school clubs to which they belong.

13. **ER** *My Personal Journal,* reproducible master 43-2. Students are asked to write about working in a group at school or in their community. They are asked whether they were a group leader or member and whether the group reached its goals and why.

14. **RF** Ask students to list characteristics of good group members versus bad group members.

15. **ER** Have students survey student or community leaders about what makes a good group member. Ask students to write a report about their findings.

16. **RT** Have students complete the following statement: "A good group member is someone who . . ."

■ Being a Good Citizen

17. **ER** Have students write a report on the following topic: "What Does It Mean to Be a Good Citizen?"

18. **ER** Have students interview a community official on what citizenship means to that person.

■ Participating in Business Meetings

19. **ER** Ask students to obtain permission to attend a school or community meeting. Have them observe how the meeting was conducted. Ask them to share their impressions about how the meeting was conducted.

20. **RT** *Parliamentary Procedure,* transparency master 43-3. Use this transparency master as a basis of discussion about parliamentary procedure. Have students conduct a mock meeting using the sample agenda.

21. **RF** *Participating in Meetings,* Activity B, SAG. Students are asked to match terms related to parliamentary procedure with their descriptions. Then they are asked to unscramble the order of business for a meeting by numbering the statements in the correct order for parliamentary procedure.

22. **ER** As a class, obtain permission to sit in on a governmental meeting such as a city council meeting or a state legislative session. Have students record their observations and discuss them in class.

Answer Key

■ Text

Review It, page 487
1. (Student response.)
2. Being a leader as a teenager will help a person assume family, religious, and community leadership roles as an adult. Using leadership skills will also help a person advance in his or her career as an adult. Understanding leadership skills will help people work better in groups.
3. (List five:) understanding the goals of the group, motivating group members to work toward group goals, setting an example for group members, problem solving, managing group resources, involving members in the activities of the group, working with committees, knowing your limitations as a leader
4. The problem should be discussed with only those concerned.
5. At school—(List four:) vocational organizations, student government, school clubs, sports teams, group projects, and committees (Students may justify other responses.)
   Away from school—(List two:) community groups, religious organizations (Students may justify other responses.)
6. Leadership experience helps you realize how much members do in a group. You can sympathize with the problems of leadership. You also know the importance of cooperation.
7. citizen
8. (Student response.)
9. parliamentary procedure
10. false
11. A standing committee is a permanent committee. A special committee is formed for one purpose only. When the purpose has been served, the special committee is disbanded.
12. C

■ Student Activity Guide

Leaders and Group Members, Activity A
A good leader: (The following numbers should be checked:) 1, 2, 4, 6, 7, 9, 10, 12, 14, 16, 17, 18. A good follower: (The following numbers should be checked:) 2, 3, 4, 6, 10.
Participating in Meetings, Activity B
1. D   3. I
2. G   4. C

5. J   9. A

6. E   10. K

7. F   11. B

8. H   12. L

Statements should be numbered as follows: a. 9. b. 1. c. 4. d. 3. e. 6. f. 12. g. 10. h. 5. i. 2. j. 7. k. 11. l. 8.

■ Teacher's Resource Guide/Binder

Chapter 43 Quiz

1. F   3. T

2. T   4. T

5. F   12. B

6. F   13. J

7. T   14. A

8. F   15. G

9. D   16. H

10. I   17. E

11. C   18. F

19. (Student response.)

20. It will help you take a more active role in meetings.

A Good Leader

- Understands goals

- Motivates the group

- Sets an example

- Is a problem-solver

- Manages the group's resources

- Involves members

- Works well with committees

- Knows his or her limitations

My Personal Journal

Write about working in a group at school or in your community. Were you a group leader or a group member? Did the group reach its goals? Why?

Parliamentary Procedure

As You Conduct Meetings, Follow These Steps

1. Call to Order

2. Reading and Approving of Minutes

3. Reports of Officers

4. Standing Committee Reports

5. Special Committee Reports

6. Unfinished Business

7. New Business

8. The Program

9. Announcements

10. Adjournment

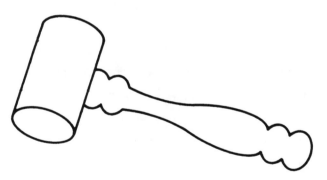

Working with a Group

Name _____

Date _____ Period _____ Score _____

CHAPTER 43 QUIZ

☐ True/False: Circle *T* if the statement is true or *F* if the statement is false.

T   F   1. Most groups are motivated more by commands than by persuasion.

T   F   2. Leaders have the responsibility of setting a good example for group members.

T   F   3. Vocational organizations are clubs that help students develop leadership skills and prepare to work in certain occupational areas.

T   F   4. To accomplish its goals, the group needs contributions from each member.

T   F   5. It is not necessary for group members to understand parliamentary procedure.

T   F   6. According to parliamentary procedure, new business is discussed before the reading and approval of the minutes.

T   F   7. Someone must second a motion before it can be discussed.

T   F   8. Before the decision on one motion has been made, someone can make a motion on another topic.

☐ Matching: Match the following terms with their definitions.

_____   9. A member of a community.

_____   10. Feeling the need or desire to do something.

_____   11. Working together as a team to reach goals.

_____   12. A group of people who work together for a special purpose.

_____   13. A fair and orderly way for leaders to conduct meetings.

_____   14. A schedule of what will take place at a meeting.

_____   15. A record of what takes place at a meeting.

_____   16. A suggestion for the group to take action.

_____   17. More than half of the members.

_____   18. Less than half of the members.

A. agenda
B. committee
C. cooperation
D. citizen
E. majority
F. minority
G. minutes
H. motion
 I. motivation
J. parliamentary procedure

☐ Essay Questions: Provide the answers you feel best show your understanding of the subject matter.

19. List leadership opportunities you might have at school and in your community.

20. Explain how understanding parliamentary procedure can help you.

Reproducible Quiz

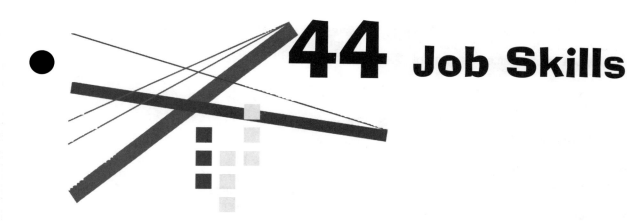

44 Job Skills

Objectives

After studying this chapter, students will be able to
■ list qualities of a good employee.
■ describe skills needed for employment.
■ explain how to apply and interview for a job.

Teaching Materials

Text, pages 488–497
   Words to Know
   Review It
   Apply It
   Think More About It
Student Activity Guide
   A. *Qualities of a Good Employee*
   B. *Finding a Job*
   C. *Personal Fact Sheet*
   D. *Job Interview*
Teacher's Resource Guide/Binder
   School and Work, transparency master 44-1
   My Personal Journal, reproducible master 44-2
   A Matter of Skill, reproducible master 44-3
   Chapter 44 Quiz

Introductory Activities

1. *School and Work*, transparency master 44-1. Use this transparency master as a basis of discussion about how school and work are similar.
2. Ask students who have jobs to describe to the class the types of skills they must have to perform their jobs effectively.

Strategies to Reteach, Reinforce, Enrich, and Extend Text Concepts

■ Qualities of a Good Employee

3. **ER** *Qualities of a Good Employee*, Activity A, SAG. Students are asked to invite a panel of employers to class or to interview some employees. They are asked to find out about various qualities related to being a good employee such as being cooperative, a hard worker, dependable, trustworthy, having a positive attitude, respecting others, handling criticism, having good grooming habits, having good reading and math skills, and using good organizational skills. The responses can be discussed in class.
4. **RF** Divide the class into small groups. Have students pretend they are employers. Ask them to prepare a list of qualities they would expect an employee to have. Have each group share its list with the class.

■ Skills Needed for Employment

5. **ER** *My Personal Journal,* reproducible master 44-2. Students are asked to write about what they believe are their job skills and which ones they would like to develop. Then they are asked "If you were an employer, would you hire you?"
6. **RF** Have students demonstrate various job-related math skills such as counting back change to a customer, figuring sales tax, taking inventory of objects, etc. Discuss the importance of learning basic math skills.

7. **EX** Have students role-play situations in which they would use communication skills on the job. Examples might include a babysitter, restaurant server, or salesperson.
8. **ER** As a class project, plan a Career Day. Have students identify careers of greatest interest to them. Contact speakers in the community. Send them a name badge with an I.D. ribbon, letter of welcome, map of the school, and list of questions prepared by the students concerning job skills. You may want to videotape the speakers for use in future classes.
9. **RT** *A Matter of Skill,* reproducible master 44-3. Students are asked to identify a job they would like to have. They are then asked to explain why they would need various skills.

■ Finding a Job

10. **ER** Have students interview someone who is in charge of hiring people. Have students ask the person what takes place during a typical interview. Have students prepare a report based on the interviews.
11. **EX** Brainstorm the following topics: A. what employers should expect from employees B. what employees should expect from employers C. reasons people get fired D. reasons people get promoted E. what to do on a job when there is nothing to do
12. **RF** List a dozen ways to lose a job. For each way listed, suggest a means for improving the situation.
13. **ER** *Finding a Job,* Activity B, SAG. Students are asked to write an article about how someone their age can find and keep a job. Students may want to submit their articles to the school newspaper or to a community newspaper for publication.
14. **RF** *Personal Fact Sheet,* Activity C, SAG. Students are asked to complete a job information sheet. This will be useful to students as they fill out job applications now and in the future.
15. **EX** *Job Interview,* Activity D, SAG. Students are asked to pretend they are on a job interview. They

are asked to respond to questions an interviewer might ask. Responses can be discussed in class.

Answer Key

■ Text

Review It, page 497
1. (Student response.)
2. (Give two guidelines:) Be tactful, avoid hurting feelings, start by saying something positive. (Students may justify other responses.)
3. (Student response. Suggested answers might include giving directions; grading papers; writing tests; listening to students, parents, and administrators; and writing notes to parents.
4. (List three:) cashier, bank teller, chemist, airline pilot (Students may justify other responses.)
5. (Student response. Suggested answers might include typing, filing, computer skills, telephone skills, and knowledge of office machinery.)
6. (List one:) to get work experience, to learn to get along with others, to earn some extra money, to learn about job responsibilities (Students may justify other responses.)
7. (Give three sources:) friends, neighbors, family members, newspaper want ads, places of business, Internet
8. references
9. B

■ Teacher's Resource Guide/Binder

Chapter 44 Quiz

1.	F	8.	T
2.	F	9.	T
3.	T	10.	T
4.	T	11.	B
5.	T	12.	D
6.	F	13.	C
7.	T		

14. (Student response.)
15. (Student response.)

School and Work

School and work are similar because

- eight hours a day are spent at both school and work

- both school and work require cooperation, courtesy, and resourcefulness

- honors, recognition, and promotion result from hard work in both places

- students who get along with their teachers usually get along with their bosses later in life

- students who do not cheat are preparing to resist corruption on the job

- adapting to new situations at school prepares students to adjust to changes at work

- accepting directions from teachers and employers helps a person succeed

My Personal Journal

Write about what you believe are your job skills. Which job skills would you like to develop? If you were an employer, would you hire you?

_____

_____

_____

_____

_____

_____

_____

_____

_____

_____

_____

_____

_____

_____

_____

_____

_____

_____

_____

_____

_____

_____

_____

A Matter of Skill

Name _____ **Date** _____ **Period**

Identify a job you would like to have. Explain why you would need the following skills. Then list specific skills you would need for the job and explain why you would need them.

Communication skills

_____

_____

_____

_____

Reading skills

_____

_____

_____

_____

Math skills

_____

_____

_____

_____

Organizational skills

_____

_____

_____

_____

Other specific skills

_____

_____

_____

_____

Job Skills

Name _____

Date _____ **Period** _____ **Score** _____

CHAPTER 44 QUIZ

☐ True/False: Circle *T* if the statement is true or *F* if the statement is false.

T F 1. People who cooperate are upset when they do not get their own way.

T F 2. Criticism is useless in helping you improve your work skills.

T F 3. Well-groomed workers are clean and wear clean clothes that are suitable for the job.

T F 4. Organizational skills are needed for every type of job.

T F 5. If you are under the age of 16, you will need to apply for a work permit.

T F 6. Neatness is not important when filling out a job application.

T F 7. Your personal fact sheet should include your social security number.

T F 8. Teachers, coaches, and former employers often make good references.

T F 9. Before going on a job interview, it is a good idea to learn as much about the company as you can.

T F 10. People often apply for several jobs before receiving a job offer.

☐ Multiple Choice: Choose the best answer and write the corresponding letter in the blank.

_____ 11. Which of the following is *not* a quality of a good employee?

A. Being punctual.
B. Having a negative attitude.
C. Being trustworthy.
D. Showing respect for others.

_____ 12. Which of the following people need to have good communication skills?

A. Babysitter.
B. Waiter or waitress.
C. Salesperson.
D. All of the above.

_____ 13. When you go on a job interview, _____.

A. arrive a few minutes after your appointment
B. wear jeans and a T-shirt
C. answer questions truthfully and with enthusiasm
D. let the interviewer know you are nervous

☐ Essay Questions: Provide the answers you feel best show your understanding of the subject matter.

14. Name a job. Then list four qualities or skills you have that would make you a good employee.

15. List six items of information you would include on your own personal fact sheet.

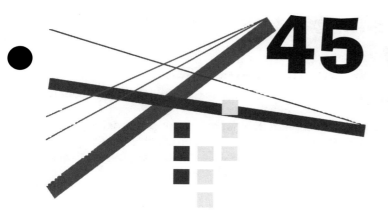

45 Career Decisions

Objectives

After studying this chapter, students will be able to
- list sources of career information.
- describe how interests, aptitudes, and abilities can help them choose careers.
- explain how their careers can affect their lifestyles.

Teaching Materials

Text, pages 498–506
- *Words to Know*
- *Review It*
- *Apply It*
- *Think More About It*

Student Activity Guide
- A. *Your Interests, Aptitudes, and Abilities*
- B. *Your Future Career*

Teachers' Resource Guide/Binder
- *Occupational Areas of Interest*, reproducible master 45-1
- *My Personal Journal*, reproducible master 45-2
- *A Career Plan*, reproducible master 45-3
- Chapter 45 Quiz

Introductory Activities

1. Ask students if they have given any thought to a career. Have them discuss any interests they might have.
2. *Occupational Areas of Interest*, reproducible master 45-1. Use this handout sheet as a basis of discussion about various types of occupations. Ask students to identify occupational areas of interest to them and name careers in these areas.

Strategies to Reteach, Reinforce, Enrich, and Extend Text Concepts

■ An Occupation or a Career?

3. **ER** Have students interview several adults about what they like best and least about working. If possible, have them tape the interviews. Students should be prepared to discuss the interviews in class.
4. **ER** Have students survey people to discover reasons they work at their particular jobs and the level of satisfaction they receive from their work. Ask students to prepare a report about the survey results.

■ Sources of Career Information

5. **ER** Ask a school guidance counselor to speak to your class about the materials available in the guidance department related to career decisions.
6. **RF** Have students outline the procedure they will follow as they research their career choices.
7. **ER** Have students research a specific job using guidance materials, library materials, and interviews. Ask them to prepare a report including information on education or training needed, duties, working conditions, special requirements, and pay.

■ Interests, Aptitudes, and Abilities

8. **ER** *My Personal Journal*, reproducible master 45-2. Students are asked to write about their future careers. They are asked how their interests, aptitudes, and abilities might contribute to their success in this career.

9. **RT** Have students distinguish between interests, aptitudes, and abilities. Ask them to explain how these relate to career success and satisfaction.

10. **EX** *Your Interests, Aptitudes, and Abilities*, Activity A, SAG. Students are asked to check statements about interests, aptitudes, and abilities that describe them. After analyzing their responses, they are asked to list four careers they feel might be right for them.

11. **ER** Ask a guidance counselor to administer an aptitude test to the class. Ask the counselor to relate each student's aptitudes to suitable occupations.

■ Training and Education for Your Career

12. **ER** Invite a panel of speakers from several types of careers to discuss the influence of school upon career preparation. Have students prepare a list of questions in advance.

13. **ER** If possible, have students spend a day or part of a day at work with a parent, adult friend, or Rotary Club member. (This could be arranged during times such as spring break, teacher's institute days, etc.) Ask students to report on the roles of the people they observed, working conditions, etc. Have students give reasons they would or would not select that particular career.

14. **ER** Have students contact a company that has a training or apprenticeship program for new employees. Ask students to interview the personnel manager about program requirements.

■ Careers Affect Lifestyles

15. **EX** Ask students to brainstorm about what they think the lifestyles of each of the following people would be like:
   A. factory worker
   B. doctor
   C. teacher
   D. lawyer
   E. store manager
   F. food service worker
   G. editor
   H. artist
   I. accountant
   J. construction worker
   (Others may be added.)

16. **ER** Invite a panel of people with various careers to class to describe how their careers have influenced their lifestyles.

■ Careers of the Future

17. **EX** *Your Future Career*, Activity B, SAG. Students are asked to pretend that it is 20 years from now and to describe their careers and lifestyles.

They are then asked about how they prepared for their careers.

■ Making a Career Plan

18. **ER** Have students interview a professional about how he or she prepared a career plan. Have students ask if they found career plans helpful.

19. **RF** *A Career Plan*, reproducible master 45-3. Students are asked to write a career plan, detailing how they could reach their career goal.

Answer Key

■ Text

Review It, page 506
1. (List three:) gardening, cutting the grass, trimming the bushes, washing windows (Students may justify other responses.)
2. false
3. (List three:) guidance counselors, libraries, friends, neighbors, relatives, people in the community, Internet
4. to find out what qualities are needed to work in specific jobs related to a certain area of interest
5. You are likely to succeed in a career for which you have aptitude. Such a career would involve skills that are easy for you to learn.
6. abilities
7. A
8. formal classes and on-the-job training
9. (List four:) where you live, who your friends are, how much money you have and how you can spend it, your working hours, your leisure time, when you can take vacations, how much time you have to spend with your family
10. Some types of jobs are available in only certain areas.
11. career plan

■ Teacher's Resource Guide/Binder

Chapter 45 Quiz

1. T		10. T
2. F		11. F
3. T		12. H
4. T		13. D
5. T		14. G
6. F		15. E
7. F		16. A
8. F		17. B
9. T		18. C

19. An ideal career is one that interests you while making the best use of your aptitudes and abilities.
20. (Student response.)

Occupational Areas of Interests

● **Artistic**

Interest in creative expression of feelings or ideas

Scientific

Interest in discovering, collecting, and analyzing information about the natural world and in applying scientific research findings to problems in medicine, life sciences, and natural sciences

Plants and Animals

Interest in activities involving plants and animals, usually in an outdoor setting

Protective

Interest in the protection of people and property

Mechanical

Interest in applying mechanical principles to practical situations, using machines, handtools, or techniques

● **Industrial**

Interest in repetitive, concrete, organized activities in a factory setting

Business Detail

Interest in organized, clearly defined activities requiring accuracy and attention to detail, primarily in an office setting

Selling

Interest in bringing others to a point of view through personal persuasion, using sales and promotion techniques

Accommodating

Interest in catering to the wishes of others, usually on a one-to-one basis

Humanitarian

Interest in helping others with their mental, spiritual, social, physical, or vocational needs

Leading-Influencing

Interest in leading and influencing others through activities involving high-level verbal or numerical abilities

● **Physical Performing**

Interest in physical activities performed before an audience

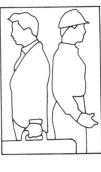

My Personal Journal

Write about your future career. How might your interests, aptitudes, and abilities contribute to your success in this career?

_____

_____

_____

_____

_____

_____

_____

_____

_____

_____

_____

_____

_____

_____

_____

_____

_____

_____

_____

_____

_____

_____

_____

_____

_____

A Career Plan

Name _____ **Date** _____ **Period** _____

A career plan is a list of steps you need to take to reach your career goal. Indicate your career goal. Then on the steps below, write how you plan to achieve that career goal. Describe extracurricular and volunteer activities, as well as part-time jobs, that might prepare you for this career.

Career goal: _____

Entry-Level Jobs

_____

_____

_____

_____

_____

_____

College

_____

_____

_____

_____

_____

High School

_____

_____

_____

_____

_____

Junior High

_____

_____

_____

_____

_____

Career Decisions

Name _____

Date _____ **Period** _____ **Score** _____

CHAPTER 45 QUIZ

☐ True/False: Circle *T* if the statement is true or *F* if the statement is false.

T   F   1. Few teenagers know what they want to do for a career.

T   F   2. A computer can tell you which career to choose.

T   F   3. Your guidance counselor at school is a good resource for career information.

T   F   4. The Occupational Outlook Handbook includes information about career opportunities in many occupations.

T   F   5. Trying new activities can help you develop new interests that can point you toward a career.

T   F   6. You were born with your abilities.

T   F   7. If you have a low aptitude for math, becoming an accountant would be a good career choice.

T   F   8. A career as a teacher's aide requires more training and education than that of a certified teacher.

T   F   9. A high school diploma is required to enter an apprenticeship program.

T   F   10. The career you choose will affect your lifestyle.

☐ Matching: Match the following terms with their definitions.

_____ 11. What someone does for a living.

_____ 12. All the smaller duties you perform throughout the day.

_____ 13. The sequence of jobs you have over a period of years.

_____ 14. Spending a day at work with someone whose career interests you.

_____ 15. The activities you enjoy and the ideas you like.

_____ 16. Skills you have developed through training and practice.

_____ 17. Where employees are trained in a skilled trade.

_____ 18. Your natural talents.

A. abilities
B. apprenticeship programs
C. aptitudes
D. career
E. interests
F. occupation
G. shadowing
H. tasks

☐ Essay Questions: Provide the answers you feel best show your understanding of the subject matter.

19. Describe an ideal career.

20. List a career in which you are interested. Describe the type of training and education you would need for that career.

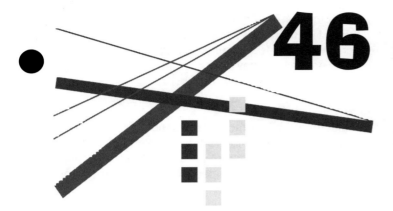

46 Careers in Family and Consumer Sciences

Objectives

After studying this chapter, students will be able to
- describe the seven family and consumer sciences career groups and give examples of jobs in each group.
- list opportunities for entrepreneurship they could explore right now.

Teaching Materials

Text, pages 507–518
  Words to Know
  Review It
  Apply It
  Think More About It
Student Activity Guide
  A. *Exploring Careers*
  B. *Becoming an Entrepreneur*
Teacher's Resource Guide/Binder
  Family and Consumer Sciences Career Cluster, transparency master 46-1
  My Personal Journal, reproducible master 46-2
  Preparing to Be an Entrepreneur, transparency master 46-3
  Blast-Off, color transparency CT-46
  Chapter 46 Quiz

Introductory Activities

1. *Blast-Off,* color transparency CT-46. Use this transparency as a basis for a discussion about careers in family and consumer sciences. Discuss specific jobs that are available in each category.
2. Ask students if they would consider starting their own business. Ask what kind of business they would like to own. Use this as the basis for a discussion on entrepreneurship.

Strategies to Reteach, Reinforce, Enrich, and Extend Text Concepts

■ Family and Consumer Sciences Careers

3. **RT** *Family and Consumer Sciences Career Cluster,* transparency master 46-1. Use this transparency on an overhead projector to illustrate the family and consumer sciences career cluster. You may want to have students identify specific careers in each area of family and consumer sciences.
4. **ER** Have students design a bulletin board illustrating the careers in family and consumer sciences.
5. **RF** Ask students who babysit to explain why babysitting would be a good way to prepare for a career in child care and human development.
6. **RT** Ask students to explain why a person with a career in family counseling must keep personal facts about their clients confidential.
7. **ER** Invite a consumer representative with a family and consumer sciences degree to describe his or her career to the class. Ask him or her to relate examples of how he or she helps to solve consumer problems.
8. **ER** Invite a panel of family and consumer sciences professionals involved in a variety of food service careers to speak to the class about how they prepared for their careers and what their job responsibilities are. Panelists may include a dietitian, a restaurant manager, a test kitchen family and consumer sciences professional, etc.
9. **RF** Ask students to list the three areas of clothing, textile, and fashion careers: Textile manufacturing, apparel production, and fashion merchandising. Under each group, have students

write as many types of careers related to that area as they can.

10. **ER** Ask an interior designer to speak to the class about how a background in design as well as a knowledge of family and consumer sciences is necessary for a career in interior design.

11. **ER** Allow your students to interview you about your career as a family and consumer sciences teacher. Describe the college courses you took and explain why you chose family and consumer sciences education as a career.

12. **RF** *Exploring Careers*, Activity A, SAG. After studying the information in the text about careers in family and consumer sciences, students are asked to complete a chart about each career group in family and consumer sciences. They are then asked to list at least three examples of careers in each group.

13. **ER** Ask a former student who is now a college student majoring in family and consumer sciences to speak to the class about the courses he or she is taking and about college life in general.

14. **ER** *My Personal Journal,* reproducible master 46-2. Students are asked to write about what they have learned about family and consumer sciences as a result of taking this course. They are then asked whether a career in family and consumer sciences would interest them.

■ Entrepreneurship

15. **RT** *Preparing to Be an Entrepreneur*, transparency master 46-3. Use this transparency master as a basis of discussion about preparing to be an entrepreneur. You may want to develop a case study about an imaginary person starting his or her own business and go through the steps with the students.

16. **ER** Invite local business owners to talk to your class about their experiences in setting up and running a business. Have students prepare a list of questions in advance.

17. **RF** *Becoming an Entrepreneur*, Activity B, SAG. Students are asked to define *entrepreneur* and to answer questions about what it would be like to become an entrepreneur.

Answer Key

■ Text

***Review It**, page 518*
1. The more you learn about each group of careers, the easier it will be to choose a career in the future.

2. (List three:) They get along well with children, children like them, they feel comfortable playing with children, they feel comfortable caring for children, they are patient, they have concern for children. (Students may justify other responses.)
3. true
4. B
5. (List three:) busperson, dishwasher, cook's helper, short order cook, stock clerk, server, host or hostess, dietitian's helper, personal food shopper, caterer's helper (Students may justify other responses.)
6. Textile manufacturing deals with the many processes of making fabrics. Apparel production involves designing and making garments. Fashion merchandising deals with buying and selling clothing and accessories.
7. true
8. (Give one example:) Children's doctors and dentists need family and consumer sciences skills to relate to children, nurses need family relations skills to serve their patients, psychologists need skills in relating with people, people in business require an understanding of consumers' needs. (Students may justify other responses.)
9. (List five:) babysitting service, children's party planning, home care service, sewing repair service, tutoring service, shopping service (Students may justify other responses.)

■ Student Activity Guide

***Becoming an Entrepreneur,** Activity B*
1. a person who starts and manages a business of his or her own
   (Questions 2 through 8 are student response.)

■ Teacher's Resource Guide/Binder

Chapter 46 Quiz

1.	F	8.	T
2.	T	9.	F
3.	T	10.	F
4.	F	11.	B
5.	F	12.	A
6.	T	13.	C
7.	F		

14. child care and human development; family counseling; management and consumerism; foods, nutrition, and wellness; clothing, textiles, and fashion; housing and interior design; family and consumer sciences education
15. (Student response.)

Family and Consumer Sciences Career Cluster

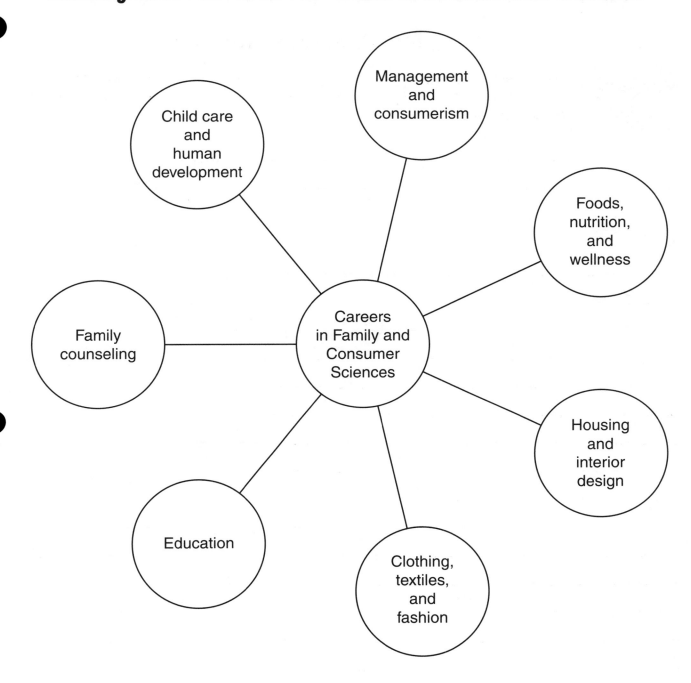

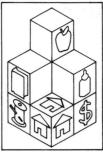

My Personal Journal

Write about what you have learned about family and consumer sciences as a result of taking this course. Would a career in a particular area of family and consumer sciences interest you? Why?

_____

_____

_____

_____

_____

_____

_____

_____

_____

_____

_____

_____

_____

_____

_____

_____

_____

_____

_____

_____

_____

_____

_____

_____

_____

_____

Preparing to Be an Entrepreneur

1. Identify your interests and skills.

2. Survey your market.

3. Make sure you have enough work and storage space.

4. Consider the costs of starting your business.

5. Decide how much work you can handle.

6. Line up employees.

7. Establish fees and estimate profits.

8. Promote your business.

9. Consult with experienced people.

Careers in Family and Consumer Sciences

Name _____

Date _____ Period _____ Score _____

☐ True/False: Circle *T* if the statement is true or *F* if the statement is false.

T F 1. Career possibilities are limited.

T F 2. Family and consumer sciences professionals may become certified by the American Association of Family and Consumer Sciences (AAFCS) by passing an exam about all areas of family and consumer sciences.

T F 3. Babysitting is a good way to begin preparing for a career in child care and human development.

T F 4. To work in family counseling requires a genuine interest in money.

T F 5. People in money management careers often counsel others on how they can increase credit purchases to go deeper into debt.

T F 6. Many people begin their careers in foods, nutrition, and wellness in the food service area because many entry-level jobs are available.

T F 7. Fashion designers do not need to have a knowledge of fabrics.

T F 8. Interior designers plan the design and furnishings of the inside of a building.

T F 9. Fewer professional family and consumer sciences professionals work in education than in any other area.

T F 10. If you choose a career outside of family and consumer sciences, you have no use for family and consumer sciences skills.

☐ Multiple Choice: Choose the best answer and write the corresponding letter in the blank.

_____ 11. Family and consumer sciences is a profession devoted to _____.
  A. cooking and sewing
  B. improving the quality of individual and family life
  C. child care
  D. buying homes

_____ 12. Entrepreneurs are people who _____.
  A. start and manage businesses of their own
  B. are lazy
  C. work for someone else
  D. are unorganized

_____ 13. Which of the following is *not* an advantage of being an entrepreneur?
  A. You make your own rules and policies.
  B. You can decide when you want to work.
  C. There are no risks involved.
  D. You have the potential to make as much money as you want.

☐ Essay Questions: Provide the answers you feel best show your understanding of the subject matter.

14. List the seven areas of family and consumer sciences careers.

15. Describe two ways you could become an entrepreneur right now.

Reproducible Quiz

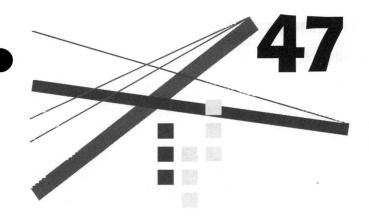

47 Balancing Family and Work

Objectives

After studying this chapter, students will be able to
- identify reasons people work.
- describe work ethic.
- explain the effects of personal life on work performance.
- explain how work influences the family.
- describe how company policies can assist families.
- suggest ways families can balance family and work demands.

Teaching Materials

Text, pages 519–528
Words to Know
Review It
Apply It
Think More About It
Student Activity Guide
A. *Family and Work Interview*
B. *The Balancing Act*
Teacher's Resource Guide/Binder
My Personal Journal, reproducible master 47-1
Family-Friendly Employer, reproducible master 47-2
Balancing Family and Work, transparency master 47-3
Chapter Quiz

Introductory Activities

1. Ask student what balancing family and work means to them.
2. Have students talk about what type of work they plan to do as adults. Discuss how they plan to balance family and work.

Strategies to Reteach, Reinforce, Enrich, and Extend Text Concepts

■ Reasons People Work

3. **ER** *My Personal Journal,* reproducible master 47-1. Students are asked to think about their future and describe why they will work.
4. **ER** *Family and Work Interview,* Activity A, SAG. Students are asked to interview a working adult with a family about his or her job, why he or she works, and the effects of work upon his or her personal life. Students can then compare responses.
5. **ER** Ask students to survey mothers who work outside of the home about the reasons they work outside of the home. Then have them interview fathers who work outside of the home about their reasons for working outside of the home. Ask students to compare survey responses.

■ Work Ethic

6. **ER** Ask a panel of employers to describe what they believe a positive work ethic is and what a negative work ethic is.
7. **RT** Discuss why doing a job to the best of your ability is part of a good work ethic.

■ Effects of Personal Life on Work

8. **RT** Have students describe how a person's personal life might affect his or her job performance.
9. **ER** Ask an employer to describe what might happen if an employee allows home life to interfere with work.

■ Demands of Work on Families

10. **RT** Have students list typical concerns of working parents.
11. **RF** Have students from dual-career families share some of the concerns their parents face in terms of child care, caring for older relatives, and caring for the home.
12. **EX** Have students estimate the economic value of housework. Have them figure out what it would cost a family to hire everything done that family members normally do.

■ Ways Employers Help Families

13. **RT** Have students define and give examples of *flextime, job sharing,* and *telecommuting*. Have them explain why these can be part of a company's family-friendly policies.
14. **EX** *Family-Friendly Employer*, reproducible master 47-2. Students are asked to pretend they are employers who are in the process of developing an employee handbook. They are asked to develop family-friendly policies for employees.

■ Balancing Family and Work Demands

15. **RT** *The Balancing Act*, Activity B, SAG. Students are asked to pretend it is 15 to 20 years from now and they have a family and job. They are asked to explain how they would balance their family and work.
16. **RF** *Balancing Family and Work*, transparency master 47-3. Use this master to brainstorm ways various demands for family and work can be balanced.
17. **ER** Invite a panel of both employers and employees to discuss balancing family and work demands.

Answer Key

■ Text

Review It, page 528
1. (Student response. Answers might include money, for needs and wants, ambition, satisfaction and fulfillment, enjoyment, and independence.)
2. Ambition
3. If you have a good work ethic, you will do the job to the best of your ability. You will arrive on time and come prepared to do the job. If you have a negative work ethic, you might take frequent breaks and be unreliable.
4. (List two:) You may lose wages; you don't accomplish as much; your work is interrupted; you may not have been available when other people needed you.
5. families in which both parents work
6. qualifications of the child care employees; number and ages of other children; activities that are planned for their children; cost
7. (Student response.)
8. B
9. (Student response.)

■ Teacher's Resource Guide/Binder

Chapter Quiz

1. T	6. T	11. J	16. D
2. T	7. F	12. F	17. H
3. F	8. T	13. E	18. G
4. T	9. I	14. B	
5. F	10. A	15. C	

19. Working parents may be concerned about the amount of time they miss spending with their children. There may be older family members who require constant care. Responsibilities concerning the home must be fulfilled.
20. delegating tasks and making schedules, setting priorities, using support systems, making use of technology in the home

My Personal Journal

Think about your life in the future. Write about why you will work. (You may want to describe economic, psychological, emotional, and other reasons.)

_____

_____

_____

_____

_____

_____

_____

_____

_____

_____

_____

_____

_____

_____

_____

_____

_____

_____

_____

_____

_____

_____

_____

_____

_____

_____

Family-Friendly Employer

Name _____ **Date** _____ **Period** _____

Pretend you are an employer. You are in the process of developing an employee handbook. Under each heading, write what your company's policy would be.

Flextime:

_____

_____

_____

_____

Job sharing:

_____

_____

_____

_____

Telecommuting:

_____

_____

_____

_____

Child care services:

_____

_____

_____

_____

Health club facilities:

_____

_____

_____

_____

Other family-friendly benefits:

_____

_____

_____

_____

Balancing Family and Work

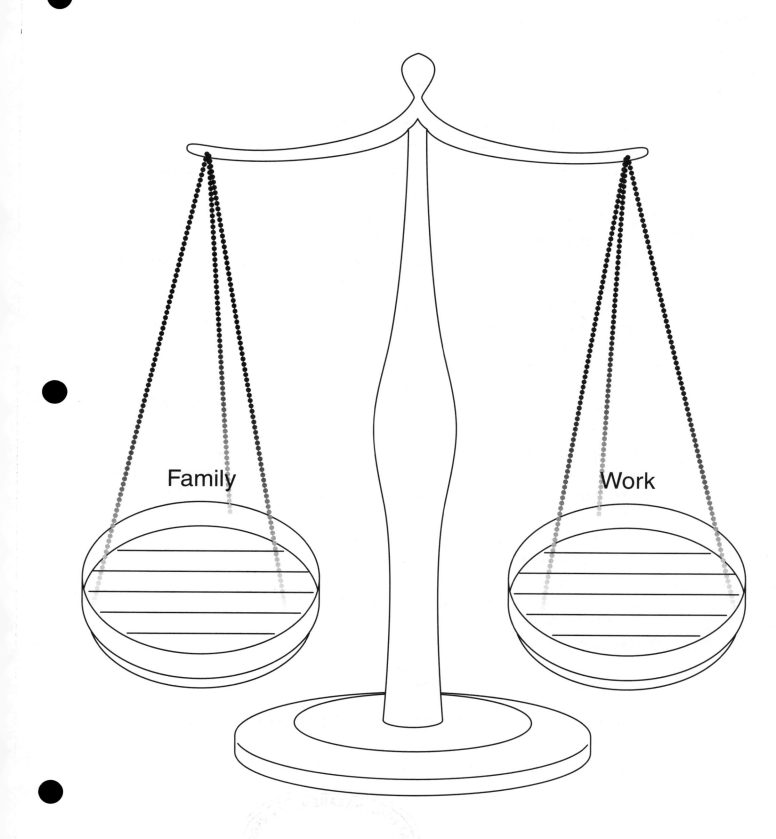

Balancing Family and Work

Name _____

Date _____ Period _____ Score _____

CHAPTER 47 QUIZ

☐ True/False: Circle *T* if the statement is true or *F* if the statement is false.

T F 1. Money is probably the most important reason people work.

T F 2. People must consider their needs and wants when they are choosing a job.

T F 3. Everyone has the same work ethic.

T F 4. Unexpected circumstances may conflict with work.

T F 5. Maintaining a home and family is a part-time job.

T F 6. Many companies that have family-friendly policies have found that such policies result in an increase in productivity and a reduction in stress.

T F 7. Balancing the demands of family and work is easy.

T F 8. Instrumental support requires the giver to do or give something to the person in need.

☐ Matching: Match the following terms and identifying phrases.

_____ 9. Effort required to accomplish an activity.

_____ 10. A desire or drive to achieve and succeed.

_____ 11. A belief or principle of good conduct in the workplace.

_____ 12. A group of people who are responsible for the care of a parent and children.

_____ 13. When homework is combined with other careers outside the home.

_____ 14. Company rules that affect the family positively.

_____ 15. Freedom to work hours that are convenient to an employee's personal situation.

_____ 16. When two people do the same job but work at different times of the day or week.

_____ 17. Using the Internet to work from home.

_____ 18. People who provide aid and assistance for individuals in the family.

A. ambition
B. family-friendly policies
C. flextime
D. job sharing
E. multiple roles
F. sandwich generation
G. support system
H. telecommuting
I. work
J. work ethic

☐ Essay Questions: Provide complete responses to the following questions or statements.

19. List three concerns working parents may have.

20. Name four methods of balancing family and work responsibilities.

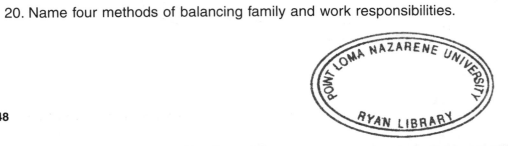
Reproducible Quiz